environment
and population

problems and solutions

INGRID WALDRON
ROBERT E. RICKLEFS

University of Pennsylvania

HOLT, RINEHART AND WINSTON, INC.

New York   Chicago   San Francisco   Atlanta
Dallas   Montreal   Toronto   London   Sydney

D0709041

preface

In this book we are concerned with human population growth and man's relationship to his environment. We explore both the problems and the possible solutions.

Biological principles and facts are crucial for understanding these issues, and we have stressed these biological aspects in order to make the book suitable for an introductory biology course. However, to develop a genuine understanding of environmental and population problems we have needed to use much material that is traditionally included in other subjects, such as physics, economics, history, sociology and psychology. Efforts to solve the problems we discuss must be based on a comprehensive understanding that focuses on the issues rather than on a traditional academic discipline. Since the problems are so urgent, we hope that this book will contribute not only to your interest in and understanding of the problems, but also to your thought and action toward solutions.

We have omitted references from the body of the text in order to make it more readable. References for the main sources of our data and for many of the ideas can be found in the annotated bibliographies at the end of each chapter and in the table and figure legends. Additional, uncited material has been used for general background, for certain specific data and to cross-check the accuracy of data in the cited material. As indicated in the text, many of the numerical data for nonindustrial countries or the entire world are only approximate estimates that indicate general magnitudes but not precise quantities.

Philadelphia, Pennsylvania

Ingrid Waldron
Robert E. Ricklefs

acknowledgements

Joseph Eyer (Biology Department, University of Pennsylvania) first introduced us to much of the data and many of the ideas presented in Chapters 11, 15, 16 and 17. We are very grateful to him for hours of interesting discussions and for allowing us to use data from his thesis before it is published. Many useful references were first brought to our attention by other students in graduate and undergraduate seminars and in the Population Study Group. Robin Gordon and Dorothy Filanowski were very helpful in the collection of data that we needed. The manuscript has been much improved by suggestions from friends, colleagues and students including Jay Mandel, Charles Snowdon, Gwendolyn Wachtel and especially Robert Socolow. We are happy to thank each one for his or her help.

contents

PART TWO / **POPULATION REGULATION**

section four / **natural processes**

section five / **human populations**

part one
man in his environment

section one

introduction

chapter 1

our future–progress or disaster?

The human population of the world is currently increasing by 2 percent each year. At this rate of growth, population doubles every 35 years. In the last 35 years the population has increased from 2.2 billion people to 3.6 billion people. Especially high rates of population increase are prevalent in the nonindustrial countries of Asia, Africa and Latin America. In the industrial countries there is high and rapidly increasing use of minerals, fuels, and so on, coupled with growing production of pollutants (Figure 1-1). This rapid population growth and technological growth has recently aroused much alarm. Where will it all lead?

One conclusion, at least, is clear: that the population growth must stop sometime within the foreseeable future. If current rates of population increase continue for about 540 years, each person will have only one square yard of land. Admittedly, at this point it is still possible to imagine technological solutions that might sustain such population densities, for example, skyscrapers floating on the seas with gardens on the roofs. But there is clearly some upper limit to the possibilities for technological solution. If population growth were to continue at the current rate for 12½ centuries, there would be about 180 billion billion people. Each person's body contains about 11 kilograms of carbon. Since there are only about 2000 billion billion kilograms of carbon in and on the whole earth, we would have reached a situation in which every earthly carbon atom was in a person and there would be no carbon atoms for plants, other animals, new people, carbon dioxide, fabrics, fuels or anything else. Such a situation is clearly impossible! We cannot conceive of a technological solution that would make it possible to reach this population size. Thus, simple chemical calculations imply that sometime within the next 12 centuries population growth *must* slow down. Our subsequent discussion will show that population increase on the earth will probably need to stop long before then, most likely within one century.

Proposals have been made that the excess people be sent to some other planet. This suggestion is heard less often now that people have seen how much expense and energy are required just to get three men as far as the moon, where they are able to survive only because of

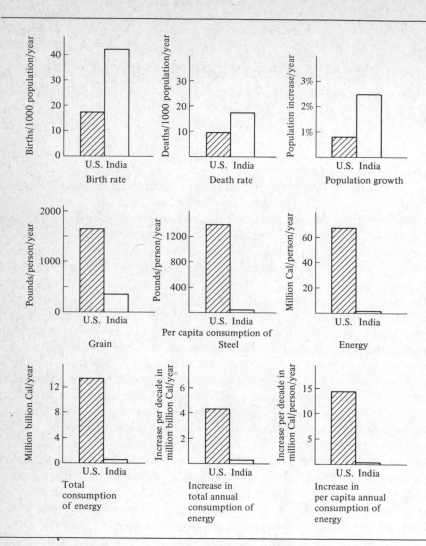

This figure illustrates the contrasting problems of high consumption of resources in industrialized countries and rapid population growth in nonindustrial countries. It is difficult to get figures on the production of waste products (pollutants), but it is reasonable to suppose that waste production is proportionately higher in countries where consumption is higher.

Note that population growth caused less than half the increase in consumption of energy (coal, gas, electricity, and so on). The increase in *per capita* consumption of energy was responsible for more than half the increase in total energy consumption in both countries. Thus, if population growth were stopped, energy consumption would continue to increase, although not quite as rapidly. All data are for the late 1960s; increases are for 1957 to 1967.

Source: U.N. *Demographic Yearbooks;* U.N. Statistical Papers, Series J, *World Energy Supplies; Studies in Family Planning,* No. 32.

resources brought with them from the earth. Any conceivable method of transport could not carry enough people far enough to reach any planet that has a reasonable temperature and the oxygen and water required for human survival.

Since emigration from the earth is impossible, there are only two ways to stop population growth: decrease the birth rate or increase the death rate. World population growth must equal the difference between the birth rate, which determines how many people enter the world population each year, and the death rate, which determines how many people leave it each year. A most important question then is whether the inevitable slowdown in population growth will come by a decrease in births or an increase in deaths.

A pessimist might project some of the current events and trends into the future and imagine that increasing death rates will end population growth as follows: "As we approach the end of the 20th century, we can expect cancer due to pollution to become a leading cause of death in industrialized countries. In Asia, Africa and Latin America, death rates may rise as more and more people suffer malnutrition and starvation. Population growth may be further reduced by declining birth rates due to poor health and consequent sterility. New wars can be expected in several regions and may lead to population decrease in some countries where fighting is most severe. One of the combatant countries may introduce germ warfare which may produce widespread epidemics of new diseases for which no cure is known."

On the other hand, an optimist can point to the possibilities for decreasing births while keeping death rates low: "Birth rates have already declined in many places. In Japan, for example, the average couple has about two children (just enough to replace themselves in a stable population). Birth rates can be expected to decrease in other places if education and medical care are improved. We also know how to decrease pollution and increase food supplies, and thus how to avoid increases in death rates. For example, the Taiwanese convert sewage to fertilizer, which decreases water pollution and increases food supplies. Cleaner subways with quieter rubber-wheeled cars and reliable service could substitute for those major air polluters, our private autos. Improved breeds of grain, rat-proof grain silos and other such changes could increase food supplies enormously if used more widely."

Many more examples of how problems could be solved will be given throughout this book. Few of the problems have easy solutions, but they all seem to have some solution which is technologically feasible, and for which resources could be available. Nevertheless, we do not necessarily think that the optimist is right and the pessimist wrong. The big question is whether people will mobilize the resources to solve the problems. If current trends of technological development, resource distribution and population growth continue, they will lead to increasingly difficult and eventually catastrophic problems. Will we continue to drift toward disasters, or will we mobilize ourselves to make the needed changes?

Detailed evidence of impending problems and possible solutions is presented in the rest of the book. The first half will deal with the problems in man's relationship to his environment. We will be concerned particularly with the contrasting potential of technology, on the one hand, to satisfy our needs and desires, and on the other hand, to disturb the environment in ways that interfere with satisfaction of our needs for clean air, water and food. The balance between benefits and threats in each case depends on how the technology is used, especially on whether sufficient consideration is given to the total effect of the technology on the environment in general and human life in particular.

As will become clear, the problems of how technology is used must be confronted directly and will not go away if we simply stop population growth. However, continued rapid population growth can make solutions more difficult, and in the long run impossible. Therefore, in the second half of the book we will discuss the conditions under which populations grow and stabilize, analyzing particularly the factors that cause decreased birth rates. This leads us to suggestions of possible methods for stopping population growth.

chapter 2

the need for ecological balance

The most important principle that ecology brings to our study of man's place in nature is the need for mechanisms that maintain ecological balance. Were it not for the natural mechanisms which restore ecological balance when it is disturbed, the environment would rapidly deteriorate under the impact of natural and man-made disturbances. Man can and does overwhelm the natural restorative mechanisms to produce long-term changes in the ecosystem. Some of these changes are desired and must be counted among the benefits of technology, for example, the elimination of pathogenic organisms that cause human disease, or the increase in food production resulting from agricultural techniques. Other changes of the natural ecosystem are unintended and undesirable, for example, the pollution of rivers or the accidental poisoning of birds by insecticides.

These unintended disruptions of the natural ecosystem can have serious repercussions for man since we derive many benefits from the natural ecosystem: edible fish from the rivers, birds that eat insect pests, natural processes that decompose waste products and provide the nutrients necessary for plant growth, and nature as a source of beauty, recreation and psychic renewal. For these reasons and many others, it is in our best interests to preserve a properly functioning ecosystem. We may be able to substitute technological processes for some of the biological processes upon which we rely, but not at the same price. Every time man has to repair or substitute for a damaged ecosystem, he must reach into his own pocket to pay the bill.

In order to preserve natural ecosystems we must understand how they function. In this chapter, we will describe first the basic natural mechanisms that maintain balance in ecosystems, and then some of the causes and consequences of man's disruptions of the ecological balance.

To Maintain Balance in Natural Systems, Materials Must Be Recycled
The Apollo space flights have dramatized the fact that we are living on a relatively small ball of matter isolated in space—the "spaceship earth." Our planet is a self-contained system. The only inputs we receive from the outside are a constant rain of light and heat (primarily

9

from our own star, the sun), the gravitational attraction exerted by the sun and other bodies in space, and occasional bits and fragments of cosmic debris. For life, energy from the light of the sun is absolutely necessary because it is the source of power for all life processes. This energy can be reused a limited number of times, but it is gradually converted to heat which cannot be used to power most biological processes. Therefore, life processes require a constant input of energy for continued existence.

Life also requires material substances—various chemical elements which are combined in thousands of intricate molecular patterns to form the matter of life. Biological substances are synthesized from inorganic molecules in the air, soil and water. Sugars are made by green plants from carbon dioxide and water. The elements in proteins (important structural and functional constituents of cells) include nitrogen and sulfur in addition to the carbon, oxygen and hydrogen that make up sugars. Additional elements form part of other molecules. For example, iron is a necessary constituent of hemoglobin. Phosphorus is a necessary part of DNA, that is, deoxyribonucleic acid, the molecule which contains genetic information or genes. Minerals such as sodium and calcium are necessary constituents of blood plasma and teeth.

There is only a limited amount of any of these elements on or near the surface of the earth. We have what is here with us now, and the amount we are gaining from outer space is minuscule. If chemical elements were consumed by living forms in the way that energy is consumed, the elements would soon become scarce and the abundance of life would decrease towards eventual extinction. Many elements are used by biological organisms in such large quantities that the earth's supply would be exhausted in a matter of decades or centuries if the elements were not returned to inorganic forms that plants can reuse. Because we live on a small planet with limited resources, recycling is a necessary feature of any system that is to persist.

The principal characteristics of cycles in nature are illustrated in the following descriptions of two of the cycles which are most important for life processes. We observe that water falls in the form of rain and snow, and that much of this water runs off the land into the seas and lakes. This water is recycled by evaporation back into the air, followed by condensation of the water vapor into rain or snow. Alternatively, some rain water is recycled via absorption by plant roots, transport through the plant and evaporation from plant leaves. At any one time, the atmosphere contains a finite amount of water vapor, enough to cover the earth to a depth of about one inch if it all fell as rain. But the average precipitation over the surface of the earth is 26 inches each year. If the water that falls from the air were not replenished by evaporation, it would be used up in much less than a year. Since the annual rainfall is nearly constant from year to year, we conclude that the water cycle is well balanced. That is, about as much water evaporates each year as falls in the form of rain and snow.

Carbon, the most common element in living substances, goes through a cycle which is basically similar to that of water. Just as sunlight drives the water cycle by providing the energy for evaporation, sunlight also powers the carbon cycle (Figure 2-1). Carbon is present

Figure 2–1 A SIMPLIFIED SCHEME OF THE CARBON CYCLE

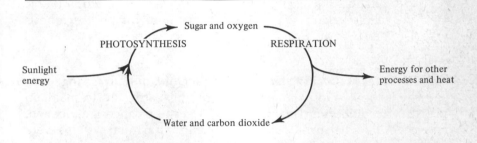

Notice how the processes of respiration and photosynthesis complement each other.

in the atmosphere and oceans as carbon dioxide, a low energy form. Green plants are capable of combining carbon with hydrogen derived from water to form high energy chemical bonds in carbohydrates such as glucose (a simple sugar). The process requires considerable energy, which plants obtain from sunlight. Pigments such as chlorophyll absorb the sunlight and convert it to a form of energy which can be used to make carbohydrates. The process by which light energy is converted into chemical energy in sugars is called photosynthesis, literally "to put together with light." Photosynthesis occurs as follows:

carbon dioxide + water + energy (sunlight)
        = glucose (with energy stored in its chemical bonds) + oxygen

The sugars that are produced in photosynthesis may be used to build other organic molecules or they may be broken down again into carbon dioxide and water by oxidation, with the concurrent release of

11

energy for other biological processes. Animals obtain their energy by oxidation. The equation for biological oxidation, or respiration, is:

glucose (with energy stored in its chemical bonds) + oxygen
= carbon dioxide + water + energy (used for chemical syntheses or motion, or given off as heat)

The equations for photosynthesis and respiration taken together exactly balance. When a gram of glucose is oxidized or "burned" to release its energy, the same amount of carbon dioxide is released as was used in photosynthesis to produce that gram of glucose. Similarly, the oxygen used in respiration equals the amount produced by photosynthesis. Thus the cycle is balanced, the nutrients required for photosynthesis are replenished by biological oxidation, and vice versa.

Natural Systems Maintain Balance in the Face of Constant Change
Recycling is the key to maintaining life on this earth, but to maintain the system in equilibrium, many other checks and balances are needed. These checks and balances would not be crucial if natural systems were fixed, never to change. Once such a system was running, it would continue indefinitely. But natural systems are constantly exposed to perturbations and they change continually in response. Over the history of the earth climates have changed drastically, continents have migrated across the globe, mountains have risen and been worn down, and new groups of animals and plants have appeared and disappeared. Even over short periods of time, there are more or less regular fluctuations with the seasons, the tides and the day-night cycle, and many unpredictable changes as well. An unusually hot August day may be only slightly annoying to you, but it may cause some insects to lay fewer eggs than usual. This affects the wasps and flies which prey on these insects, and in turn affects the birds which prey on the wasps and flies.

Despite perturbations of this nature, the ecosystem is able to maintain itself in balance because organisms and populations can respond appropriately to changes in their environment. Frequently, organisms make responses which tend to restore their condition to its original state. For example, in cold weather you shiver, which produces more heat and restores body temperature. When oxygen is low, as it is at high altitudes, you breathe faster and thus maintain oxygen levels in your body tissues. These biological responses are analogous to the response of a driver whose car is hit by a sudden gust of wind blowing across the road (an environmental perturbation). To restore the car to its intended course, the driver must turn the steering wheel in the appropriate direction, but not too far (or the car will end up in the ditch on the other side of the road), and not too late (turning the wheel after the car was in the ditch would not help either).

Natural systems counter environmental change with four different kinds of response: regulatory, acclimatory, developmental and evolutionary. The first three responses represent changes which may occur in individuals, and the first two are reversible. Evolutionary responses involve changes in the genetic makeup of populations, changes in characteristics that are fixed in individuals.

Regulatory responses cope with short-term changes in environmental conditions such as temperature. In hot weather the normal human response is to remove a layer or two of clothing, move into the shade and, if it is very hot, to perspire. These responses are structural (clothing), behavioral (movement) and physiological (loss of water through the skin). If the temperature were to drop suddenly, or if you were to walk into an air-conditioned room, these responses would quickly be reversed.

Acclimatory changes occur over longer periods of time and although they are reversible, the reverses require time. The "sun tan," a response to high intensity sunlight, is a good example of acclimatory change. The tan results from the deposition of melanin pigment granules in the superficial layers of the skin. These granules absorb light and dissipate it as heat, thereby preventing ultraviolet radiation from penetrating more deeply into the skin and causing damage to the cells. It requires several days to form a good protective tan and more to lose it. Similarly, when you go to high altitudes where there is less oxygen to breathe, it takes several days or weeks before you are able to perform activities as if at sea level. The acclimatory response involves an increase in the number of red blood cells and a change in the blood hemoglobin to a form that takes up oxygen more readily.

Developmental responses result from the interaction between a growing organism and its environment, and are often nonreversible. Plants grow in the direction of needed sunlight; if a plant is long exposed to light from one side only, it may acquire a permanently asymmetrical shape. Children who are poorly nourished usually attain small stature, which in turn acts to reduce their nutritional requirements as adults.

Populations also respond by evolving, or adjusting their basic genetic makeup to meet new environmental conditions. Individuals do not evolve; rather one kind of individual is replaced in a population by another kind that is better suited to the new conditions. This process of differential reproduction and survival is known as natural selection. Genetic variation among individuals in the population forms the basis for evolution, for without variation there can be no choice for natural selection to act upon. The theory of natural selection put forth by Charles Darwin more than a century ago is based on a sequence of observations and logical arguments: within populations different individuals possess different traits; many of these traits are passed from parent to offspring; some traits are more fit than others, that is, individuals with these traits leave more progeny; thus, these traits will be increasingly common in subsequent generations, as the progeny of the fittest individuals gradually replace less fit individuals in the population. The fitness of a given trait is meaningful only in the context of the environment in which it exists. For example, the genetic defect which results in sickle-cell anemia in man is generally detrimental, because the anemia results in the death of a large portion of those who inherit the trait from both parents and a small portion of those who inherit the trait from only one parent. In many tropical areas, however, the trait is beneficial for a person who inherits it from only one parent, since such a person is less susceptible to malaria because his red blood cells are more resistant to infection by the parasite that causes malaria. Thus in tropical countries with endemic malaria, an individual is most likely to survive and reproduce if he has one gene for sickle-cell anemia. Therefore, the gene has become relatively common in such areas. The example of "industrial melanism" presented in Box 2-1 clearly demonstrates natural selection and the evolutionary changes that it has produced in a moth population during the industrial revolution in England.

Time, or rate of environmental change, is the most important factor determining whether responses will be regulatory, acclimatory, developmental or evolutionary. Obviously, changes that occur within the lifetime of individuals do not permit evolutionary responses that require many generations. The most rapid fluctuations can be countered only by regulatory responses.

The Balance of Natural Systems Is Often Overwhelmed by Man's Disruptions

Man's activities have often disrupted the natural balances which have been so finely and painstakingly tuned by the natural responses of animals and plants. Perhaps the most dramatic effect of our disruptions has been the extinction of a considerable number of species, including even species that were once extremely numerous, such as the passenger pigeon. We must now face even the fearsome possibility that we will so disrupt our environment that we will eventually cause our own extinction.

Certainly this would be an unexpected and unintended conse-

Box 2–1 **AN EXAMPLE OF EVOLUTION: INDUSTRIAL MELANISM IN THE PEPPERED MOTH** *BISTON BETULARIA*

In early 19th century England, most peppered moths were grey with black speckles. They spent the day resting on lichen-covered tree trunks of similar appearance. Butterfly collectors found only a few dark or melanic, individuals. During the 1800s England became industrialized and manufacturing areas suffered from rather severe air pollution. At the same time in industrializing areas, collectors noted that the melanic form of the peppered moth was becoming increasingly common. By now the melanic form may comprise more than 95 percent of the population. Where there has been relatively little pollution, the light form still prevails.

During the early 1950s an English physician, H. B. D. Kettlewell, began to investigate the change in color of peppered moths. He first established by breeding experiments that the change was in fact genetic and that evolution had occurred in the population. It seemed likely that some feature of the woods around industrial areas favored the occurrence of the dark form of the moth over the light form. To investigate this possibility, Dr. Kettlewell raised large numbers of light and dark moths, marked them and then released them into the woods in polluted and unpolluted areas. He later sampled the woods with traps containing lights to attract the moths. The relative proportions of the two forms among recaptured moths were as follows:

AREA	LIGHT FORM	DARK FORM
Dorset (unpolluted woods)		
Released	496	473
Recaptured	62	30
Percent recaptured	12.5	6.3
Birmingham (polluted woods)		
Released	201	601
Recaptured	34	205
Percent recaptured	16.0	34.1

In the unpolluted woods a higher proportion of the light form was recaptured, and in the forests around polluted areas a higher proportion of the dark form was recaptured. The differences in survival of the two forms in two different environments clearly

15

established that natural selection was responsible for the occurrence of industrial melanism.

Dr. Kettlewell also wished to determine the selective agents involved. Exactly what aspect of the environment was responsible for the evolutionary change? He observed that in polluted woods, the tree trunks were blackened and devoid of the lichens which usually occurred in unpolluted areas. This observation suggested that in polluted areas the darker forms of the moth may have blended in better with the backgrounds on which they rested than the light forms did. This would conceal them more effectively from predators and hence confer greater survival. To test this, Kettlewell placed equal numbers of individuals of the two forms on tree trunks in polluted and unpolluted woods and then hid behind a blind to watch them carefully. It was discovered very quickly that several species of birds regularly searched the trunks of trees looking for moths and other insects, and that these birds more readily discovered the form which did not properly match its background color. Over a period of observation, Dr. Kettlewell tabulated the following numbers of moths taken by birds:

	LIGHT FORM	DARK FORM
Unpolluted woods	26	164
Polluted woods	43	15

The results were consistent with the release-recapture experiment, and indicate that dark forms survive better in industrial areas because they are less conspicuous to predatory birds.

Industrial melanism illustrates the type of evolutionary response which may occur over long periods of time when slow changes take place in the environment. The populations required many decades to complete the response, to complete the replacement of light by dark forms in polluted areas. Of particular interest is the recent finding that in the woods around Manchester, an industrial city that has recently adopted stringent air pollution control measures, the grey-speckled forms are beginning to increase in number in the moth populations. The agents of selection are insectivorous birds, but the background against which the moth spends the day is a critical aspect of the environment. This example clearly demonstrates how the interaction between the organism and its environment determines fitness.

quence of our activities, but we have a long record of producing unexpected and unintended consequences. The ships and airplanes that provide the basis for international commerce and travel have unintentionally also provided a means of dispersal for many pest species to new areas where they can multiply unchecked by the predators that control them in their original locale. The heat from electric power plants and the nutrients from sewage have had the unexpected effect of promoting the growth of some undesirable species and eliminating some desirable species from our lakes and rivers. DDT has reduced the populations of malaria-carrying mosquitos and some crop pests, but it has also poisoned useful birds and fish (Box 2–2). The by-products of combustion and industrial processes foul the air to the point that they damage crops and exacerbate human lung disease. The list of unpredicted and undesired side effects of man's technology is long indeed. In retospect, we see that many of these side effects were predictable and avoidable. It is to be hoped that attitudes are changing now, so that better predictions will become the basis for planning to avoid the worst consequences of man's powerful ability to disrupt the ecosystem.

How is it possible that man has been able to disrupt a balanced system which has adjusted to perturbations for so long? The obvious answer is that man has the power to manipulate his environment far beyond that of any other species, but this is only a superficial answer because we are then led to ask how it is that man has acquired this power. Basically, this power arises from man's unique propensity for cultural evolution. One may think of culture as analogous to the genetics of the population: culture is a body of information, influencing behavior and habit, which is characteristic of a population. Culture, however, differs from genetic information in three very basic ways which enable cultural responses to occur much more rapidly than genetic evolutionary responses.

First, culture may pass to genetically unrelated members of the population through learning. Thus, cultural changes may be acquired by a large portion of the population in a relatively short period of time, whereas genetic changes require a gradual replacement of one genotype by another through differences in fecundity and mortality. Second, culture is transmitted less faithfully than genetic information, the particular means of communication used being rather prone to error. Genetic transmission of information is based on the biochemical replication of large molecules, and error occurs at the rate of only one in several thousands or even one in several millions of times for each trait. Culture, on the other hand, is transmitted in verbal and written form and is subject to a high rate of error, so there is a broad base of variability for cultural selection to act upon.

Box 2-2 **THE CLEAR LAKE STORY**

Clear Lake in Northern California is 19 miles long and 7 miles wide. For many years the lake has been an important resort area, famous for its water skiing and fishing. At times during the summer months, large numbers of midges, locally known as "gnats," were attracted to the lights around the lake. Although the midges are related to mosquitos, they are not blood-sucking. Nevertheless they were bothersome to the vacationers because of their presence in large numbers. As early as 1916, investigations were made into the life history of the gnat to find ways in which the outbreaks might be controlled. Experiments with larvicides and ovicides failed to produce control programs prior to World War II. Many species of fish were found to eat large numbers of gnat larvae but not in sufficient quantity to control the population.

After the war DDT, and a similar chemical DDD, became available as insecticides. Studies indicated that DDD would offer the most effective control and be least toxic to other forms of wildlife. In September 1949, DDD was applied to Clear Lake at the level of 0.014 parts of insecticide per million parts of water (ppm). This dose killed an estimated 99 percent of the midge larvae, and for the next two years very few adult midges were reported around the lake. However, in 1951, larvae were again found, and they increased over the next several years until in September 1954, another application of DDD to the lake killed 99 percent of the midges. In December, local residents began to find western grebes, diving birds which nested around the lake, dead on its shores. Midge populations recovered more rapidly after the 1954 application than after the 1949 application. Another treatment of DDD, given in September 1957, was less successful in its effects. Officials suspected that the gnats were evolving resistance to the insecticide. In December of that year, more western grebes were found dead. Several weeks later, two dying grebes were sent to the California Department of Fish and Game Disease Laboratory, but no infectious disease was found. Fat samples were submitted to the California Department of Agriculture's Bureau of Chemistry for routine analysis, and to the astonishment of many wildlife officials, they were found to contain the unusually high concentration of 1600 ppm DDD.

Although this high concentration of DDD came as a surprise at the time, it is clear now how biological processes concentrated the DDD. DDD is much more soluble in fat than in water, so when DDD is sprayed on a lake, it is rapidly absorbed into the fatty parts of living organisms. When a fish eats plants containing DDD, it cannot excrete the DDD rapidly and it has only poor ability to break the DDD down chemically, so most of the DDD gets stored in the fish's fat. Most of the other molecules from the plant are metabolized and excreted, so the fish ends up with a higher concentration of DDD in its fat than the plants had (see Figure 7–1, pg. 70). When a grebe eats the fish, this process is repeated and the grebe will have an even higher concentration of DDD. The consequence at Clear Lake was that grebes, once numbering over one thousand breeding pairs, have not bred successfully at Clear Lake since 1950, and not more than 25 pairs inhabited the lake by 1960. The concentration of DDD residues in the game fish was as high as 2000 ppm in the fat tissues of the white catfish and largemouth bass, about 100,000 times the concentration of the original application of insecticide. In the edible flesh, residues were as high as 100 ppm, far above permissible levels set by the U.S. Department of Agriculture for human consumption.

The result of the midge control program at Clear Lake has been to breed a DDD-resistant strain of midge which still poses a threat to the tourist industry, to all but eliminate at least one species of waterbird from the lake, and to place in jeopardy the lake's most important asset, its fishery. All this came as a surprise. The designers of the control program had not counted on the ability of the midge to evolve resistance to a very toxic insecticide, nor had they foreseen that DDD residues would accumulate to such high levels in other members of the lake's fauna, to the point of killing one species and rendering many others completely useless to man. However, we have shown how these consequences could have been predicted using biological principles and careful thought. Such predictions are not easy because the system of natural checks and balances is so complicated that any attempt to impose human controls must have manifold effects. Nevertheless, we must strive to make accurate predictions and use them in planning.

Third, and most important, are changes brought about through man's reasoning and imagination. Genetic mutations are biochemical mistakes. They alter the morphology, behavior or physiology of the organism, but they are so far removed from their ultimate effect on the organism that they are not directed or purposeful. We may liken mutations to typing errors. The latter are caused by slips of the fingers, unrelated to the sense of what is being typed. Often such errors are not so bad that they critically alter the meaning of the message. Some errors, however, may be extremely disadvantageous to their propagator, as in the case of the man who mixed his d's and q's and introduced Queen Victoria at a banquet as "our queer old dean." Through reasoning and imagination man is able to make cultural changes in direct response to environmental conditions. That is, we seek solutions to our problems through directed changes in our culture, whereas natural selection must sift through random errors in search of one that might prove useful.

For these reasons—rapid transmission of culture among generations by learning, high rate of error, and directed change—cultural evolution proceeds much more quickly than genetic evolution, so much so that natural systems which rely on the latter are often unable to keep pace. Only organisms with very short generation times and high rates of reproduction are capable of genetic evolution which is sufficiently rapid to keep pace with our cultural evolution. For example, some strains of bacteria have been able to evolve considerable resistance to the antibiotics which we use to cure disease by killing bacteria. Widespread use of penicillin has created a new environment which selectively favors bacteria with the rare mutations that enable them to grow unaffected by this antibiotic. Because of the extremely short generation time and high rate of reproduction, bacteria with the penicillin-resistance mutations have rapidly replaced nonresistant bacteria in populations of disease organisms. Similarly, when an insecticide has been widely used for several years or decades, insects often evolve resistance to the insecticide. In predicting all the manifold effects of a technology, we will need to anticipate not only the failure of natural systems to adjust, but also this kind of all-too-successful adjustment.

In the past, our high rate of cultural change has made it possible to supply the needs of growing human populations (Chapter 15). In the future, rapid cultural evolution could provide solutions to our most pressing environmental problems. However, if we are to benefit rather than suffer from our ability to produce large and rapid changes in our environment, we must improve our ability to predict the important effects of each change we make, and we must evaluate more carefully the relative costs and benefits of particular changes in the natural environment. On this basis, we must develop technologies that are in harmony with the natural world.

BIBLIOGRAPHY

Commoner, B. 1966. *Science and Survival.* New York: The Viking Press, Inc. [describes how man disrupts his environment, and analyzes the role of science in this].

Cox, G., ed. 1969.   *Readings in Conservation Ecology.*   New York: Appleton-Century-Crofts [an excellent source book with many original papers on conservation, pollution and ecology, including one by Hunt and Bischoff on Clear Lake].

Kettlewell, H. B. D. 1959.   Darwin's Missing Evidence.   *Scientific American,* March 1959 [an account of industrial melanism by the man who made the study].

Maynard-Smith, J. 1958.   *The Theory of Evolution.* Baltimore: Penguin Books, Inc. [the most lucid account of evolution and natural selection].

section two

food

chapter 3

food needs, shortages and surpluses

We have argued that human beings must achieve balance with their environment if they expect to continue to obtain the food, oxygen and clean water that they need to survive. This chapter outlines food needs and the whole range of problems we face in meeting these needs. Chapters 4 through 7 describe the biological processes in food production, the environmental imbalances that result from agriculture and ways to restore needed ecological balance. Chapter 8 concludes our discussion of food with an evaluation of the overall possibilities for increasing food supply to meet increasing needs.

Food Needs

The atoms in our bodies come from the food we eat, the water we drink and the air we breathe. We must eat certain atoms (like iron) which our cells incorporate into complex and essential molecules (like hemoglobin). We must also eat certain complex molecules which our bodies need but our cells are unable to synthesize, for example, the vitamins and the essential amino acids. Amino acids are used to construct proteins in much the same way that letters are used to construct words. Proteins are molecules that play a crucial role in the structure of the body, the contraction of muscles and the chemical processes of metabolism. The "essential" amino acids are the ones our cells cannot synthesize.

Our food also provides the energy we need for muscular contraction, for the synthesis of body constituents and for many other vital processes. Energy is released from food by oxidation, a process which is basically analogous to burning fuel (Figure 2–1), but is much more carefully regulated and occurs at much lower temperatures. Most of this energy is obtained from carbohydrates such as sugar and starch, although fat and proteins may also be metabolized for energy. When molecules are metabolized for energy, most of their atoms are not incorporated into the body, but rather are given off as waste products like carbon dioxide.

The amount of food a person needs for energy and/or incorporation into his body varies depending on his level of activity, his rate of development, and his size. Average requirements do, however, provide a useful basis for estimating world food needs now and in the future. The average person needs about 2400 Calories of energy, 60 grams (just over two ounces) of protein, and small amounts of about a dozen vitamins and minerals such as iron, iodine, calcium and salt. Ideally, at least one-third of the protein should come from animal sources (meat, milk, eggs, fish) or from legumes (beans, peas), since the proteins in these foods have the essential amino acids in just about the needed ratios, whereas the proteins in cereal grains are deficient in one or more of the essential amino acids. A daily diet of 2½ eggs and 1½ pounds of wheat would fulfill protein and caloric requirements, although some minerals and vitamins would be deficient.

Many People Are Undernourished . . .

Roughly half the people in the world suffer from inadequate nutrition. Protein deficits are most common. About one-third of the world's people do not get enough of the proteins that contain adequate proportions of all the essential amino acids. Approximately one-quarter of the world's population does not receive adequate Calories. Although these estimates are inexact, they indicate a nutrition problem of considerable magnitude.

The main victims of inadequate nutrition are the poor and the young. Rapidly growing children have high protein needs that can only be met if high protein foods like milk are available. Many children suffer from severe protein deficiencies, especially in cities where women abandon traditional customs of prolonged nursing and poverty precludes the substitution of cow's milk. Protein deficiencies in early childhood may lead to irreversible brain damage and permanently lowered mental capacities. Children weakened by malnutrition commonly succumb to disease; measles is often fatal. Infection can lead to worsened malnutrition, for example, when parasites compete with their human host for the limited supply of food.

Even in the United States, where many people overeat, undernourishment is common among the poor. One-third of the people in families with incomes less than $1650 a year had inadequate vitamin A, about 10 percent had inadequate vitamin B_1, and 20 percent inadequate vitamin B_2. In addition, more than one-tenth had low blood protein levels; and one-quarter had anemia, probably due to iron deficiency.

. . . while the United States and Other Countries Have Food Surpluses!

Even though hunger and diet deficiencies are so prevalent, "overproduction" is commonly said to be the main problem for agriculture in the United States, and food "surpluses" are controlled by government programs. How can there be food surpluses, when the food deficits are so great? Put simply, the farmer wants to sell his food for a profit, while the undernourished are generally too poor to pay profitable prices for more food. So there is too much food to be sold at a profit, not too much food for human needs. Thus it is clear that people are hungry not only because there are biological limitations on the amount of food we can grow, but also because our economic institutions fail to distribute the food we can grow to those who need it.

How big are these surpluses? We present estimates for the United States only, although Canada, some European countries and even some Asian countries also complain of surpluses. For several years around 1966, the United States exported enough food aid to provide the minimum caloric requirements for 100 million people, out of a world population that was roughly 3½ billion people. During these years of bad weather and low production in Asia, the United States shipped roughly 20 million tons of grain a year. Food aid shipments have decreased recently because crops have improved in Asia and because stored United States surpluses have been reduced to levels that approximate reasonable emergency stores.

Production of surpluses is prevented by another program that pays farmers about $1 billion per year *not* to grow crops on about 60 million acres of farmland. This idle land is about one-seventh of the total cropland in the United States. Even if 10 million acres were left idle for conservation purposes, the other 50 million could produce close to 40 million tons of grain a year. This would be enough to make up about half the caloric deficits for all undernourished people in the world today.

The simultaneous existence of undernourishment and programs to control food "surpluses" illustrates that the problems of providing adequate food are political and economic, as much as they are problems of agricultural technique and material resources. Adequate food can be supplied, but it will not be supplied unless there are changes in economic organization. For example, hunger among the poor can only be eliminated if everyone has a job with an adequate wage (0 percent unemployed instead of 6 percent in the United States in 1971), or if governments make food available to everyone who needs it. Such policies could eliminate hunger throughout the world, although only with international cooperation.

Many people argue against such proposals because they believe that improved diets, by improving health, will increase population growth and thus aggravate food problems in the long run. Note that these arguments are never made by someone who is himself in dan-

27

ger of starving to death. Furthermore, experience has shown that increased population growth need not result from food aid. Taiwan, for example, received more food aid per capita than any other Asian country, while its birth rate was falling rapidly and its rate of population growth declined. The decline resulted from social and economic changes that motivated people to want and to have smaller families (Chapter 18). Food aid can contribute to such changes. For example, couples that now have large numbers of sons in the hope that at least one will survive to support them in their old age are likely to have fewer children, if adequate food increases childhood survival. Food aid can also help a country raise its own food, for example, when it is used to pay workers who are building a dam or digging irrigation ditches. So food aid can be more than a temporary stopgap. It can contribute to a permanent solution of hunger problems, by supporting projects for increased food production and by contributing to the social change that results in lower birth rates.

What Malthus Did Not Know
In 1798 Malthus predicted that human populations would increase by a constant multiple each year, whereas food production would increase by a constant addition which would not be sufficient to keep pace with population growth. Consequently population growth would be halted by "famine, pestilence and war." The last assertion may yet turn out to be right, but it need not, since the initial premises have been shown by history to be inaccurate. Taiwan is but one example of a prosperous country where birth rates have decreased, and population has increased less rapidly than Malthus' prediction of constant multiplication. (Further evidence and explanations are given in the second half of this book.) Furthermore, food production can increase more rapidly than the fixed yearly additions predicted by Malthus, and has increased slightly more rapidly than population during the last two decades. An example of the kind of development that can lead to very rapid increases in food production is given next.

The Green Revolution
Hopes for a "Green Revolution" of vastly increased food production are centered on new high-yielding breeds of wheat and rice. In tropical and subtropical climates, these new breeds can yield 30–100 percent more than traditional breeds. Such dramatic increases have motivated many peasant farmers to change from their traditional agriculture to the new breeds and the new techniques they require. Acreage devoted to the new breeds has increased rapidly from less than 1 percent of cropland in Asia outside of China in 1966 to about

10 percent in 1970. The higher yields of the new breeds resulted in a harvest 5–10 percent bigger than it would have been otherwise. This was enough grain to feed roughly 50 million people.

One of the main advantages of the new breeds is their favorable response to fertilizer. Heavy heads of grain grow in response to high doses of fertilizer. The thin stems of traditional breeds break under the weight, so growth is stopped. The new breeds have stronger, thicker stems. Thus, high yields are possible, although only if fertilizer is available to provide the mineral nutrients needed for the increased growth. (In Chapter 5 we discuss the possibilities and problems of providing fertilizer.) Another advantage of the new breeds is that they use the available sunlight energy more efficiently. For example, because the stalks are shorter a higher proportion of the energy is used to synthesize edible grain, and less to synthesize inedible stalk. Also, because the new breeds mature faster, it has become possible to raise two crops a year in many regions.

Double-cropping and heavier use of fertilizer increase the demand for water. Hence water has become the limiting resource for agriculture in many areas. The new wheat grows well only on irrigated land, although efforts are being made to develop breeds for dryland use. The new rice does well only where flooding of rice paddies is controlled so that the short-stemmed plants do not drown. Furthermore, in humid regions the new rice is susceptible to a kind of bacterial infection called rice blight. The new breeds appear to be more susceptible to disease than traditional varieties that have had years of natural selection for resistance. (Methods of protecting crops without endangering the environment will be discussed in Chapter 7.)

Clearly, there is an impressive list of biological problems to be solved if the food potential of these new breeds is to be realized. Other problems that have impeded increases in food production include inadequate storage and marketing facilities, and a lack of technically trained agricultural workers to advise the farmers.

Equally difficult economic and political problems have developed. More land could be planted with improved breeds, were it not that small farmers who want to adopt the new breeds often cannot get the cash or credit to purchase the seeds and fertilizer. In India and Pakistan these small farmers have protested with riots and political disturbances against their inability to obtain a share of the increasing prosperity that the new seeds have brought to larger farmers. Laborers have also protested when their wages have not increased, or when they have been replaced on the farm by tractors bought with increased profits from new breeds. Some tenants have been evicted by landlords who found it more profitable to till the land themselves, now that yields have risen. The dissension over who should profit from the new

29

grains has also affected pricing policy. Grain prices have been high and this has encouraged farmers to invest in the new seeds, fertilizer and irrigation pumps. But high prices mean that poor people cannot afford to buy as much food. Several governments that have supported high prices in order to encourage high food production, find themselves with surplus grain which they cannot sell at the price they paid. Some of these governments are exporting grains to the highest bidder to minimize their losses. Such "surplus" grain is exported from countries where many are undernourished!

Each of the problems associated with the Green Revolution can be solved, at least partially. But will they be? If they are, food supplies in many tropical countries could be increased by at least one-quarter. Other ways to increase food production will be discussed in the next five chapters. In Chapter 8 we will show that, if wisely executed, these methods could supply the increased food to give us time (at least 30 years) in which to stop population growth. If we fail, massive famine may become our modern means of population control.

BIBLIOGRAPHY

Brown, L. R. 1970. *Seeds of Change*. New York: Frederick A. Praeger, Inc. [re "Green Revolution" and foreign aid].

Dalrymple, D. G. 1969. *Technological Change in Agriculture: Effects and Implications for the Developing Nations*. Washington: USDA & AID [an astute analysis of problems and potentials of the "Green Revolution"].

Pyke, M. 1970. *Man and Food*. New York: McGraw Hill, Inc. [very good discussions of nutrition and malnutrition].

chapter 4

energy in the ecosystem

The energy in our food is the driving force for all our life processes. Without it the chemical and physical processes which make up what we call life could not occur. The source of new energy for living beings on the earth is sunlight. A continuous inflow of new energy is needed for life processes, since each time the energy is used, some of it is converted to heat energy which is no longer useful for most biological processes. In this chapter, we explain why energy cannot be reused indefinitely, estimate total plant growth and its relation to the rate of inflow of sunlight, discuss the inefficiencies in animals' use of the energy in their food and present several practical implications for increasing food supplies.

Laws of Physics Apply to Biological Processes
Energy is defined as the capacity to do work. Work is defined as changes in motion: for example, a jet plane taking off, a heart beating or molecules moving faster in a substance when it is heated up. Energy can be measured in Calories, a familiar unit because it is used in diet information. A Calorie of energy in any form is equivalent to the heat energy required to raise the temperature of one kilogram of water one degree Centigrade. (This is the large Calorie, often called the kilocalorie. A kilocalorie is 1000 times larger than the small calorie which is spelled with a small "c.") We have already mentioned a variety of forms of energy: light, heat, the energy stored in chemical bonds.

Several rules always apply to the conversion of energy from one form to another. These are the Laws of Thermodynamics. Two of the laws are of particular interest here. First, energy is neither created nor destroyed. Energy may be converted from one form to another, but the total amount of energy always remains the same. There is only one exception of practical importance, that is, the conversion of matter to energy in nuclear reactions. Otherwise, the total amount of energy remains constant.

The second law of thermodynamics is more subtle and can be stated in a variety of ways. The most relevant formulation for our purposes is: whenever energy is converted from one form to another (for example, electrical energy is converted to light energy in a light bulb), some of the energy is always converted to heat energy (so the light bulb gets hot, and there is less light energy coming out than electrical energy going in). In other words, all energy conversions are inefficient in that some of the energy ends up as heat energy, which is random motion of molecules and in most cases not useful for the work to be done. Biological energy conversions have the same kind of inefficiency as all others. For example, when energy stored in chemical bonds is converted to the energy of motion in muscles, heat is produced (which is why shivering helps you to keep warm). The heat energy produced during inefficient energy transformations in plants and animals cannot be used to accomplish most kinds of biological work. Instead the heat energy is given off and eventually radiated out into space. At the same time, new energy is constantly supplied to biological systems by the inflow of sunlight energy, which plants convert to chemical energy in the process called photosynthesis. This chemical energy is then used by the plants and the animals which eat them to power the biological processes involved in maintenance and reproduction.

Energy Limits on Total Plant Production
Only a small fraction of the sun's energy is ever used by plants in photosynthesis. About one-third of the sun's energy is reflected back by clouds, and another 20 percent is reflected, scattered or absorbed by dust and other particles in the atmosphere. Thus, only about half of the sunshine that arrives at the outer atmosphere reaches the surface of the earth and is available to plant life.

Of the sunlight energy that reaches the surface of the earth, less than 1 percent is used in photosynthesis. One reason is that much of the sunshine that falls on plants is not used for photosynthesis, but instead is reflected, or absorbed and converted to heat which evaporates water from plant surfaces. It is also true that much of the sun's energy that reaches the earth's surface does not reach plant surfaces. Water reflects and absorbs much light, with the consequence that plant productivity tends to be low wherever plants grow in water (Table 4–1). Another reason that plant productivity is low in aquatic regions is that mineral nutrients tend to be scarce. In desert regions plant productivity is extremely low since the lack of water limits plant growth to sparse vegetation. Because much of the desert surface is not covered by plants, a high percentage of sunshine falls on rock or soil and is not utilized by plants. Thus it is clear that the total plant productivity of the earth is currently nowhere near the upper limit that would be set by the availability of sunshine. Productivity could be increased by watering the desert and by fertilizing aquatic regions.

Table 4–1 NET PRIMARY PRODUCTION FOR THE MAJOR
ECOSYSTEMS OF THE EARTH

ECOSYSTEM	AREA (MILLION MILLION SQUARE METERS)	ANNUAL MEAN NET PRIMARY PRODUCTIVITY (CALORIES PER SQUARE METER PER YEAR)	WORLD NET PRIMARY PRODUCTION (MILLION BILLION CALORIES PER YEAR)
Lake and stream	2	2250	5
Swamp and marsh	2	9000	18
Tropical forest	20	9000	180
Temperate forest	18	5850	105
Boreal forest	12	3600	43
Woodland and shrubland	7	2700	19
Savannah	15	3150	47
Temperate grassland	9	2250	20
Tundra and alpine	8	630	5
Desert scrub	18	315	6
Desert, rock and ice	24	15	1
Agricultural land	14	2900	41
TOTAL LAND	149	3300	490
Open ocean	332	560	190
Continental shelf	27	1600	43
Attached algae and estuaries	2	9000	18
TOTAL OCEAN	361	700	250
TOTAL FOR EARTH	510	1440	740

Net primary productivity is defined as the energy stored in newly synthesized
plant tisses. Productivity estimates for some of the regions may err by as much
as 50 percent, but the basic picture of relative and total productivities is substantially correct.

Source: The data were adapted from R. H. Whittaker. 1970. *Communities and Ecosystems.* New York: Crowell-Collier and Macmillan, Inc. (By multiplying his data
in dry grams of production by 4.5 Calories per dry gram.)

Some instances where these theoretical possibilities seem feasible and
desirable will be discussed in subsequent chapters.

Inefficiencies in the Biological Use of Energy

As would be expected on the basis of the second law of thermodynamics, the photosynthetic conversion of light energy to chemical

energy is inefficient. This inefficiency is one reason that the total amount of chemical energy stored in a plant's molecules is considerably less than the total light energy captured by the plant's chlorophyll. The other reason is that much of the sugar produced by photosynthesis is used by the plant as a source of energy for its own life processes. The energy for maintaining the plant is released as the sugar molecules are broken down into molecules with less chemical energy, usually carbon dioxide and water. The proportion of the chemical energy produced during photosynthesis which is used for metabolic processes varies from about 20 to 75 percent. Thus, the chemical energy stored in a plant and available to an animal that eats it is about 80 to 25 percent of all the chemical energy produced by photosynthesis in that plant. The energy stored in the plant and available to consumers is called the net primary productivity (as in Table 4–1).

Animal use of chemical energy is also inefficient. Little of the food consumed by animals is converted into animal tissue (Figure 4–1). Some of the food is never digested. For example, plant fibers, wood, hair and insect exoskeletons are indigestible for most animals. Such

Figure 4–1 SCHEMATIC DIAGRAM OF ONE LINK IN THE FOOD CHAIN

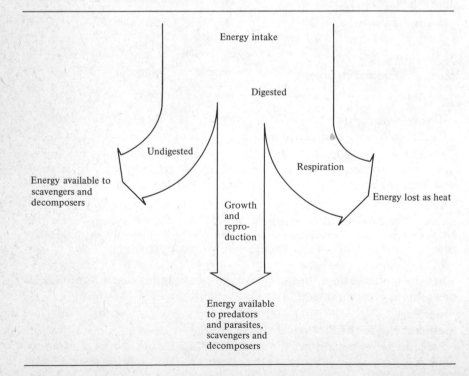

undigested material is excreted and becomes food for bacteria and fungi that are specialized to digest and assimilate these materials. The fraction of the food energy which is digested varies between 10 and 80 percent. Generally, animal tissues are assimilated with efficiencies of 60 percent or more, most leafy vegetables at 30–40 percent and wood at 10–20 percent efficiency.

Material that is digested is metabolized to provide energy for life processes or is incorporated into animal tissue. The metabolic or respired energy is eventually converted to unusable heat energy. The rest of the energy in the digested food is available for growth and reproduction, that is, for building more animal tissue. In general, about 10 percent of the chemical energy in the food consumed is stored as chemical energy in the molecules of the new tissues produced during growth and reproduction (Figure 4–2). The percent tends to be lower for warm-blooded animals, since their high level of activity requires energy that might otherwise have been used for growth and reproduction. For inactive, cold-blooded animals that eat highly digestible food, as much as a third of the energy in the food consumed may be stored in high energy molecules in new tissue.

Only the energy stored during growth and reproduction of an animal is available to a predator that eats the animal. As a result, people who eat cows can obtain less than one-fifth of the energy that was stored in the food the cows ate. Put another way, the corn fed to a cow would supply the energy requirements for at least five times as many people if it were fed to the people directly rather than via an inefficient converter, the cow. Although direct consumption of the corn would provide energy more efficiently, the corn has inadequate proportions of some essential amino acids and would require supplementation to provide a nutritionally adequate diet. Methods of achieving this are discussed in Chapter 8.

Energy Transfer in Food Chains Is Inefficient

A simple predatory food chain is the one just discussed: corn is eaten by cows which are eaten by people. A more typically complex predatory food chain is illustrated in Figure 7–1 (see pg. 70). In any such food chain, less energy is available to the carnivore (man) than to the herbivore (cow), since the herbivore stores only a small fraction of the energy available in the food it eats. Since the carnivores, like the herbivores, fail to digest some of the food they eat, and during metabolic processes convert some of the useful chemical energy in their digested food to relatively unusable heat energy, there is less energy stored in the carnivore population than in the herbivore population. Thus, very generally, the higher an animal is in the food chain, the less the energy

Figure 4–2 ENERGY FLOW FOR DIFFERENT KINDS OF ANIMALS

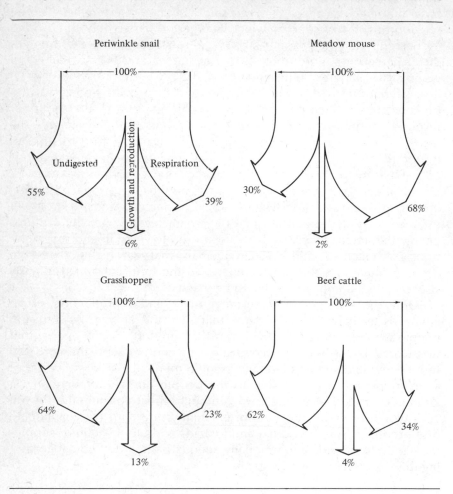

Active, warm-blooded animals like the meadow mouse tend to have high respiration. Grass eaters like the cow and grasshopper are unable to digest much of the food they eat. If cows are fed corn rather than grass, digestion is more complete and the growth and assimilation efficiency may exceed 10 percent.

Source: Data are from Golley, F. B. 1960. Energy dynamics of a food chain of an old-field community. *Ecological Monographs 30:* 187–206; Odum, E. P. and A. E. Smalley. 1959. Comparison of population energy flow of a herbivorous and a deposit-feeding invertebrate in a salt marsh ecosystem. *P.N.A.S. 45:* 617–622; and Phillipson, J. 1966. *Ecological Energetics.* London: Edward Arnold and Co.

available to him, because more of the energy originally captured by plants has been lost by inefficient intermediates. Because of this, man can obtain a larger proportion of the total productivity of the earth by eating plants than by eating animals. In most poor countries, this ecological principle is well-embodied in the prevalent diets, which consist predominantly of grain or tubers.

When man can neither consume nor efficiently replace natural primary producers, the wisest policy may be to harvest higher levels in the food chain. For example, the only plants that will grow on much dry and hilly land are leaves and grasses with too much cellulose for us to digest. Ruminants, such as cows and sheep, have bacteria and protozoa in their stomachs which can convert this cellulose to food we can digest. In such regions, the food available to humans is increased by raising cows and sheep. Another case in which it is more practicable to eat animals, despite the losses due to food chain ineffi-ciency, is the phytoplankton, the small floating plants in oceans and lakes. These are difficult to harvest profitably, and to a large extent indigestible for humans. These plants are naturally converted by way of the food chain to forms we can use, namely fish and aquatic mam-mals. Most of the fish large enough for commercial fishing are carni-vores. Using 10 percent as a rough estimate of the efficiency of energy transfer at each step in the food chain, we calculate that roughly $1/10 \times 1/10 = 1/100$ of marine plant productivity is available to people who eat carnivorous fish. Even less of the total productivity is available if we eat carnivorous fish which prey on other carnivores rather than on herbivores. This is one reason why man harvests less than 3 percent of his food from the sea, although nearly a third of the earth's primary production occurs in the sea.

We turn now from a discussion of the predatory part of the food chain (in which food is eaten by progressively larger consumers) to a discussion of the decomposer or detritus part of the food chain. A substantial amount of food is not "eaten" in the strict sense but is "decomposed" by bacteria, and fungi such as mushrooms. This path of the food chain usually begins with the death of organisms, or parts of organisms (shedding of leaves or hair, for example) or with food that cannot be digested and merely passes through the digestive tract of an animal. Energy that enters the detritus segment of the food chain may find its way back into the predator segments because microorganisms are eaten by very small predators, which are food for slightly larger predators, and so on.

Surveys have shown that herbivores consume only about 10 per-cent of green leaves in forests, or 1.5–2.5 percent of total net produc-tivity. The rest of the plant net productivity is processed as detritus. Man obtains little food either directly or indirectly from the detritus segment of the food chain. Bacteria have high respiratory rates, so much of the energy in their food is released as heat and little is stored in tissue where it would be available to predators. Furthermore, bacteria are so small that they are difficult to harvest. On the other hand, the other major class of decomposers, the fungi, might become an increasingly important source of food. Mushrooms farmed on sewage and other wastes could serve to reclaim a useful proportion of high energy molecules and proteins in the wastes and convert them to edible material. A less direct contribution of the decomposers to our food production is their activity in releasing mineral nutrients for plant growth, a function we will describe in the next chapter.

Finally, we wish to emphasize that total world plant productivity does not place any very immediate limits on the human population that can be supported. The average person consumes less than 2400 Calories daily or 876,000 Calories annually. Thus, the 3.6 billion people in the world consume about 3.1 million billion Calories annually. This is less than 1 percent of terrestrial plant productivity and less than a tenth of the caloric content of plants grown on agricultural land (Table 4–1). There are several reasons why such a small portion of agricultural productivity is consumed by humans. Insects, rodents and birds eat a significant fraction of agricultural produce. Some primary production is consumed by humans only after inefficient conversion by domesticated animals. For grain and vegetable products that are consumed directly, much of the plant is inedible.

In conclusion, the limited amount of sun's energy arriving each year at the earth's surface does not set any very immediate limits on food production for humans. Some of the inefficiences in utilizing the sun's energy seem to be unavoidable consequences of properties of the physical world, and others are pervasive properties of biological organisms. But many of the inefficiencies in energy use could be changed by human effort, for example by increasing nutrients in some bodies of water and by watering the desert, by breeding plants to have a higher proportion of edible matter and to capture more of the sunlight incident on them (as in the new breeds of the Green Revolution), and by eating more plants and less meat to eliminate intervening inefficient energy conversion by animals.

BIBLIOGRAPHY

Cloud, P. E., Jr., ed. 1969. *Resources and Man.* San Francisco: W. H. Freeman and Company [contains excellent discussions and recommendations regarding man's prospects for food, mineral and energy resources].

Kormondy, E. T. 1969. *Concepts of Ecology.* Englewood Cliffs: Prentice-Hall, Inc. [a good introduction to basic ecological principles].

Phillipson, J. 1966. *Ecological Energetics.* London: Edward Arnold and Co. [a brief, readable introduction to the basic patterns of primary production, consumption and decomposition in the ecosystem].

Ryther, J. J. H. 1969.   Photosynthesis and fish production in the sea. *Science*
    166: 72–76.
Scientific American.   September, 1970.   The Biosphere [a useful issue with
    11 articles on energy, nutrient cycling and human ecology].

chapter 5

nutrient cycles

We have seen that chemical energy is not retained in the ecosystem, but rather is degraded to heat energy, which cannot be used by life processes and which is eventually radiated back out into space. The nutrients which form the substance of life behave much differently. Unlike energy, which the sun continuously provides, nutrients are forever limited to those now present near the surface of the earth. Minerals and other required substances cannot be permanently removed from the pool of available nutrients without adverse effects on the organic productivity of the earth. A well-functioning ecosystem must recycle these nutrients and return them to a form in which they are once again available for use by plants. Natural biological communities fulfill this requirement. Nutrients are alternately incorporated into living matter by green plants, and released by metabolic breakdown processes primarily in animals and microorganisms.

Carbon and oxygen may be recycled quickly through the complementary processes of photosynthesis and respiration Figure 2–1, pg. 11). Each year photosynthesis in land plants produces oxygen equal to about one ten-thousandth of the total oxygen in the atmosphere, so the global pool of oxygen is quite large relative to the rate of recycling.

Compounds containing most of the other elements—nitrogen, phosphorus, sulfur and so on—are decomposed in steps by specialized microorganisms. Ecologists often state that the role of these "decomposer" organisms is to make nutrients available for plant growth. However, it must be understood that bacteria decompose certain organic compounds for the same purpose that animals decompose carbon compounds: to release energy for use in their own metabolic processes. We will expand upon this in the discussion of some specific cycles.

In this chapter we will consider the cycles of three nutrients, carbon, nitrogen and phosphorus, on a world scale. These are, next to hydrogen and oxygen, the most abundant elements in living tissues. Carbon, nitrogen and phosphorus are probably more important determinants of the abundance of plant growth than any other nutrients. Water, another crucial factor limiting plant growth, will be discussed in the next chapter.

The Carbon Cycle

The carbon cycle is presented diagrammatically in Figure 5–1. Its basic features include three major pools of carbon near the surface of the earth: (a) carbon compounds in living organisms and dead organic matter, (b) carbon dioxide in the atmosphere and dissolved in the oceans and (c) calcium carbonate sediments (limestones). The latter pool is very large but becomes available for life processes at a very slow rate through erosion.

Figure 5–1 THE CARBON CYCLE

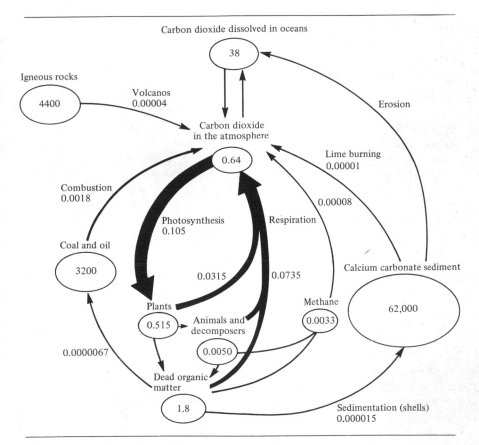

All values are in billion billion grams of carbon and rates are per year. Worldwide estimates such as these may easily err by a factor of 2, but the data are sufficiently accurate to give a good idea of which stores and processes are quantitatively most important.

Source: Data primarily from H. J. M. Bowen. 1966. *Trace Elements in Biochemistry.* New York: Academic Press, Inc. Adapted with permission.

Living systems annually cycle about 0.25 to 0.3 percent of the carbon available in the atmosphere and the oceans; hence the total pool is recycled every three to four hundred years. The exchange of carbon between the atmosphere and the oceans is not rapid, and over short periods they may be considered as separate pools. The atmospheric pool of carbon dioxide is much smaller relative to terrestrial plant production than is the oceanic pool relative to marine plant production. Hence atmospheric carbon dioxide is recycled much more rapidly, on the average after only eight years in the atmosphere. The average time in the atmosphere can be calculated as follows: terrestrial net productivity is 490 million billion Calories per year (Table 4–1, pg. 33) which equals 110 million billion dry grams of plant matter or about 55 million billion grams of carbon incorporated into growing plants; adding 40 percent for respiratory losses by plants gives 77 million billion grams of carbon or about 12 percent of atmospheric carbon incorporated by photosynthesis yearly, which is equivalent to an average lifetime of eight years for atmospheric carbon dioxide.

During many periods of the earth's history, a portion of organic production has not been returned to carbon dioxide. For millions of years organic sediments were laid down at the bottoms of shallow seas under conditions which did not permit total decomposition. This organic matter gradually changed into the beds of coal and oil, from which we are now recovering the chemical energy that decomposers were not able to exploit millions of years ago. These deposits contain approximately 3200 billion billion grams of carbon, about 50,000 times the total net annual productivity of the earth at the present time. Since only a relatively small percent of the earth's productivity at any one time was ever deposited in coal and oil-forming sediments, the accumulation of fossil fuels required many millions of years.

Our combustion of coal, oil and gas burns these carbon reserves at a rate of about five million billion grams per year, which adds carbon dioxide at about 2 percent the rate of respiration of plants, animals and microorganisms. The excess production of carbon dioxide since the industrial revolution has caused the content of carbon dioxide in the air to rise about 10 percent: from 290 to 330 parts per million, between 1900 and 1960. The effect of this change is not clear, but many scientists are worried that it will increase the "greenhouse effect," or the retention of heat in the atmosphere, and thus raise the temperature of the earth. Carbon dioxide and glass behave similarly in that they are transparent to visible light but reflect infrared radiation. In a greenhouse, light enters through the glass roof and is absorbed by the plants and soil. The absorbed light is converted to heat which is then reradiated as infrared light. But since this cannot pass back through the glass, it is retained in the greenhouse and increases the temperature of the air. Carbon dioxide in the atmosphere works in the same way. If a temperature rise is caused by the increased carbon dioxide, it could increase the melting of the great reserves of ice on the surface of the earth, thus raise ocean levels and flood many coastal regions. Conversely, the tremendous amounts of particulate matter which our combustion processes are pouring into the atmosphere may increase the reflection of sunlight by the atmosphere, and thus reduce the temperature of the earth by reducing the amount of sunlight that reaches the earth. Scientists have not yet accurately predicted future trends.

The Nitrogen Cycle

The nitrogen cycle is illustrated in Figure 5–2. Nitrogen is a constituent of organic molecules such as proteins and DNA. Animals, fungi and bacteria can metabolize these molecules for energy and excrete the nitrogen from them in the form of ammonia or chemically related compounds such as urea. Although relatively little energy is available from the ammonia, some bacteria are specialized to obtain energy by metabolizing ammonia to nitrite, and others obtain energy by metabolizing nitrite to nitrate.

Plants can absorb nitrate and ammonium from the soil water and can incorporate nitrogen from these compounds into organic molecules like protein. The largest pool of nitrogen is the gaseous nitrogen in the atmosphere, but this molecular nitrogen cannot be used by most plants. Only certain kinds of bacteria and blue-green algae can "fix" nitrogen from the atmosphere and convert it to organic forms. Although energetically expensive, nitrogen fixation is advantageous to a plant in soils and waters that are deficient in nitrates or ammonium. It is difficult to measure how rapidly nitrogen fixation occurs, but it probably approaches the rate at which nitrates are converted to nitrogen gas or about one-hundredth of the total nitrogen incorporation by plants. Nitrogen fixation has assumed great importance in modern agriculture as a natural method of increasing the nitrogen content of soils. Leguminous plants (peas and alfalfa, for example) contain in their roots bacteria that fix nitrogen and produce a net increase in usable soil nitrogen. Alfalfa crops are frequently rotated with other crops such as corn in order to maintain soil fertility. Nitrogen-fixing blue-green algae that grow in rice paddies serve to increase the usable nitrogen available to the rice plants.

Farmers use several other methods to restore nitrates to cropland soil. For example, ammonia or nitrates are a major component of most

Figure 5–2 THE NITROGEN CYCLE

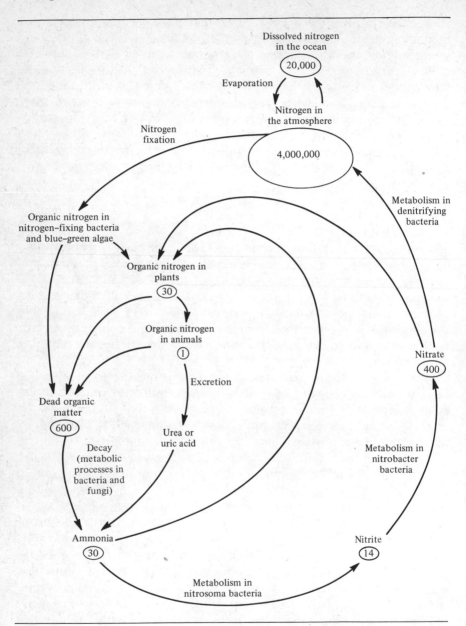

The numbers indicate approximately how much nitrogen there is in each form (in million billion grams). Very little is known about the rates of nitrogen transfer. Only the major processes in the natural, biological nitrogen cycle are shown.

Several human activities have a major impact on the nitrogen cycle. Fertilizer factories remove nitrogen from the air and incorporate it in ammonium and nitrate compounds that are spread on croplands. Some of the nitrogen in the fertilizer returns to the air, by evaporation of ammonia or by wind erosion of soil particles to which fertilizer has adhered. When dust artificial fertilizers. One pound of fertilizer can add enough of scarce nutrients to support production of ten additional pounds of grain, for the new breeds used in the Green Revolution. It is necessary to use fertilizers to restore nitrogen content of the soil artificially because people do not generally return their wastes and their bodies to their cropland, but rather flush much of their garbage and excreta into rivers. This disrupts the local nitrogen cycle, causing enrichment of the waters and impoverishment of the land. The amount of nitrogen removed by harvest from croplands is greater than the nitrogen in the food actually eaten by humans, and less than that in the total plant growth on agricultural land. On this basis, we can estimate that the nitrogen removed from croplands worldwide must be between 2 and 20 times as much as is added in fertilizers. The actual nitrogen restored to the soil by fertilizers is even less, since roughly a third of the nitrogen in artificial fertilizer is washed into streams or lost to the air before it can be taken up by growing plants. The inadequate return of nitrogen to the soil is not due to any scarcity of raw materials, since nitrogenous fertilizers are manufactured from abundant raw materials such as the nitrogen in the air. There is even unused manufacturing capacity at the present time, but farmers whose land is being depleted of nitrogen lack the resources to pay for the fertilizer that the idle equipment could produce.

Other means of restoring nitrogen to cropland more nearly mimic the natural nitrogen cycle and have a variety of advantages over the use of manufactured fertilizers. These alternatives all involve the return of dead and decaying material to the soil. As decay proceeds, nutrients are released slowly and steadily so that most of them are absorbed promptly by growing plants and are not washed out of the soil by rainwater runoff. Furthermore, the decaying material gives the soil a more open, porous texture which permits easier absorption

---

Figure 5–2   (continued)

settles out of the air and when rain falls with dissolved ammonia, some of the nitrogen is returned to the soil or to the oceans. Human activity speeds up the flow of nitrogen from land to water in two ways. First, we take nitrogen-containing food from the land and return nitrogen-containing excretory wastes and garbage to the rivers. Second, the nitrogen in fertilizer tends to be washed into rivers rather rapidly because cultivation of a field often increases soil erosion, and because fertilizer is typically applied in large, infrequent loads which cannot be absorbed immediately by the plants. This fertilizer is easily washed out of the soil, especially when the soil lacks decaying organic material that could adsorb the mineral nutrients.

Source: Data primarily from H. J. M. Bowen. 1966. *Trace Elements in Biochemistry.* New York: Academic Press, Inc. Adapted with permission. Supplemented by C. C. Delwiche. 1970. The Nitrogen Cycle, *Scientific American,* September, pp. 137–146.

of water and oxygen. The increased supply of oxygen for the roots enhances the uptake of mineral nutrients, since the oxygen is needed for the metabolic processes which supply the energy to pump mineral nutrients into the plant. A time-honored practice with all these advantages is the use of barnyard manure as fertilizer. A variety of techniques for decontaminating and concentrating sewage for use as fertilizer have been employed in places like Taiwan and Chicago and have the advantage that they prevent overfertilization of the rivers at the same time that they fertilize the soil. (See the section on eutrophication that follows on pg. 47.)

The Phosphorus Cycle

Phosphorus, like nitrogen and carbon, is required by man in substantial amounts. Phosphorus is a major constituent of DNA, the molecule which carries the genetic code. It is also incorporated into structural lipids which are used to build cell membranes, and it is important in the energy transfer systems of the cell. Phosphorus salts form a major component of bones and teeth. Phosphorus is incorporated at about one-tenth the amount of nitrogen in the synthesis of protoplasm.

Phosphorus is returned to inorganic pools by bacterial decomposition of dead organic matter and by excretion of phosphate salts along with other metabolic wastes. The phosphorus cycle is simpler than the nitrogen cycle, largely because biological decomposition requires only one step which is completed by phosphatizing bacteria.

Under certain conditions phosphates do not dissolve in water, but rather precipitate to form sediments which are not immediately available to the ecosystem. These sediments may eventually form phosphate rock, which is returned naturally to the ecosystem through mountain building and erosion. Phosphate rocks also provide the raw materials for fertilizers and for various chemical products, particularly detergents. Phosphate reserves are large enough to supply abundant raw materials for these uses for many centuries into the future.

The problem with phosphate is primarily one of disposal rather than supply. Through sewage and agricultural runoff, detergents and fertilizers contribute large quantities of phosphorus to the rivers and lakes of some regions in industrial countries. The largest contribution of phosphates comes from detergents and other products in the sewage. Runoff from cultivated agricultural lands is about one-fifth the contribution of sewage wastes. Although man's contribution of phosphorus to fresh waters in the United States is less than one-thousandth of that contributed by natural erosion, the concentration of man's imputs may produce a substantial effect locally. The phosphorus concentration in streams flowing through forested areas is roughly one-tenth of the phosphorus concentration in streams flowing past agricultural lands or urban areas.

Eutrophication

By augmenting the natural flow of nutrients into rivers and lakes through the disposal of sewage from urban areas and the runoff of fertilizers from croplands, man has upset natural nutrient cycles and substantially altered some ecosystems. Our fertilization of fresh waters in the United States has greatly increased the rate of "eutrophication" of some of our lakes. Eutrophic literally means "well-nourished." Natural bodies of water may be classified between two extreme types. On the one hand, oligotrophic lakes are poor in nutrients and harbor little plant and animal life; but they have clear water and are aesthetically pleasing. At the other extreme are the eutrophic lakes which are rich in nutrients and support large amounts of natural life. These lakes often are excellent fisheries, but occasionally their high productivity results in rapid algal growths, called "blooms." During an algal bloom, algae often grow more rapidly than they can be consumed by fish and other herbivores. This results in masses of decaying plants which frequently produce foul odors and are aesthetically undesirable. Algal blooms may also indirectly lead to fish die-offs. The bacteria which consume the dead algae at the end of a bloom deplete the water of the oxygen required by the fish. The rich growth of algae in the surface layers of eutrophic lakes prevents the penetration of light to the depths of the lake, and thus prevents photosynthetic activity that could replenish the oxygen consumed in the bacterial decomposition of dead organic matter. Therefore, the depths of eutrophic lakes are frequently devoid of oxygen and cannot support fish and other animal life.

Eutrophication is a natural process which all lakes pass through during their life history. Lakes, after all, are sedimentation basins that eventually fill up and become marshes, then fields, and finally forested areas. During the process of eutrophication, organic materials which are washed into the lake settle to the bottom, and nutrients in them are released by bacteria and decomposer organisms. The nutrient-enriched waters in turn support heavy growths of plant and animal life. The natural process of eutrophication is very slow, generally occurring over thousands of years, and even longer for some lakes. This is in contrast to the rapid changes man's activities may cause. One example, the eutrophication of the Great Lakes, is described in Box 5–1.

The most bothersome aspect of eutrophication is the occasional immense growth of algae and rooted vegetation which clogs boating channels, makes water "mucky" and undesirable for swimming and

Box 5–1 **EUTROPHICATION OF GREAT LAKES**

LAKE	VOLUME OF WATER (CUBIC MILES)	DRAIN-AGE AREA (SQUARE MILES)	DRAIN-AGE AREA PER VOLUME	DISSOLVED SOLIDS (PARTS PER MILLION) 1900	DISSOLVED SOLIDS (PARTS PER MILLION) 1960	DISSOLVED OXYGEN 1960 (PERCENT OF SATURATION)
Superior	2935	81,000	27.6	60	60	100, all depths
Huron	849	74,000	88.2	105	110	100, all depths
Michigan	1180	67,900	57.5	130	150	Near 100, all depths
Ontario	393	32,100	81.7	140	185	50–60, winter
Erie	116	40,000	345.0	140	180	10–50

Source: Data from A. M. Beeton, "Eutrophication of the St. Lawrence Great Lakes," *Limnology and Oceanography, 10:* 240–54 (1965).

Because of man's activities, dissolved nutrients have increased in Lakes Michigan, Ontario and Erie since the turn of the century. For its volume, Lake Erie receives the greatest amount of runoff of the five lakes; it has several major cities discharging sewage at its edge; and consequently it has a very high concentration of dissolved nutrients. Lakes Superior and Huron, besides having smaller drainage basins relative to their volumes, are surrounded to a large extent, particularly in Canada, by forested lands which release relatively small amounts of nutrients from their soils. Lake Ontario owes most of its pollution to the flow of water into it from Lake Erie. Lake Michigan is also relatively rich among the lakes because of its proximity to the large metropolitan area of Chicago and the agricultural areas of Michigan and Wisconsin.

Where dissolved solids are high, there is more bacterial decay and therefore less dissolved oxygen. Lake Erie, the most eutrophic of the five Great Lakes, is inhabited primarily by perch, smelt and carp, all characteristic of rich waters with low oxygen content. The dominant fish of Lakes Superior, Huron and Michigan belong to the salmonid group which is characteristic of clear waters. Several kinds of commercially important fish: lake herring, whitefish, sauger, walleyes and pike, have all but disappeared from Lake Erie during this century. Because other species have replaced them, the total fish catch has not decreased, but the new species: carp, yellow perch and smelt, are considered to be less desirable.

This change in fish, the heavy growth of algae stimulated by abundant nutrients, and the large amount of decaying matter are a most undesirable set of changes for Lake Erie. These changes will be reversed only slowly, even with effective programs to reduce the flow of sewage and nutrients from agricultural lands into Lake Erie. Large deposits of organic matter on the bottom of the lake can be expected to continue to provide nutrients for much algal growth and bacterial decay even after the inflow of nutrients is stopped.

---

often results in foul-smelling mats of decaying organisms. Attempts to control this problem have taken several approaches. One has been to treat the symptoms by destroying the vegetation itself. This is usually accomplished with copper sulfate for algal control and sodium arsenate for rooted plants. Of course, both poisons are very toxic and affect other life in the water as well. In addition, the use of such poisons produces quantities of dead vegetation which are then consumed by bacteria, which deplete dissolved oxygen and may create unpleasant odors. A second approach is to harvest the plant growth, thereby removing large amounts of nutrients in the form of plant tissues. Mechanical harvesting of microscopic phytoplankton is very expensive and harvested vegetation presents a difficult disposal problem in some areas. A more promising approach is to import animals that feed on aquatic plants. For example, alligator weed has been controlled in parts of Florida by flea beetles which were imported from Argentina.

In many situations, the soundest approach will be to eliminate the sources of nutrients to rivers and lakes by processing sewage and using it to fertilize croplands, or by reducing the use of artificial fertilizers, detergents and other products that introduce large quantities of nutrients to our waters. A considerable controversy has arisen as to which inflows are most important to control. In particular, some ecologists have accused the phosphates in detergents of being the chief villain in eutrophication, while other researchers (especially those employed in the chemical industry) have worked to exculpate phosphates.

To approach this problem, we must first ask: what nutrient is limiting for aquatic plant growth? If algae grow until they have used up all the available phosphates, then phosphate is the limiting nutrient. If more phosphates are added, then more algae should grow, since other nutrients and sunlight are presumed to be available in excess. Phosphate does appear to be the limiting nutrient in many lakes, especially where there are blue-green algae which can convert the abundant dissolved nitrogen from the air into nitrogen compounds which plants can use. On the other hand, in estuaries and other coastal waters, there are apparently very few nitrogen-fixing blue-green algae, and nitrate is often the limiting nutrient.

In very eutrophic lakes, high phosphate may support so much algal growth that other nutrients may become limiting. For example, in algal blooms, rapid photosynthesis sometimes depletes the supply of dissolved carbon dioxide. Bacterial metabolism of organic compounds in sewage enriches the supply of carbon dioxide and will thus enhance algal growth in these situations. Phosphate is sometimes the limiting nutrient for the bacteria which are supplying the carbon dioxide which is limiting for algal growth. In this situation additions of phosphate will indirectly increase algal growth.

Where phosphate is directly or indirectly the limiting nutrient for plant growth, it is obvious that reductions in phosphate will reduce eutrophication. Even where phosphate is not now the limiting nutrient, it may be advisable to control plant growth by reducing phosphate sufficiently so that it becomes the limiting nutrient. Phosphorus may be a particularly easy nutrient to control since, unlike nitrogen and carbon, it does not exist in gaseous form and therefore control programs need not be concerned with atmospheric concentrations. Since detergents supply roughly one-third of the phosphates entering our waters, one reasonable control measure would be the reduction of phosphates in detergents, as has already been required in Canada and in some areas of the United States. It should be noted, however, that the substitutes proposed by industry to replace phosphates in detergents may have more serious consequences for the environment and human health than the phosphates they replace. For example, nitrilotriacetic acid, or NTA, may be converted to nitrosamines which are known to be carcinogenic in some cases. Furthermore, NTA and its degradation products contain nitrogen which may aggravate eutrophication in coastal waters where nitrate is the limiting nutrient.

Nutrient Cycles and Tropical Agriculture

A large portion of the world's land lies within the tropics. It seems contradictory that the natural vegetation of the tropics, especially of the humid areas, is the most productive on earth (see Table 4–1, pg. 33), and yet the inhabitants of the tropics are among the most poorly nourished in the world. Why is it that the tropics fail to produce the food required to feed its peoples? Part of the reason is that the tropical climate poses special difficulties for agriculture, and relatively little research has been done to develop the technology to overcome these difficulties. The paucity of research is aggravated by the diversity of conditions within the tropics, and consequent differences in technology needed. Our discussion does not, for the most part, deal with this diversity, but rather generalizes about the equatorial forest regions of West Africa.

Forest soils in the tropics differ from those in temperate zones because the high temperatures result in rapid decomposition of dead organic material throughout the year. Rapid decay results in rapid release of mineral nutrients, most of which are absorbed promptly by the forest plants. Because of the rapid decomposition and rapid uptake of mineral nutrients, relatively less of the nutrients are in the soil and relatively more are in the vegetation in tropical forests, as compared to temperate forests. When the land is cleared, burning of the cleared vegetation will return most of the nutrients from the plants to the soil, but nitrogen is lost in the form of gaseous nitrogen oxides. After clearing, the soil is exposed directly to strong sunlight which hastens decay and the release of nutrients in soluble form. The soil is also exposed directly to heavy rainfall which rapidly leaches soluble nutrients from the soil. Low initial levels of nitrogen in the soil combined with rapid decomposition and leaching mean that there is not enough nitrogen for good crops, especially for protein-rich crops. After clearing, some types of tropical soils are even baked into cement-hard surfaces called laterites. Laterite may be impossible to cultivate, and weathering processes and the natural vegetation may require many centuries to restore the soils to their original condition.

Through much of the tropics, these problems are solved by the indigenous "slash-and-burn" method of agriculture. The forest is cleared and burned in small patches and rapidly growing crops are planted first so that exposure of the soil is minimized and mineral nutrients are quickly absorbed into living plants where they cannot be washed away. After about three years of use the land is abandoned for about ten years while the forest regrows. During the long fallow period between crops, nitrate content is restored by nitrogen-fixing bacteria, and the trees' tap roots pull up minerals such as phosphorus from deep subsoil layers to surface layers. The primary disadvantage to this method is that so little of the land can be used for crops in any given year, because of the long fallow period. If population increases and the land must be cultivated more frequently, then the forest fallow may be replaced by grass, especially in dry regions (Chapter 15). The land then becomes less fertile and more difficult to cultivate.

One alternative is to grow perennial crops, such as fruit trees and coffee, which do not require frequent land clearing. Perennial crops, however, rarely achieve the level of food productivity exhibited by temperate annuals such as wheat and corn. Another alternative is the use of fertilizers, mulches and other techniques to maintain high soil fertility with continuous cropping. Such techniques have been successfully used in the tropics (Table 5–1) but are not yet widespread partly because tropical farmers often lack the resources to purchase fertilizers and other materials, and partly because the necessary

51

research to develop techniques appropriate to particular regions has in most cases not been done yet.

Table 5–1 CONTRIBUTION OF MULCH AND FERTILIZER TO MAINTENANCE OF SOIL FERTILITY

| | CLEAN WEEDED | | MULCHED | |
year	*without fertilizer*	*fertilized since 1953*	*without fertilizer*	*fertilized since 1953*
1947–1948	1032	—	1127	—
1953–1954	200	440	1117	1434
1955–1956	186	797	1464	1977
1956–1957	124	706	986	1344

These plots in the Congo were continuously planted to cotton, and soil fertility has been estimated in terms of cotton yield (given in kilograms of harvested cotton per hectare). One plot had no treatment; one had cut grasses mulched into the soil; one received inorganic fertilizer containing 150 kg. of bicalcium phosphate, 250 kg. of sodium nitrate and 50 kg. of potassium sulphate per hectare per year after 1953; and one had both fertilizer and mulching. The decaying material in mulches adsorbs soil nutrients so they are not washed out of the soil and increases soil porosity so water and oxygen percolate in to plant roots more readily and yields are improved. The high productivity in 1955–1956 was probably due to unusually favorable climate in that year.

Source: From F. Jurion and J. Henry, *Can Primitive Farming Be Modernized?* (Congo: National Institute for Agricultural Studies, 1969). Reprinted by permission of the Royal Library of Belgium.

BIBLIOGRAPHY

Commoner, B. 1970. Threats to the integrity of the nitrogen cycle: nitrogen compounds in soil, water, atmosphere and precipitation. S. F. Singer, ed. *Global Effects of Environmental Pollution.* New York: Springer-Verlag. pp. 70–95.

Jurion, F. and J. Henry. 1969. *Can Primitive Farming Be Modernized?* National Institute for Agricultural Studies, Congo [re tropical agriculture].

Likens, G. E., ed. 1972. *Nutrients and Eutrophication, Symposium Volume 1.* Lawrence, Kansas: American Society of Limnology and Oceanography, Allen Press.

Ovington, T. D. 1965. Organic production, turnover, and mineral cycling in woodlands. *Biological Reviews 40:* 295–336.

Whittaker, R. H. 1970. *Communities and Ecosystems.* New York:Crowell-Collier and Macmillan [good general discussion of mineral cycles].

chapter 6

water

Plants and animals are most abundant and diverse in the humid tropics where water is plentiful; life is sparse or absent in arid desert regions. Like other living organisms, we require water to maintain proper physiological function and to flush the toxic waste products of metabolism out of our bodies. We use even larger quantities of water for our agriculture and industry. Water is often reused over and over again: for the generation of electric power, for recreation, for human consumption, for industry, for irrigation.

If water could be reused indefinitely, then there would be no reason to worry about inadequate water supplies. However, two factors limit the reuse of water. First, in many situations water is used for flushing out wastes, so the water leaves the user carrying contaminants that may make it unsuitable for other uses. In these situations reuse depends on cleaning the contaminants out of the water. The second major factor which limits recycling of water is evaporation. A large proportion of the water used in irrigation, for example, is transpired (that is, evaporated) by plants and escapes as water vapor to the atmosphere. This water is eventually returned to lakes and rivers by precipitation, but this process is slow and does not make up the local and immediate losses due to the evaporation. Thus evaporation does not prevent recycling, but it does slow down the recycling and returns water to different locations from where it was lost.

On the other hand, it should be remembered that evaporation and precipitation processes have a useful side, since evaporation leaves most contaminants behind and precipitation provides a constant supply of fresh, clean water. Indeed, our basic source of fresh water is provided by evaporation and precipitation which move water from the abundant but salty reservoir, the oceans, to our land and rivers. When we want to use water at a rate faster than it is supplied by this natural cycle, we must either clean water for reuse or substitute a man-made process (desalinization) for the evaporation–precipitation part of the natural cycle. Note that the rate of supply of fresh water, not the total quantity of water, is crucial. In this chapter we will describe water use relative to supply for the United States, water pollutants and methods for removing them, and finally the potential usefulness of desalinization processes.

53

Water Use: The United States

In Table 6–1 we show how water is used in the United States. Water use in hydroelectric power plants is not included since usage is brief

Table 6–1 THE USE OF WATER IN THE UNITED STATES
IN 1960

USE	BILLIONS OF GALLONS PER DAY
Domestic	11
Irrigation and livestock	112
Industrial	145
Commercial	4
Public	4
TOTAL	275

Source: Data are from the *United States Water Atlas* for 1960 prepared by the Water Information Center, Inc.

Table 6–2 WATER REQUIREMENTS FOR THE PRODUCTION
OF VARIOUS FOOD PRODUCTS

PRODUCTS	FOOD VALUE (CALORIES PER POUND)	PERCENT WATER	WATER REQUIREMENTS *pounds of water per pound of food*	*gallons per 1000 Calories*
Wheat	1480	11–14	500–760	40–60
Maize (corn)	1580	74	690	83
Potato	279	80	75	32
Tomato	95	94	72	91
Orange	131	85	275	250
Meat	1350	55	20,000–50,000	1850–4400
Milk	300	87	4200	1700

One gallon of water weighs 8.32 pounds.

Source: Data from G. Young, "Dry Lands and Desalted Water," *Science 167:* 339–343 (1970); P. Ehrlich and A. Ehrlich, *Population, Resources, Environment* (San Francisco: W. H. Freeman and Company, 1970); and U.S. Department of Agriculture *Home and Garden Bulletin* No. 72.

and passage through the turbines of a hydroelectric power-generating plant has relatively little effect on the quality of the water. Hydroelectric power plants use more water—two trillion gallons per day—than all other economic sectors put together.

We actually drink only a small proportion of the total domestic water supply, about two quarts (0.5 gallon) per person per day, compared to our per capita home consumption of 40 to 60 gallons per day. Most of the water is used for bathing, washing, flushing wastes, and watering lawns and gardens.

Agricultural production requires vast amounts of water to satisfy the rapid evaporative losses of plants. Nearly 40 percent of water use is for irrigation. Crops require anywhere from 75 pounds of water per pound of fresh yield (potatoes) to about 750 pounds (wheat and most other grains) to more than 2000 pounds (rice). It is perhaps more significant to compare water requirements with respect to the energy produced for human consumption. Potatoes are one of the best crops from the standpoint of water; grains require twice as much water per Calorie of food energy (Table 6–2). Animal products such as meat and milk require much more water per pound of product because of the extra link in the food chain. Thus, a steer may eat 30 pounds of alfalfa per day which requires 24,000 pounds of water to produce. If the steer is butchered at the age of two years and produces 700 pounds of meat, the total water required is 24,000 pounds times 730 days divided by 700 pounds of meat, or about 25,000 pounds of water per pound of meat. To produce a quart of milk requires about 1000 gallons of water. Similarly, water requirements are much higher for animal products like butter or wool and leather than for plant products like margarine or cotton. Thus, consumption of plant products instead of animal products places less strain on agricultural water supplies and may be a critical factor in regions with low rainfall.

Industrial consumption of water is very high. It is difficult to obtain estimates of the water used to produce manufactured products. Three large chemical plants from which we were able to obtain information used 3, 11, and 112 pounds of water per pound of chemical product. Paul and Anne Ehrlich estimate that the production of one automobile requires the use of at least 100,000 gallons of water. If the average automobile weighs 3300 pounds, water use would be 30 gallons (250 pounds) of water per pound of final product.

The per capita consumption of water in the United States has risen from about 500 gallons per person per day at the turn of the century to more than 1300 gallons per person per day at the present time (excluding water used for hydroelectric power). During the same period the population of the United States increased from 80 million to 210 million. Thus population growth and increased consumption per capita contributed about equally to the increase in total water use. Population growth is likely to be slower in the future (Chapter 17), while per capita use will probably continue to rise rapidly as more of our food is grown under irrigation and as we use more and more manufactured products.

Is water likely to be a limiting factor on the growth of the population of the United States? About 1.3 trillion gallons per day run off the land; the rest is lost through evaporation and transpiration. Since per capita water use is presently 1300 gallons per day, the total runoff should support about a billion people at the present rate of use, about five times the present population. Higher estimates result if we take into account the fact that water may be used repeatedly. On the other hand, estimates of supportable population are reduced when we consider that per capita consumption of water is likely to continue to increase and that minimum flows in rivers are more critical than average flows.

The efficiency with which water is used is the other crucial factor in predicting how many people our water supply can support. As is the case for most ecological questions, the factors influencing efficiency of water use are fairly subtle and complex. For example, deforestation or paving over an area generally leads to more rapid runoff of rainwater, so that less water soaks down to ground stores of water where it is available throughout the year as needed, and more water rushes into the ocean where it is not available for use until after another cycle of evaporation and precipitation. Another factor leading to decreased efficiency in water use is the increasing migration of the people of the United States to arid regions. Not only is it expensive to construct aqueducts and other facilities for carrying water to these regions, but also evaporative losses in transit are often large and agricultural losses of water are especially high, because the dry desert air results in higher rates of evaporation from food plants and croplands. Since all natural waters carry small amounts of salt, salt accumulates rapidly when evaporation is high, unless extra water is available to run off through the soil and wash out the salt. Since high concentrations of salt in the soil kill plants, this extra water must be supplied. Box 6–1 gives further examples of complex difficulties that can arise in irrigation. There are obvious advantages to desert living, particularly an abundance of sunshine for human pleasure and for high agricultural productivity. But it should be recognized that these advantages are achieved at the cost of inefficient water use, or conversely that more efficient water use could be achieved by forgoing these advantages and shifting human population centers and agriculture to wetter regions.

Box 6–1 **THE ASWAN DAM**

In Egypt, the Nile River is the lifeblood of the arid country through which it flows. Once each year for a short period the Nile used to flood, carrying nutrient rich silt over its banks into the surrounding six or so million acres of land which for centuries has provided the agricultural base for Egyptian civilizations. However, because the flooding of the Nile is seasonal, the area could yield but one crop per year. The Egyptian population is growing so rapidly that it is expected to double in the next 25 years, so there is a clear need for increased capacity to grow food.

More than a decade ago, the Egyptian government began to build the Aswan Dam on the Nile in southern Egypt, above the rich agricultural lands. Lake Nasser was intended to store sufficient water to bring under cultivation over one million acres of new land and to permit year-round irrigation and multiple cropping over a 500-mile stretch of the river. However, agricultural water supplies have not increased, due to unexpectedly high losses from Lake Nasser. Official plans failed to take into account high evaporation due to higher wind speeds over an open body of water and seepage through porous sandstone to inaccessible underground stores. Furthermore, the Nile no longer overflows its banks to deposit its millions of tons of silt and nutrients each year. Before long the soil will require artificial fertilization to maintain crop production. Changes in the flow of the Nile have had deleterious effects on the fisheries of parts of the Mediterranean which relied heavily on the outwash of the nutrient-rich silts. These silts are now being deposited in Lake Nasser at such a rate that it is expected to fill up within a few centuries. Most, if not all, of these problems were anticipated by opponents of the plan to build the Aswan Dam.

Perennial irrigation creates another problem: an increase in schistosomiasis or bilharzia, a disease which is caused by the blood fluke. The blood fluke is a parasitic worm which, as an adult, inhabits the blood vessels of the liver, intestines and urinary bladder in humans and some other mammals. There the flukes and their toxic products cause abscesses, hemorrhage, blockage of blood vessels and a whole array of uncomfortable and incapacitating symptoms. The eggs of the fluke are released via the urine or feces into water where they hatch. They must then enter certain kinds of snail which live only in wet conditions, which is why increased irrigation has led to spread of schistosomiasis. In the

57

snail, the juvenile stages of the fluke develop into a form which can penetrate the skin of people who wade or swim in the water or the surface of the mouth and throat of people who drink the water. The prevalence of schistosomiasis can be reduced by interrupting development at any point in the life cycle of the fluke: by preventing infected feces and urine from reaching the water, by killing the snails, by providing clean water for human use or by killing the adult fluke in the human with a drug. None of these methods is easy to carry out, but a multipronged attack has been mounted with considerable effectiveness around Shanghai and could presumably work in Egypt.

We conclude that there is enough water in the United States to support a considerable increase in population, provided the costs of increasing the supply are met. These costs would include the expense of more and better treatment plants to improve water purification for increased reuse of water, the expense of constructing more dams to store water for use during dry seasons and aqueducts to carry water to regions where water is scarce, and possibly the expense of desalinization.

Water Pollutants and Ways to Remove Them so Water Can Be Reused
As population centers continue to grow, they will place heavy demands on water use. In many parts of the United States, water use currently exceeds the total runoff, indicating that water is already used more than once on the average and/or that underground water stores are being depleted. For multiple use, the water which flows out of certain sectors must be of sufficient quality to be used by other sectors. To some extent this can be achieved by careful planning of the sequence in which water is used for various purposes. For example, pilot experiments have shown that water use in homes can be reduced by about 40 percent if water from the bath and laundry is used for flushing the toilets. The cost of the necessary filters and storage tank is $500 per home and would be less if mass produced. In many situations it is not possible to arrange the sequence of uses so neatly, and much more extensive cleaning of the water will be necessary. The cleaning process is much complicated by the variety of pollutants that find their way into the water and the variety of methods needed for removing them.

Probably the largest quantity of water pollutants are organic molecules from dead and decaying biological matter. If added to streams in small quantities, organic matter is broken down by bacteria which metabolize it for energy (Chapter 4). Thus a stream is self-purifying, if the load of sewage is not too large. However when too much organic matter is added, so much bacterial growth is stimulated that their metabolism uses up much of the oxygen in the water. Many types of bacteria cannot grow without oxygen, so the breakdown of organic material slows down when oxygen is depleted. This is of such importance that organic pollution is commonly measured in units of "biological oxygen demand" (abbreviated BOD).

One of the main functions of sewage treatment is to reduce the quantity of organic material in the effluent. Primary sewage treatment relies solely on physical methods of removing wastes from water: large particles are removed with screens, grease and scum are skimmed off and suspended particles settle out to form a sludge. This process reduces biological oxygen demand pollutants in the water by about a third. About two-thirds of communities in the United States also use secondary treatment on their sewage. In secondary treatment the sewage is aerated and a variety of other procedures are used to hasten bacterial breakdown of organic compounds while the sewage is in the sewage plant. This removes 75–90 percent of the biological oxygen demand pollutants.

Several serious problems remain however. First, there is the problem of how to dispose of the sludge. Incineration or dumping in the ocean are common, but to some extent just serve to shift the pollution problem to a new locale. Treatment and use as fertilizer is ecologically sound and not very expensive, although generally not actually profitable economically. The second problem is what to do about the large quantities of phosphorus and nitrogen that are released by the decay processes and remain in the water after secondary sewage treatment. These nutrients can provide the basis for rapid algal growth downstream from the sewage plant with all the attendant problems of eutrophication (Chapter 5). Ecologically, the most appealing solution is to use the treated water to irrigate and fertilize surrounding land. This approach has been used successfully on agricultural land and for reclaiming the spoils banks around strip mines. Another alternative is to subject the water to tertiary treatment in which chemical treatment, charcoal filtration, or other advanced methods can further clean the water. Tertiary treatment has been used in some areas of extreme water scarcity to allow complete recycling of water, but is not yet widely used, primarily because of its expense.

Specialized types of tertiary treatment will be needed to remove toxic materials such as arsenic and mercury, which are increasing in concentration in our rivers and lakes. Arsenic is a well-known poison which is finding its way into rivers in substantial amounts. Recent studies in the area of Lawrence, Kansas have demonstrated that the

Box 6–2 **A CASE HISTORY—WATER USE IN PHILADELPHIA**

The City of Philadelphia is considered to have one of the most advanced water commissions among large cities in the United States. The city, with just over two million people, uses about 125 billion gallons of water a year, which it gets primarily from the Delaware River and from one major contributary to the Delaware River. About 5 million persons live within the Delaware River Basin and another 15 million live just outside the basin in areas (primarily New York City) to which water is exported.

The Delaware River Basin encompasses 12,800 square miles with an annual precipitation of about 44 inches, for a total inflow of about 9800 billion gallons of water per year. About 4800 billion gallons per year flow out of the mouth of the Delaware; at least 4900 billion gallons per year evaporate from water surfaces, plants and so on; and about 300 billion gallons per year are shipped to New York and New Jersey for use there. This suggests that the annual outflow exceeds the annual inflow by more than 200 billion gallons a year, which may represent gradual decreases in the basin's ground water reserves of 15 trillion gallons. (Much more rapid loss of ground water is occurring in some arid regions of the United States, such as Arizona.) During periods of drought, ground water is the main source of water flow into rivers. This basal flow during dry periods is important in two respects. First, waste materials are dumped into rivers regardless of their flow rates. During dry periods, when river flow is low, the concentration of pollutants in the water increases proportionately. Second, the flow of water out of the Delaware is necessary to keep salty ocean water from backing up to the intake for Philadelphia's water system. During the extremely dry period of the early 1960s, river flow was less than one-tenth of average, and the salty water moved upstream from its normal boundary 79 miles from the mouth of the river to a position 100 miles from the river mouth and 10 miles short of the intake for one of the three water treatment plants in Philadelphia.

Considerable waste has been dumped into the rivers by the time they reach Philadelphia, so the water treatment plants use quantities of chlorine to kill microorganisms, lime to adjust the acidity, alum to precipitate sediments and carbon to filter the water. So much chlorine is added that a fish put into a bowl filled with city drinking water will usually die! To distribute this water, the city maintains more than 3200 miles of water pipes, about a tenth of which were installed prior to 1900 and are plagued by leaks.

Most sewage is treated at one of three plants before being returned to the river. With heavy rainfall, the flow of sewage is too much for the treatment plants to handle, and much of the sewage is discharged into the river untreated. This cause of untreated sewage could be eliminated by separate storm sewers or by basins to store heavy runoff for later treatment. Considerable industrial waste is also dumped into the rivers untreated. Two of the city's sewage plants give only primary treatment; the other gives secondary treatment as well. Some of the sludge is incinerated and some dumped in the ocean off southern New Jersey. Problems are clear, as are possible solutions. An agreement has been reached by most communities and factories in the region to spend about $200 million to improve treatment of wastes.

---

small amounts of arsenic in detergents and presoaks (10–70 parts per million) have resulted in arsenic values of 2 to 8 parts per billion in the Kansas River. This is close to the U.S. Public Health Service recommended maximum of 10 parts per billion as a drinking water standard. The effects of arsenic may not be felt for many years after the beginning of exposure to it.

Mercury is another heavy metal poison. Mercury is concentrated by food chains and has already taken its toll of human lives. In Minamata City, Japan, at least 46 people have died from eating fish and shellfish that had accumulated mercury from the wastes discharged by a local chemical plant. Recently the State of Michigan closed down the Wyandotte Chemicals Corporation, a chlorine and caustic soda plant which was dumping small amounts of mercury into the Detroit River. The reason? Tests of fish flesh in Lake St. Clair and Lake Erie revealed concentrations of mercury up to 7 parts per million, 14 times the maximum level deemed safe to eat. United States and Canadian fish and wildlife officials banned fishing completely in Lake St. Clair and partially in Lake Erie, an action which brought lawsuits from commercial fishermen against several chemical companies. The action against Wyandotte may have been in part a political move to cash in on the current "environment" issue, as the contribution of mercury by Wyandotte was a trifle compared to the total pollution. The incident does demonstrate the increased sensitivity of the government and the public to problems of environmental pollution.

Since mercury and other heavy metals are not broken down once they reach the environment, the best hope for avoiding risks is to prevent them from entering the environment. To do this, factories should reclaim the metals from their waste water and we should decrease uses (such as mercury fungicides on seeds) which almost unavoidably lead to heavy metals entering the environment. The strategy of preventing pollutants from entering natural waters is probably the best way of coping with a variety of other major pollutants, for example, oil from tanker spills and ship bilge, and heat from power plants. In addition we should try to minimize the flow into the environment of a great variety of manufactured compounds of unknown effect. One example are the polychlorinated biphenyls (PCB's), which until recently were added to plastics, paint and rubber, and which still are used in electrical equipment and cooling systems. PCB's have been found in high concentrations in some fish and fish-eating birds, some eggs and milk, and the fat of some humans. PCB's are similar in chemical structure to DDT, and apparently resemble DDT also in their persistence and in causing at least some similar disruptions of physiology (Chapter 7).

Desalinization of Water: A Potential Source of Abundant but Expensive Water

In a world where food is in short supply, it is natural to look to unfarmed deserts and to the occasional agricultural oases which have been produced in these areas by irrigation. Many deserts are near the ocean, and one can visualize billions of gallons of pure water flowing from nuclear desalinization plants to grow crops to feed the hungry world. Pipe dream, or reality? The crucial question is costs, and estimates differ. The Atomic Energy Commission (AEC) of the United States is putting forward an optimistic view. Other independent researchers have a more sober outlook.

The desalting process is usually a simple distillation process. Salt water is heated and the resulting water vapor is cooled and condensed into fresh water. One good source of heat is the waste heat produced by power plants, heat which is usually discharged into the environment as thermal pollution. The concentrated hot brine which is the residue of the distillation process can be diluted with salt water and then piped back into the sea. Simple, but expensive.

Currently, the cheapest desalted water costs more than 75 cents per 1000 gallons, as compared to the 5 to 10 cents per 1000 gallons cost which is usual for agricultural water in the United States if the source of irrigation is relatively close. Small cities in arid parts of the country often pay 50 to 70 cents per 1000 gallons. People can afford to pay high prices for domestic water in order to live in arid parts of the country with desirable climates; a family of four uses only about 250 gallons of water per day, which at $1 per thousand gallons is only 25 cents per day, or about $90 per year, hardly a prohibitive price. But farmers use much more water and the increased cost per gallon represents a much larger added expense for them. Can desalted water be produced at sufficiently low prices to be attractive to agriculture, or will it be profitable only for the development of cities in arid areas?

Most optimistic projections of costs of desalted water involve the construction of "agro-industrial complexes" in which a single plant simultaneously produces desalted water for agriculture and electricity for industry. In this way, the heat from power production can be used to distill the salt water, and a portion of the high cost of desalted water can be defrayed by the profits from the sale of electricity to industry. A typical plan on the drawing boards and apparently feasible within the next ten years involves a nuclear desalting plant that would produce a billion gallons of water per day, enough to irrigate 320,000 acres of land. The agriculture supported by the plant would feed at most three million people, more realistically, half that many. The steam produced in the process would be used to generate 1585 megawatts of electricity for industry. The initial investment for such a plant would run about $1.8 billion and annual operating costs would be about $250 million. It should be pointed out that much of the cost of the desalted water would be for interest on the financing of the desalting plant. Prices would be 10 cents per 1000 gallons if no interest were paid, but 24 cents per 1000 gallons at a typical interest rate of 10 percent. The latter price is too high for profitable use in farming under current economic conditions.

The Los Angeles Metropolitan Water District has considered building a 150 million gallon per day nuclear desalting plant. The original proposal by the Bechtel Corporation required $444 million in construction costs and would have produced water at 25 cents per 1000 gallons. By the time the plans were completed in 1968, the estimated construction costs had climbed to $765 million and the cost of water to between 40 and 50 cents per 1000 gallons. The project was dropped because it was economically impractical. As Clawson and his colleagues remarked, "If desalting of sea water is not economic in southern California today—where alternative water must be brought long distances at high cost, where electricity surely has a ready market, and where much of the water would go to agriculture—then where is large-scale desalting of sea water economic? If it is not economic at an interest rate of 3.5 percent, and at the lifetime capacity factor for both water and power of 90 percent, assumed for this venture, then what are the prospects under less generous assumptions?"[1]

In summary, it is not possible at this time, or in the near future, to bring the cost estimates for desalted water into line with prices that farmers are willing to pay, except in isolated instances. However, research on desalinization may bring lower costs. Furthermore, irrigation costs are currently less than 2 percent of the retail price of food in the United States, so even a fivefold increase in water prices need not produce a very big increase in food costs for the consumer. Agriculture is generally practiced where it is most profitable, so *any* increase in the total agricultural production of the earth is likely to bring some increased cost for food. Industries and domestic consumers generally use less water than agriculture and can therefore afford to pay higher prices for water, so desalinization may soon play an important role in the industrialization and population settlement of arid areas.

BIBLIOGRAPHY

Bradley, C. 1962. Human water needs and water use in America. *Science 138*: 489–91.

Clawson, M., H. H. Landsberg, and L. T. Alexander. 1969. Desalted water for agriculture: Is it economic? *Science 164*: 1141–48 [a thorough critique of desalinization and agro-industrial complexes].

Ehrlich, P. R. and A. H. Ehrlich. 1970. *Population, Resources, Environment.* San Francisco: W. H. Freeman and Company [Chapter 5 contains information on agro-industrial complexes].

Goldwater, L. J. 1971. Mercury in the environment. *Scientific American* May: 15–21.

Wagner, R. H. 1971. *Environment and Man.* New York: W. W. Norton & Co., Inc. [a good general introduction].

Young, G. 1970. Dry lands and desalted water. *Science 167*: 339–43. [presents an optimistic viewpoint].

[1] Marion Clawson, Hans H. Landsberg, and Lyle T. Alexander, "Desalted Water for Agriculture: Is It Economic," *Science 164*: 1141–1148 (1969).

chapter 7

pesticides

The Use of Pesticides Has Produced Significant Benefits

A pesticide is a chemical that poisons pests. A pest is any organism that constitutes a significant nuisance to people. Judgments may differ about whether a particular nuisance is significant or even really a nuisance. Spiders are commonly killed, although biologists think these insect-eaters are predominantly helpful to man.

There is, however, little dispute about the need to control the locusts, beetles, rats, sparrows, molds, bacteria, viruses and other creatures that compete with us for our food supply. They consume food that would otherwise be available for hungry people and they damage crop plants so the plants grow poorly or not at all. Weeds compete with food plants for sunlight, water and minerals and thus also rank as significant pests. Losses due to all pests are probably between a quarter and a half of world crops. Before harvest, losses are commonly 10 percent to insects, 10 percent to weeds, and 10 percent to viral, bacterial and fungal infections. After harvest, insects and rodents may each destroy 10 percent of the stored grain.

Another major group of pests are the animals that transmit disease organisms. Many of these are blood-sucking insects such as the mosquitos which carry the protozoa that cause malaria and the fleas which carry the bactera that cause plague. Rats are considered pests not only because they carry fleas, but also because they carry *Salmonella* and other disease organisms from garbage into human food they contact.

There is good reason, then, for efforts to reduce the numbers of these pests, including efforts to poison them with pesticides. One spectacular success has been the use of DDT to kill malaria-carrying mosquitos. In many tropical countries DDT-spraying campaigns have made a major contribution to the virtual elimination of malaria and the resultant 30 percent decrease in death rates. Agricultural use of pesticides is widespread in industrial countries, although not so spectacularly successful. (Table 7–1 gives the categories, names and quantities used for the major pesticides in the United States.) In this country in 1966, approximately ⅛ of the crop land was treated with insecticides and ¼ was treated with herbicides (used primary as weedkillers). Half of the farm use of insecticides was on cotton crops, where treat-

Table 7-1 PRODUCTION AND USE OF PESTICIDES IN
THE UNITED STATES

	MILLION POUNDS		
	produced in U.S. 1967	*used in U.S.* 1966	*used by farmers in U.S. (excluding Alaska and Hawaii)* 1966
Fungicides (mold preventatives, and so on)	167	125	33
Herbicides (weedkillers, etc.)			
2,4-D & 2,4,5-T	111	85	41
other herbicides	237	142	83
Total herbicide	348	227	124
Insecticides (including fumigants)			
Chlorinated hydrocarbons			
DDT	103	50	27
Aldrin-toxaphene group	120	78	53
others	?	?	9
Organophosphates			
parathion	45	?	16
others	?	?	24
Carbamates	?	?	13
Other chemicals	?	?	53
Total insecticide	504	329	195
Total pesticide	**1019**	**681**	**353**

Source: Data from U.S. Department of Agriculture. 1970. "Quantities of Pesticides Used by Farmers in 1966," *Agricultural Economic Report* No. 179, Economic Research Service, U.S. Government Printing Office; "Cleaning Our Environment, The Chemical Basis for Action," American Chemical Society (1969).

ment increases yields by about a half. Somewhat less than half of the farm use of herbicides was on corn, where treatment increases yields by about a quarter and decreases the need for labor to control weeds. In nonindustrial countries the yields per acre are less than half of those in industrial countries; a significant part of this difference is due to the 90 percent lower levels of pesticide use.

Problem: Pesticides Are Sometimes Ineffective

However, serious problems mar this story of the benefits due to pesticides. Many insects have shown increasing resistance to insecticides. After seven years of widespread use of DDT, 200 times as much DDT was needed to kill houseflies collected from Illinois farms. The lethal dose for boll worms has increased several thousandfold during the last decade. To a biologist, the general trend of increasing resistance is quite predictable. Widespread pesticide use confers definite advantages to any animal that happens to have a gene that codes for an enzyme that can convert the poison to a less toxic molecule. These animals are more likely to survive and reproduce than others that lack such resistance genes. Therefore this genetic trait will become widespread in the population. Because so many insects have evolved high resistance, several of the pesticides that have been widely used for more than two decades have now become relatively ineffective in protecting some crops. This is one of the major reasons that DDT use in the United States declined by half during the decade of the sixties.

Insecticides kill not only boll weevils and house flies, but also honey bees and insects that eat pests. Use of pesticides can sometimes increase the populations of pest insects by killing their natural predators. Consider the cottony cushion scale insect that sucks sap from citrus trees. This insect was under control in California, until widespread use of DDT caused a major outbreak. The scale insect increased in numbers because it was less sensitive to DDT than was the beetle that ate it. The outbreak was brought under control by ending use of DDT in citrus orchards, so the predator population could increase and once again keep the cottony cushion scale under control.

Problem: Pesticides Harm Other Organisms in the Environment

Insecticides damage other animals besides insects because they affect chemical processes which are widespread throughout the animal kingdom. For example, in many animal nervous systems, the communication between some nerve cells depends on the chemical, acetylcholine. Electrical activity in a nerve cell stimulates it to secrete acetylcholine, which flows a tiny distance to the next nerve cell where it excites electrical activity in that nerve cell. Similarly, a nerve cell which innervates a muscle releases acetylcholine which flows across a tiny gap to excite electrical activity and contraction in the muscle. Once this has been accomplished, the acetylcholine is destroyed by an enzyme, acetylcholinesterase. This enzyme is inactivated by carbamate insecticides (for example, carbaryl) and by organophosphate insecticides (for example, parathion). When the acetylcholinesterase enzyme is inactivated, acetylcholine accumulates. This leads to hyperactivity of the nerve and muscle cells, often accompanied by uncontrollable muscle spasms and convulsions. For example, inhalation of an organophosphate poison increases the activity of nerves to the salivary glands and to the muscles that constrict the windpipe, and thus can lead to death by choking. That these chemicals can be highly toxic to man is suggested by the fact that they are chemically closely related to nerve gases, but in the United States less than 30 deaths annually have been caused by accidental poisoning with organophosphate insecticides.

The chlorinated hydrocarbon compounds are the other important group of insecticides. Typical of them is DDT, which causes hyperactivity in the nervous system, apparently by disrupting the flow of electrical charges in nerve cells. Deaths of vertebrates due to these insecticides have most commonly followed widespread government spraying programs. An example are the spraying programs which use DDT to kill the bark beetles that carry the fungus that plugs the water-conducting vessels of elms and thus causes Dutch elm disease. Heavy spraying of elms has resulted in contamination of organic debris below the trees, with consequent contamination of earthworms and convulsive deaths among the robins that ate the earthworms.

Not all the dangers from pesticides are predictable from knowledge of their primary mode of action. Their effects extend in unpredictable ways to all sorts of life processes. One dramatic example comes from the history of the herbicides, 2,4,5-T and 2,4-D. These are synthetic mimics of the natural plant hormone, auxin. They cause uncoordinated growth leading to death when they are applied to susceptible weed plants. They also cause trees and shrubs to drop their leaves, and have been widely used as defoliants in the war in Vietnam. Spraying with these compounds not only disrupts Vietnamese ecology; it may also cause direct damage to human health. 2,4,5-T administered to pregnant mice and other rodents causes congenital defects in their offspring. While human beings might be affected quite differently from mice, it seems possible that the 2,4,5-T content of drinking water in heavily sprayed parts of South Vietnam may have been high enough to cause the increase reported there in babies with congenital defects.

It is not unusual that the experiments that revealed the birth defects were performed 20 years after 2,4,5-T came into general use, nor that restrictions in use did not follow immediately on these experiments. The experimental results reached the Food and Drug Administration in October 1968. No public announcement was made until October 1969, when restrictions on 2,4,5-T use were proposed for January 1970. Planned restrictions were postponed for four months to allow an investigation of Dow Chemical Company's claim that the birth defects were due not to 2,4,5-T but rather to a contaminant, dioxin. By April 1970 it had been established that both 2,4,5-T and dioxin caused birth defects. The federal government restricted domestic use of 2,4,5-T to pasture, range and forest land, and the military suspended use in Vietnam. However the ban against use on food crops was not actually in force as late as August 1971 because the law allows for further delays while appeals from other companies are being decided. More stringent restrictions on domestic use of 2,4,5-T were felt to be unnecessary since 2,4,5-T in soil is almost entirely decomposed within five months. However, scanty data on the much more dangerous dioxin compound indicate that less than 20 percent of dioxin has been degraded after five months in soil. One final note: use of 2,4-D has not been restricted yet, despite accumulating evidence that 2,4-D can also cause congenital abnormalities.

Many people are now worried that further serious "side effects" of pesticides will be discovered, and that some of these may be due to persistent chemicals that will remain in the environment long after their use is stopped. Certainly persistence is a problem with the pesticides that contain heavy metals, such as mercury-containing fungicides used on seeds and arsenic-containing herbicides used to kill weeds in United States cotton fields and to kill rice plants in Vietnam. These heavy metals have already caused some human and other poisonings as well as persistent soil infertility in some orchards. The metal ions do not decompose. The only reasonable method of control is to keep them from moving into ecosystems.

Most modern pesticides are organic compounds, not containing heavy metals. Some, like the organophosphates and carbamates, are decomposed within a few weeks by chemical reactions in soil microorganisms and elsewhere. Others, like the chlorinated hydrocarbons, are degraded only very slowly. After one year, soil retains 60–90 percent of its original DDT content in the form of DDT or its slightly less toxic chemical relatives, DDD or DDE. Even when pesticide residues have disappeared, they are not necessarily safely out of the way. Aldrin, for instance, is converted to the more toxic dieldrin in the soil. When DDD quickly disappeared from the waters of Clear Lake, it had been picked up by the living plants and animals (Box 2-2, pg. 18).

Because the chlorinated hydrocarbons are much more soluble in fat than in water, living organisms tend to absorb them and store them in their fatty parts. When an organism containing DDT is eaten, much of the DDT is stored in the fat of the consumer, since DDT is excreted rather slowly and metabolized very slowly. Many of the other molecules in the food are metabolized for energy, and during metabolism are broken down into waste products which are excreted. In consequence the food eaten during a lifetime may weigh ten times the body weight of the eater (Chapter 4). Since the proportion of DDT molecules incorporated into the body is much higher than for other food mole-

Figure 7–1 PART OF THE FOOD WEB FOR A LONG ISLAND, NEW YORK ESTUARY

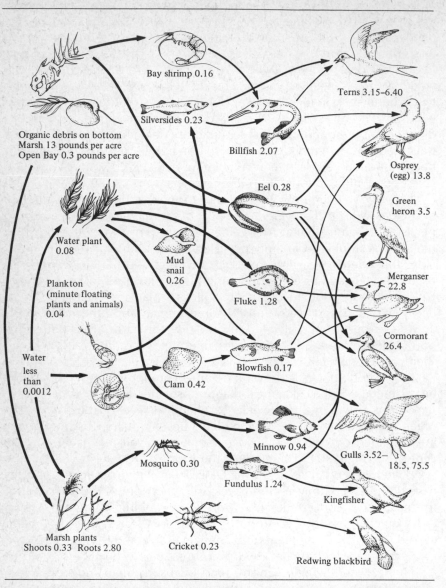

Bay shrimp 0.16

Terns 3.15–6.40

Silversides 0.23

Billfish 2.07

Organic debris on bottom
Marsh 13 pounds per acre
Open Bay 0.3 pounds per acre

Eel 0.28

Osprey (egg) 13.8

Green heron 3.5

Water plant 0.08

Mud snail 0.26

Plankton (minute floating plants and animals) 0.04

Fluke 1.28

Merganser 22.8

Water less than 0.0012

Blowfish 0.17

Cormorant 26.4

Clam 0.42

Minnow 0.94

Gulls 3.52– 18.5, 75.5

Mosquito 0.30

Fundulus 1.24

Kingfisher

Marsh plants
Shoots 0.33 Roots 2.80

Cricket 0.23

Redwing blackbird

Many of the plants and animals are illustrated, with arrows indicating the flow of nutrients. The marsh had been sprayed with DDT for 20 years to control mosquitos. Significant levels of DDT had accumulated, as indicated by the numbers (which give parts per million by weight for DDT + DDD + DDE in the whole organism). The higher concentration of DDT in animals higher up in the food web is explained in the text.

Source: From "Toxic Substances and Ecological Cycles" by George W. Woodwell. Copyright © 1967 by *Scientific American, Inc.* All rights reserved. Adapted with permission.

cules, DDT is usually more concentrated in the consumer than in his food (Figure 7-1).

Since fish- and meat-eaters generally have the highest concentrations of stored DDT and other chlorinated hydrocarbons, it is not surprising to find that the most severe effects on vertebrate wildlife populations have been among certain predators. Beginning around 1947, during the early years of widespread use of chlorinated hydrocarbons, hawks, eagles and some other birds that prey on vertebrates suffered severe failures in reproduction and consequent declines in population. In part the failure was due to thinner eggshells and consequent breakage. Thinner eggshells were found to have higher concentrations of DDT and DDE. Experimental birds responded to injections of DDE by producing thin-shelled eggs. Delayed breeding has also been caused by the chlorinated hydrocarbons. When these chemicals are fed to birds, the liver produces more of an enzyme which inactivates a female sex hormone, estrogen. Both the hormone and liver enzymes are known to be active in human beings; there is however no evidence yet that human beings are affected by current levels of DDT intake.

Problem: Possible Harmful Effects on People Have Not Been Adequately Evaluated

There is no conclusive evidence that current average intake of any pesticide is harming human health or reproduction. On the other hand, conclusive evidence to the contrary is also lacking. This is partly due to lack of study and partly due to the difficulty of detecting health impairments that may be serious for only a small segment of the population, and then perhaps only after prolonged exposure. We will briefly describe three representative studies to indicate the difficulties.

In the first study, 35 workers from a DDT factory were found to have no "ill effects attributable to exposure to DDT" despite 11–19 years of daily intake at 400 times the average in the United States. Such negative findings are however inconclusive, since a relatively high incidence of diabetes and some other abnormalities that were observed were attributed to statistical fluctuations due to the small size of the group. Furthermore, only men currently employed were included in the study. Any worker who might have become too sick to work because of DDT exposure was not included in the sample.

The second study seems to show a relationship between DDT and cancer, but must be judged equally inconclusive. Autopsies showed higher levels of stored DDT + DDE + DDD in the fat of individuals who died of various cancers than in controls. However, it is not known whether the correlation between DDT and cancer deaths is due to DDT causing cancer, or to cancer somehow lowering the body's ability to dispose of DDT, or to some unmeasured third variable, such as age, which might result both in more stored DDT and in more cancer deaths.

It has been possible to avoid such ambiguities in experiments where mice were fed diets with and without DDT added. These studies showed that DDT at high doses can cause cancers in mice. The problem in interpreting this type of study is that it is impossible to extrapolate with confidence from the effects of high doses on a relatively small number of mice, to the effects of prolonged low doses on a large number of humans. For DDT, carcinogenic doses per unit body weight in mice were about 100–1000 times higher than the average dietary intake for humans in the United States. (Many breastfed babies in the United States get doses as high as 1/10 of the lowest carcinogenic dose of DDT, since DDT is carried into milk with the fat that is mobilized for milk production. Legal limits on DDT in cows' milk are lower than the average DDT content of mother's milk in the United States. Animal fat generally contains high levels of DDT, concentrated from the food the animal has eaten. Vegetarians have roughly 75 percent lower DDT intake than the general population. Nondietary intake is negligible except for those exposed at work and careless users of home sprays.)

It should be stressed that the three studies described are among the most informative available. The difficulties in interpreting them can be overcome only by investing considerably larger resources in more complete studies. More definitive conclusions could come from studying much larger numbers of workers with high exposure, contacting former as well as current workers, carrying out pesticide residue analyses for a large sample of autopsies with adequate records of all possibly relevant variables, and testing effects of a wide range of dose levels on a variety of animals. The funding to make possible such extensive testing would seem worthwhile, since the current alternative is to conduct a poorly controlled experiment on our entire population.

To summarize the problems with pesticides: they commonly kill useful insects and occasionally kill other nonpest animals; they occasionally interfere with a wide variety of natural processes ranging from growth of orchard trees to reproduction of birds; accidental overexposures are practically the only cases of demonstrated adverse effects on human health, but testing has certainly not been adequate to exclude the possibility of other harmful effects.

Safer Alternatives Are Available and More Could Be Developed
There are alternatives to pesticides which avoid some of the problems. An obvious example is the use of metal storage containers for grain.

These can be made rat-proof, and waterproof so that the grain is too dry for fungus growth, and even airtight so that no oxygen-requiring pests can survive. Improved methods of cultivation can also eliminate certain pests, such as the European corn borer. This insect overwinters as a larva in cornstalks and cannot emerge as an adult moth in the spring if the stalks have been plowed under. Inspection and quarantine procedures can slow down the introduction of new pests. The significance of these procedures is suggested by the fact that 100 important pest species (including the boll weevil and gypsy moth) were imported into the United States between the Civil War and the Plant Quarantine Act of 1912; about 30 important pests have been imported since then.

Imported species often become significant pests when predators, parasites and diseases that reduced their numbers in their native habitat are not imported along with them. Purposeful importation of these "natural enemies" has played a major role in bringing some pest populations under control. The beetle that eats cottony cushion scale was imported for control purposes after an accidental introduction of the scale insect to the United States. Prickly pear cactus was cleared from vast areas of Australia by an imported moth with a hearty appetite for prickly pear. Insects and parasites are particularly useful in this kind of biological control, since they tend to have narrow food preferences which prevent them from attacking species that people want to maintain. The advantages of biological control over pesticides include reduced danger to human health, lower cost, since the imported species reproduces itself, and a built-in tendency to overcome evolution of resistance on the part of the pest by counter-evolution of attack on the part of the imported species. Sometimes it is not necessary to import a predator or parasite, but only to improve conditions for a local species. A prosaic example is the farmer who feeds his barn cats during lean periods, so they will be there to control rat and mice populations when they start to increase.

A number of major plant diseases and plant-eating insects have been brought under control by breeding plant varieties with genetic resistance to the pest. In a few spectacular cases, insect populations have been eliminated by the release of large numbers of sterilized males. If the insect population is relatively small and isolated (for example, on an island) and if the females mate infrequently, then the numerous sterilized males can monopolize the mating with females and reproduction is prevented. Chemical attractants that simulate the odor of food or virgin females can be used to attract insects to traps containing poisons or sterilants. Such traps have also been used effectively to determine the numbers of particular pest species, so that insecticide use can be limited to areas of actual infestation.

Even when pesticide use is limited to times and places where it is needed, much pesticide is wasted by current methods of spraying and dusting. More than half the pesticide never hits the target plants. If less wasteful application procedures were used and if applications were limited to times and places of actual infestation, the quantity of insecticides used could be decreased severalfold and thus all the problems discussed in the previous sections could be reduced. Part of the reason that farmers and others continue such wasteful practices as airplane spraying without prior pest-testing is that such methods reduce labor costs more than enough to offset costs for extra materials. Such calculations of immediate profitability by individual farmers leave out of account the costs that others pay for the farmer's excessive use of pesticides, such as the danger to wildlife and human health. Their calculations also omit the costs that develop over the years, for example, the increasing resistance to common pesticides.

Similar considerations of individual profit have also slowed progress in developing alternatives to pesticide use. Many of the alternatives do not involve a salable product. Consider, for example, the practices of inspection and quarantine, plowing stubble under, and importing predators or parasites that reproduce themselves once established. Naturally enough, industry has shown little interest in developing such techniques; almost all of their $60 million or more annual research budget is spent on developing new chemicals. In contrast, more than 60 percent of the federal government's $40 million research program on pest control is devoted to alternatives to pesticides. The alternatives proposed are safer, and many will be cheaper than pesticides, but we should expect industry to continue to concentrate on pesticides since they are likely to be more profitable, especially as long as industry does not have to pay for the damage its products may cause once they enter our environment.

There is an additional problem in developing biological methods of pest control. In general an imported predator or a method of cultivation is effective against only one or a few pest species. This specificity is an advantage since it avoids the more general damage pesticides may cause. However such specificity means that considerable research is needed to develop an effective program to protect even one kind of plant. One to two dozen different organisms cause significant damage to a crop like rice or corn or potatoes. Research will be required not only to find methods of controlling each of these, but also to make sure that the methods are compatible with each other. Pesticides would continue to play a role in an optimum "integrated control" program, but types would be selected to complement other control techniques and quantities used would be much smaller.

Policy Proposals

It should be obvious by now that "Ban DDT!" may be a catchy slogan, but it is too simplistic to be a useful policy. The outcome of such a ban will almost certainly be an acceleration of the current shift to organophosphate and carbamate pesticides. These are less long-lasting, but the organophosphates are more toxic to mammals and to predatory insects. The effects of repeated exposure to low doses is not known. Any policy to limit use of DDT needs to be supplemented by policies to develop safer alternatives. Furthermore, it would seem reasonable to limit DDT use rather than ban it, since there are important programs (for example, malaria control) where alternative control measures can not be effective immediately.

This raises the question of how to limit the use of each pesticide to situations where it will benefit society more than it will cost. Two major approaches have been proposed. Each has serious problems. In the first approach the free market mechanisms would be improved by adding *all* costs of pesticide use to the costs paid by the user, for example, by adding to pesticide prices a tax equivalent to the amount of damage to be expected from its use. It would be difficult to estimate how much this tax should be, because we know so little about what the damages are and because it is difficult to attach a price tag to a human death or the extinction of a species. Furthermore, although a tax based on estimated total costs would decrease pesticide use, there is no reason to assume that the most profitable uses, which would tend to continue, would be the ones most beneficial to society. The alternative is to develop regulation programs. Our lack of confidence in this alternative is based on past experience, of which the 2,4,5-T incident described above is more or less typical. Despite the fact that the law explicitly requires proof of safety before registration of a pesticide for use, such incidents often reveal an unspoken assumption that chemicals, like people, are innocent until proven guilty. This point of view is fostered by close relations between industry and regulatory agency personnel and it is not likely to change unless others of us can organize into an effective political counterforce.

Even if we achieve the political change that would bring effective regulatory agencies, we cannot expect to escape damaging effects of chemicals unless we slow the rate at which we introduce new products into our environment. Not only are hundreds of different chemicals used as pesticides in the United States, but the products sold also contain an unknown number of dangerous contaminants like dioxin. The unmanageability of this situation is one of the bases for our belief that we need a new definition of the good life, a definition that recognizes that a high standard of living should not be equated with maximum consumption of goods. We present this idea more fully in Chapter 11.

BIBLIOGRAPHY

Headley, J. C. and J. N. Lewis 1967. *The Pesticide Problem: An Economic Approach to Public Policy.* Baltimore: The Johns Hopkins Press [the most well-balanced presentation we found; the general reader can easily omit the technical economics chapters].

Huffaker, C. B. 1970. Life against life—Nature's pest control scheme. *Environmental Research, 3:* 162–175 [a readable, detailed account of some alternatives to pesticides].

Peakall, D. B. 1970. Pesticides and the reproduction of birds. *Scientific American,* April: 73–78.

Rudd, R. L. 1964. *Pesticides and the Living Landscape.* Madison: Univ. of Wisconsin Press [concentrates on the biological aspects of problems of pesticides].

U.S. Dept. of Health, Education, and Welfare. 1969. *Report of the secretary's commission on pesticides and their relationship to environmental health* [repetitious, disorganized and generally unreadable, but the best compendium of data; this gives summaries and references for the three studies described in this chapter on effects of pesticides on human health].

chapter 8

food supplies in the future

In the preceding chapters we have discussed the major needs for plant growth: energy, mineral nutrients and water. We have described how increased efficiency in the use of these inputs could increase the food available for people. For example, water use is more efficient if agriculture is developed in humid regions where evaporative losses are lower. Increased recycling of sewage increases the supply of mineral nutrients available for growing food. New breeds of plants that use sunlight, fertilizer and/or water more efficiently have already contributed significantly to increases in food production. Reductions of insect, rat and weed populations increase the amount of food available for human consumption. Programs to translate such principles into the reality of increased food are currently widespread.

How to Supply Adequate Calories: Yields Per Acre
Can Be Increased

One urgent goal is to increase the yield per acre in nonindustrial countries. The possibility of a considerable increase is suggested by the fact that yields in nonindustrial countries average only about one-third of those in industrial countries. The caloric value of food crops harvested from an acre in India averages less than 5000 Calories/day compared to more than 10,000 Calories/day in Japan.

The differences in yield are closely related to differences in the inputs the farmer is able to supply. Fertilizer use per acre is about ten times as high in Western Europe, Japan and Taiwan as in the rest of Asia, South America and Africa. Pesticide use per acre is about five times as high in Japan as in Europe and the United States where use is about eight times as high as in Latin America, Africa and India. Much more research has been done to develop high productivity breeds for temperate climates than for tropical. If farmers in nonindustrial countries were supplied with better seed, more fertilizer, and so on, yields could rise markedly.

Farmers in industrial countries also use much more machinery than those in nonindustrial countries. These machines contribute a great deal to productivity per farmer, but they make a limited contribution to productivity per acre. Rapid and extensive mechanization of agriculture is generally an unwise policy for nonindustrial countries, because labor is abundant and capital is scarce. If a farmhand is displaced by a machine, he often joins the ranks of the unemployed. In contrast, the capital not invested in agricultural machinery is sorely needed for other projects. Therefore, mechanization is generally only justified when it can increase food production per acre, for example, when soil must be prepared rapidly in order to grow two crops within a limited rainy season, or when clay soils are too heavy to be turned without a tractor or when pumps are needed for irrigation.

We should not overemphasize the importance of the tangible inputs. Intangible factors such as technical knowledge and organization' will be at least as important and at least as difficult to supply. We have already emphasized the importance of research to develop breeds and techniques that are adapted to the specific soils and climates where they are to be used. Attempts to transfer technology without this adaptive research have failed repeatedly. Furthermore, technical advice to individual farmers is needed. Again the farmers of nonindustrial countries have woefully smaller resources than the farmers of industrial countries. For example, both India and the Philippines have one agricultural research worker for every 70,000 agricultural workers, compared to one for every 1400 in Japan. India and the Philippines have one extension worker for every 1000 farms, compared to one for every 450 farms in Japan. Furthermore, illiteracy is generally much higher in nonindustrial countries so that communication of information and advice is considerably less efficient. Unless these technical deficiencies are remedied, it will be difficult to make good use of whatever tangible inputs do become available.

A further critical need is for organization that can get the resources to the place where they are needed at the time they are needed. This problem is especially severe since one failure can cancel out all the successes up to that point. If irrigation pumps cannot be repaired for lack of one part, a harvest may fail entirely. In India during recent bumper harvests due to good weather and the new breeds of grain, available storage space was totally inadequate and much grain was lost to birds, rats and molds which could not be kept out of makeshift stores. To avoid such problems is difficult because of the time-lag between recognizing a need, planning for it and successful execution of the plan. Large-scale irrigation projects are rarely operative within less than a decade of initial planning. Longer delays often arise in completing the canals to individual fields and in developing optimal regulation of flow rates.

Attention must also be paid to the crucial problem of providing better incentives to encourage peasant farmers to try new and improved technology. A tenant farmer who pays a large and fixed percentage of his crop as rent is generally unwilling to invest in improving productivity because the landowner, through increased rent collections, acquires a very high proportion of the net income produced by the tenant's efforts. Similarly a tenant who can easily be evicted is reluctant to invest in land improvements that he may not be there to profit from. If a farmer's crop is barely large enough to meet minimal needs for survival so that he has no savings, the farmer is unlikely to abandon his time-tested traditional methods, unless he is assured of support in case an innovation fails or unless he sees his neighbors having marked success with the innovation. If credit is not available at reasonably low cost, the farmer is unlikely to invest in improvements unless they can yield very large returns that can pay high interest costs and still leave him a profit. Profit as a motive, however, seems to lead to irresolvable contradictions. Fertilizer prices low enough to make their use profitable for peasant farmers are often not high enough to be profitable for manufacturers. Food prices high enough to make new investments profitable for farmers are often too high to be paid by the hungry poor. These problems could be solved if governments assumed responsibility for providing adequate income to all or for purchasing food from producers and redistributing it to those who need it. Existing programs such as the full-employment programs of Communist countries and the U.S. Food Stamp Plan indicate some of the possibilities and the problems.

In summary, a program to improve yields per acre would require investment of considerable material resources, technical knowledge and planning effort. But such a program could provide adequate Calories for the growing world population for the next decade or two. (This estimate together with estimates for related programs is illustrated in Figure 8–1.) To finance such a program, the rich countries will need to supply the poor countries with capital worth about $10 billion/year. This cost is small when compared to the $80 billion/year U.S. military budget or the $50 billion/year U.S.S.R. military budget. This comparison of budgets suggests that the necessary material and human resources could be made available, but only if we can accomplish the necessary reordering of priorities together with the requisite social and political reorganization.

Cultivated Area Could Also Be Increased

In our discussion thus far we have concentrated on how to increase yields per acre. Increases in area cultivated have also been important in the past and will no doubt continue to be so in the future. Only

Figure 8–1 THE BIOLOGICAL POTENTIAL FOR PROVIDING ADEQUATE CALORIES FOR THE GROWING WORLD POPULATION

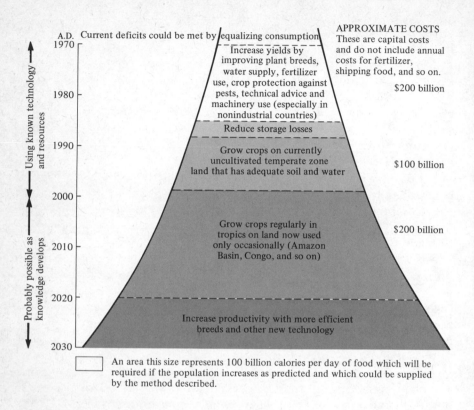

An area this size represents 100 billion calories per day of food which will be required if the population increases as predicted and which could be supplied by the method described.

This figure indicates programs that would make it possible to feed the growing world population with a diet containing minimum Calories, even if population growth continued at current rates for half a century. We refer here to the biological possibilities of growing enough food and disregard the question of political feasibility. The entire capital costs for the programs listed would be approximately equal to the military expenditures made in four years by the United States and the U.S.S.R.

Although physically possible, the feat would not be easy or pleasant. Much land now in forests would have to be used for crops; people from Asia would have to be moved to areas having new land or massive shipments of food to Asia would be required; much better technical planning will be needed to avoid fiascos such as soil ruined by salt deposited by poorly managed irrigation waters; the diets available would be minimal and monotonous grain diets; political and economic problems that keep food and other resources from reaching poor people would have to be overcome, and so on.

Estimates of the maximum population it would be possible to feed range from 5 billion people, assuming political organization remains unchanged, to 200 billion, assuming optimum use of resources and new technology. We find it extremely unlikely that the earth could support more than 30 billion about 10 percent of the world's land is now cultivated (Table 8-1). The amount of cultivated area could probably be doubled, although not very rapidly. Almost two-thirds of the potential new arable land is in the humid tropics of Africa and South America where yields obtained with current technology are not high. Much research will be necessary to solve problems such as low nutrient levels in the soil, heavy rainfalls that wash out nutrients and pack down soil, and insect pests that flourish unhampered by winter cold.

Table 8–1 UTILIZATION OF WORLD LAND

	BILLION ACRES
Cultivated land	3½
Pasture	7
Forest	10
Other	12½
(about one-third is built on and about two-thirds is desert and wasteland)	
Total land area (excluding Greenland and Antarctica)	33

Source: U.N. Food and Agriculture Organization, 1969, *Production Yearbook.*

In temperate regions, the development of new land will be slowed, not by the lack of technology, but rather by the fact that most of the unused potentially arable land is in areas that already have adequate farm acreage per capita, most notably North America. Much of this land is now forested, and its conversion to farm land would require more efficient and sparing use of wood in the United States. For example, more of our paper would have to be made from recycled waste paper and from waste products such as the fiber from sugar cane. Also, the clearing of forest land would have to be carefully planned in order to avoid soil erosion and the loss of important recreational areas.

In general, exploitation of new land can be successful only when initial plans give careful attention to the entire ecology of the situation.

Figure 8–1 (continued)

people, even at minimum subsistence levels. We would reach that population after a century of population growth at the current rate.

Source: Data compiled from President's Science Advisory Committee. 1967. *The World Food Problem*, Report of the Panel on the World Food Supply. Washington: U.S. Government Printing Office, and numerous other sources.

Otherwise, fiascos like the Dustbowl can all too easily be repeated. During the wet years of the 1920s, the sod was plowed up because it was more profitable to raise grain than cattle, but during the dry years of the 1930s, grain crops failed and the soil was exposed to wind erosion. Because the protective sod covering had been plowed up, tons of top soil were blown out of the Dustbowl with disastrous consequences for farmers and for soil fertility.

If we can achieve the kind of planning and social organization needed to avoid mistakes like the Dustbowl, the material resources of new land with the sunshine and water that fall on it could support a considerable increase in food production. After allowance is made for all the various problems in expanding cultivated acreage, it seems likely that 0.4 billion acres of temperate land and 1 billion acres of tropical land could be brought under cultivation. In combination with the increases in yield discussed earlier, these increases in acreage could supply minimum Calories for the additional people to be expected if population growth continues at the current rate until 2020 (Figure 8–1).

In conclusion, we have the physical and biological resources to supply adequate food Calories for the immediate future. The crucial question is how those resources will be used.

How to Supply the Protein Needed

If an adult eats enough grain to satisfy his caloric requirements, his protein requirements are generally satisfied by the protein in that grain. The main exceptions to this generalization are pregnant or lactating women who need exceptionally large amounts of protein for synthesizing embryonic tissue or milk. Children also synthesize new tissue at a rapid rate and thus also need more of certain essential amino acids than they can obtain from an all grain diet.

Since grain proteins have adequate amounts of most amino acids, the cheapest way to correct protein deficiencies for grain-eaters is to add small quantities of the deficient amino acids. Then the body can use not only the added amino acids, but also more of the other amino acids which are naturally available in the grain. (When the supply of any essential amino acid is inadequate, the body cannot use the other amino acids which are available, since protein synthesis is blocked by the absence of even one of the necessary amino acid constituents.) Rice, wheat or corn can be made nutritionally adequate for a child by adding ½ penny worth of amino acids and less than ¹⁄₁₀ penny worth of minerals and vitamins to each pound of grain. Programs to fortify wheat flour in India with lysine (the amino acid most deficient in wheat) have met with rapid success because they improve nutrition without requiring any change in food habits. Such fortification programs, combined with programs to supply minimum requirements for food Calories, could bring adequate nutrition to the 60 percent of the world's population who eat mainly grain. Although fortification programs could meet protein requirements, other possibilities should also be developed. For example, the protein content of grains could be improved by better use of fertilizer and by better plant breeds that would incorporate some of the recently discovered genes which produce higher content of specific required amino acids.

Many tropical people get the bulk of their Calories from starchy foods like cassava or plantains which are extremely low in proteins. Dietary deficits of proteins are in this case too great to be reasonably supplied by amino acid supplements. Animal or legume proteins are necessary. Even when not strictly necessary, animal foods are desired by most people. Furthermore, as explained in Chapter 4, cows and other ruminants are useful for converting indigestible leaves and grass to food we can digest. Pigs can serve a similar function in converting refuse to edible food.

Productivity of herds and flocks in nonindustrial countries averages about one-third of productivity in industrial countries. Much of the difference is due to lack of veterinary care and to deficiencies in feeding, sometimes deficiencies in minor elements that render the animals susceptible to disease. Improved veterinary care could eliminate at least 50 percent of the reduction in weight gain which is caused by disease, and could thus produce a 25 percent increase in animal protein available in nonindustrial countries. Control of herd size to prevent overgrazing could also improve productivity and save the soil. Another way that meat production could be increased in the tropics, particularly in Africa, is to make use of herds of native animals. These animals are better adapted to the heat than temperate-bred animals like the cow, they are more resistant to local diseases and they eat a much wider range of the available plants than do domestic animals. (A familiar example is the hippopotamus who uses water plants for food.) Perhaps the most serious problem in exploiting unconventional meat sources is the reluctance of people to change their food habits. Even relatively cosmopolitan Westerners find dog and horse meat unpalatable, although other peoples eat these meats with relish.

Estimates of the maximum fish supply are based on known fish resources and on algal growth rates and food chain inefficiencies. These estimates suggest that the ocean catch could be doubled, provided that productivity is not lowered by pollution, or by dredging and filling marshy breeding grounds or by overfishing. Overfishing removes so many individuals that few are left to grow up to be caught in next year's crop. Overfishing has already produced large declines in some catches, for example the sardine catch off the California coast. Freshwater fish production could increase fivefold, provided that pollution is kept under control and fish culture techniques are used. For example, carefully controlled sewage flows can be used to increase plant growth and thus fish production, but unregulated sewage flows can lead to excessive plant growth, decay, and decreased oxygen and fish production.

In recent years, approximately one-third of the fish catch has been converted to fish meal. Much of the fish meal is produced in South America and Africa. More than 90 percent of their fish meal is shipped to Europe and the United States for use as high quality protein supplements in animal feeds. There are two ways in which this works counter to the goal of providing minimum nutritional requirements for all people. First, it moves protein from areas where many people do not get enough animal protein to areas where consumption of animal proteins averages 50 percent to 200 percent higher than nutritional requirements (in Europe and North America, respectively). Second, 80 percent or more of the protein is lost to human consumption since the farm animals incorporate less than 20 percent of the protein in their food into protein in the meat, milk and eggs they produce. Nevertheless, the fish meal is exported because European farmers can pay more for this protein than can the many protein-deficient people living in Africa and Latin America. If fish meal were eaten where it is produced, animal protein intake would increase by 20 percent in Africa and 100 percent in Latin America.

An equal amount of protein is shipped from nonindustrial to industrial countries in oilseed pressings which are also used as animal feed. Oilseed pressings are the cakes that remain after oil has been removed from peanuts, cotton seeds and so on. The oil is also exported to industrial countries for production of margarine. If the proteins now being fed to animals in industrial countries are to become available to those who need them most, some way must be found of making human need a more effective demand than high profit farming. We also need to discover how to use fish meal and oilseed pressings in ways that are palatable to humans who need them. Food habits change slowly, but successful uses have already been found for protein concentrates from fish meal as a supplement to flour, and for soybean milk as Vitasoy, a popular soft drink in Hong Kong.

More research is needed to develop other processes for producing protein concentrates, as well as palatable ways of using these concentrates. In one new process, protein is produced by bacteria or yeasts grown on waste products containing carbon and hydrogen, supplemented with inorganic nitrogen. Processes have been developed for using paper mill wastes, refinery wastes and molasses. Most of these processes are just emerging from the pilot project stage; an estimated $50 million more in research will be needed. Eventually these processes for culturing microbes should be able to produce protein at 20 cents/pound in quantities approximating current human protein consumption. Cultures of bacteria can also yield individual amino acids and vitamins that can be used as supplements to correct specific deficiencies. A second promising process under development is the extraction of protein from indigestible leaves by a rather simple technique: pulping with water, pressing, mixing with steam and skimming off the protein. Costs are expected to run under 10 cents/pound of protein. This process could be particularly useful where tubers are the main source of food, since much of the plant protein is not in the tuber, but rather in the leaves.

In conclusion, with known technology we could supply adequate protein to a population double the current size. We would reach this size population after 35 years at the current rate of population growth. Existing protein deficits could be abolished by more equitable distribution of foods. For grain consumers, protein needs can be met cheaply by amino acid or protein concentrate supplements. Adequate material for supplements could be available from fish meal, oilseed press cakes, and bacterial cultures. Animal protein available for consumption could be doubled. As with the estimates of possible caloric increases, these are only estimates of what is biologically possible. It should be clear from the preceding paragraphs that these biological possibilities will only be fulfilled if there is a tremendous redirection of human and material resources toward the goal of supplying all food needs.

To Have Adequate Food Will Require Both Increased Production and Decreased Population Growth

Although we have argued that enough food could be provided for the human population even after 30–50 years of unabated population growth, we do not mean to imply that we need not worry about population growth until that time. As we will show in the second half of this book, any humane program for reducing birth rates is likely to take that long to stop population growth. So we must begin now if population size is to be stabilized by then. Furthermore, the sooner we begin efforts to slow population growth, the smaller the stable population size we will reach and the easier it will be to solve the problems of supplying food and of providing fuel and mineral resources (Chapters 9 and 10).

On the other hand, efforts to slow population growth will not substitute for efforts to increase the food supply. Even if population growth were reduced to zero over the next 30 years, the world population would still have increased from somewhat less than 4 billion to approximately 5 billion. (If population growth continued at current rates, we would reach 6½ billion people.) Thus, even with immediate and effective efforts to reduce birth rates, increases in food supply will be necessary.

In conclusion, increasing hunger and malnutrition can be avoided only if we work strenuously and effectively both to increase food supply and to reduce population growth.

BIBLIOGRAPHY

Borgstrom, G. 1969. *Too Many*. New York: Crowell-Collier and Macmillan, Inc. [Borgstrom raises many important and interesting points; however, his figures are not entirely reliable, as can be discovered by comparing estimates of related quantities].

President's Science Advisory Committee. 1967. *The World Food Problem*. Report of the Panel on the World Food Supply. Washington: U.S. Gov't. Printing Office [volume I gives a general introduction; volume II gives an extremely useful compendium of data supporting the generalizations in volume I].

section three

resources, industrial production and standard of living

chapter 9

fuel, power and pollutants

We have seen in earlier chapters that energy drives all life processes. This is also true of man's industry, commerce and domestic needs. In this chapter we shall examine patterns of energy consumption, the sources of energy, future prospects for energy resources and the consequences energy use has for the environment.

Energy Consumption

Energy comes from many different sources: coal, oil, gas, water and wind power, nuclear power and the sun. The total consumption of energy from different sources is best measured in terms of Calories, as we have done for the natural flow of energy in the ecosystem. Energy consumption is correlated with affluence as measured by Gross National Product, the annual production of consumable goods, services and capital goods (Figure 9–1). The United States is by far the wealthiest nation both in terms of its Gross National Product and in terms of its consumption of energy. The United States, with 6 percent of the world population, consumed 35 percent of the world production of energy in 1967. Our per capita consumption of energy is nearly twice as great as in any other large country except Canada; it is eight times the world average, and tens of times greater than the per capita consumption in most of the nonindustrial countries.

There have recently been large percentage increases in energy consumption in some regions where consumption was low initially (most notably Asia). However, the largest absolute increase in per capita energy consumption occurred in North America where initial levels were highest (Table 9–1). Thus, growth in different regions has not been acting to reduce inequalities in energy consumption.

Between 1957 and 1967 the world's per capita consumption of energy increased by 31 percent. World population grew 23 percent. Therefore, the 59 percent increase in total energy consumption was due more to increased per capita consumption than to population growth.

Coal has been the major source of energy in the world, but it is becoming relatively less important compared to petroleum and natural

Figure 9–1 THE RELATIONSHIP BETWEEN PER CAPITA GROSS
NATIONAL PRODUCT (GNP) AND PER CAPITA
ENERGY CONSUMPTION IN 1966

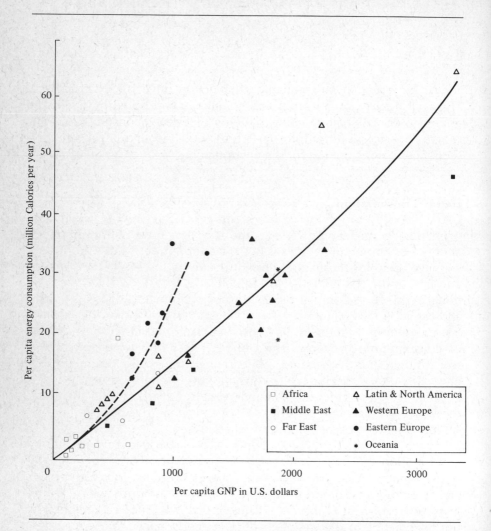

The solid line indicates the general trend for private market economies. The dashed line indicates the trend for the centrally planned economies of Eastern Europe.

Source: P. Ehrlich and A. Ehrlich. 1970. *Population, Resources, Environment* San Francisco: W. H. Freeman & Co.; U.N. Dept. of Economic and Social Affairs. 1969. *World Energy Supplies*, 1964–1967. *Statistical Papers, Series J, No. 12.*

Table 9–1 PER CAPITA CONSUMPTION OF ENERGY AND
RATE OF INCREASE IN ENERGY CONSUMPTION
IN DIFFERENT REGIONS OF THE WORLD

REGION	PER CAPITA ENERGY CONSUMP-TION (MILLION CALORIES PER PERSON) 1967	INCREASE IN PER CAPITA ENERGY CONSUMP-TION (MILLION CALORIES PER PERSON) 1957–1967	PERCENT INCREASE IN PER CAPITA ENERGY CONSUMP-TION 1957–1967	PERCENT INCREASE IN TOTAL ENERGY CONSUMP-TION 1957–1967
Africa	2.0	0.2	14	54
Far East	2.6	1.2	81	134
Western Asia	3.7	1.7	82	132
South America	4.3	1.0	29	70
Caribbean America	6.9	1.5	27	77
Western Europe	21.7	4.7	28	40
Oceania	25.0	5.9	31	62
North America	66.5	14.5	28	49
World	11.3	2.7	31	59

Source: Data from U.N. Dept. of Economic and Social Affairs. 1969. *World Energy Supplies*, 1964–1967, *Statistical Papers, Series J. No. 12.*

gas (Table 9-2). Current rates of increase in energy consumption indicate that world consumption of oil and natural gas will double every 10 years (6.9 percent increase per year) while consumption of coal will double every 20 years (3.6 percent increase per year). One half of all the petroleum production in the world up to 1968 occurred in the preceding 12 years, whereas half the coal production occurred in the preceding 31 years.

A more complete breakdown of the production and use of energy in the United States is presented in Figure 9–2. Electricity, including that produced from fossil fuels, accounts for about one-tenth of the total energy consumption. The major primary consumers of energy are the transportation sector, residential and commercial heating, the iron and steel industry and electric power utilities. Gasoline consumption by automobiles accounts for over 10 percent of all the energy consumed in the United States. The contribution of automobiles to energy demand and the associated environmental problems is even larger than this, since we should add the energy required to produce more than

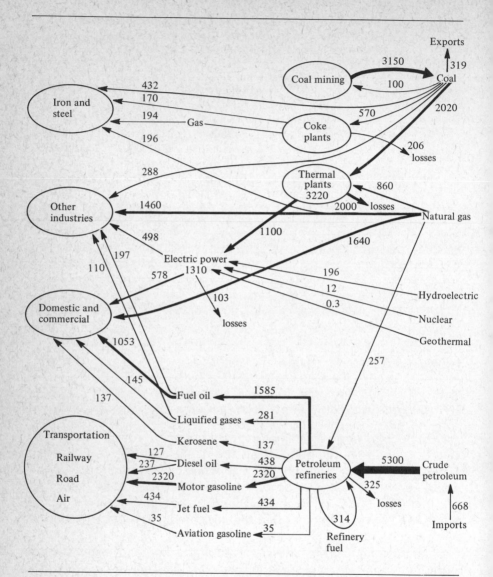

Figure 9–2 THE PRODUCTION AND USE OF ENERGY IN
THE UNITED STATES, 1968

All values are in trillion Calories per year. Most pathways with less than
100 trillion Calories per year are not included. Coal, natural gas and crude
petroleum are primary fuels. Thermal plants, coke plants and petroleum refiner-
ies are energy conversion sectors. Iron, steel and other industries, domestic and
commercial users, and transportation are final demand.

Source: Data from Organization for Economic Cooperation and Development.
1970. Statistics of Energy, 1954–1968. Paris. OECD.

Table 9–2 WORLD ENERGY CONSUMPTION, 1957 AND 1967,
IN TRILLIONS OF CALORIES PER YEAR

	TOTAL	SOLID FUEL, PRIMARILY COAL	LIQUID FUEL, PRIMARILY PETROLEUM AND ITS BY-PRODUCTS	NATURAL GAS	OTHERS, INCLUDING HYDRO-ELECTRIC, NUCLEAR PRODUCED ELECTRICITY AND GEOTHERMAL
1957	24,300	13,300 (55)	7,350 (30)	3,200 (13)	470 (2)
1967	38,600	15,000 (39)	15,300 (40)	7,500 (19)	900 (2)

Percent of total consumption is given in parentheses. Total production of electricity, including steam plants burning coal oil and natural gas, was 3200 trillion Calories in 1967.

Source: Data from U.N. Department of Economic and Social Affairs. 1969. *World Energy Supplies, 1964–1967, Statistical Papers, Series J, No. 12.*

eight million passenger cars per year and to produce the raw materials used, including 20 percent of all the steel produced in this country, half of all the lead and two-thirds of all the rubber.

The Sources of Energy
The surface of the earth is bathed with energy from the sun at the rate of 1000 billion billion Calories per year, about 25,000 times that which is used by man. Yet we do not use the abundant energy of the sun directly except in a few small experimental devices such as solar furnaces. The reason is simply that the energy of the sun is spread so thinly over the surface of the earth. Using available collecting devices, with an efficiency of roughly 10 percent, an apparatus the size of Vermont would be needed to meet current energy needs of the United States. Although this is physically possible, the cost of the requisite materials and equipment is so high that such a project seems likely to be impractical. However, current tests of new collecting devices indicate that it may be possible to attain 25 percent efficiency for the conversion of sunlight to electricity, so costs may be reduced enough to make solar energy competitive in many desert regions. Within ten years it may become

feasible to provide most of the heat, hot water and air-conditioning for most new, single-family homes by using solar energy trapped by collecting devices built into the roof and walls of the house. These residential energy uses currently constitute over 10 percent of United States' energy consumption.

The diffuse energy of the sun is naturally accumulated over time by photosynthesis and plant growth. A forest represents an accumulation of the productivity of its trees over many years. Coal represents the sun's energy concentrated by plants and then by geological processes over thousands and even millions of years. The discovery of oil and natural gas during the middle of the last century added yet another concentrated energy source which is relatively easy to exploit and transport in relation to the power which it yields.

The sun's energy is also concentrated geographically through the evaporation of water, followed by condensation, precipitation and run-off into rivers which may be tapped for hydroelectric power. Water power, like solar power, has several major advantages. Heat is not added to the ecosystem as it is when fuels are burned. Pollutants are not injected into the atmosphere. The United States presently has a hydroelectric generating power capacity that can supply about 2 percent of our energy demands, with a potential capacity four times that amount.

Tidal power, harnessed by dams with generator plants in suitable tidal basins, takes advantage of the movement of water caused by the rotation of the earth and the gravitational pull of the sun and moon. It is unfortunate that there are so few coastal areas of the world which have tide ranges and tidal basins suitable for the exploitation of tidal power, for it provides energy efficiently with little pollution.

In some areas geothermal power, from steam which is produced either naturally or artificially in the hot depths of the earth's crust, is a very important source of energy. Again, geothermal power is a relatively minor source of electricity and heat, except in parts of Italy, Iceland and California, where natural steam is abundant.

Nuclear Energy

Our recently developed ability to use nuclear or atomic energy opens up an enormous new source of power. Nuclear energy is currently regarded by many as the ultimate and complete solution to all energy supply problems. Others view its accompanying radiation problems as the final straw to break the back of the environmental camel. Perhaps even more threatening to man's future is the possibility of massive use of nuclear energy for bombing in some future war.

At present, atomic reactors provide a small part of our total energy, but the rate of growth of atomic power is sufficiently large that by the turn of the century it may become a major source of energy in the United States, provided certain assumptions about nuclear energy and its technology are correct. The process that currently provides the energy in atomic reactors is fission, the splitting apart of the nucleus of the atom. This releases enormous amounts of energy since it taps the very strong forces that hold the protons and neutrons together in the nucleus of an atom. Much smaller amounts of energy are released by burning coal and oil, since burning taps only the much weaker forces which bind atoms together. Fission of one gram of uranium-235 (the kind of uranium that can be induced to undergo fission) releases 19 million Calories of heat, which is equivalent to the heat released by burning 2.2 million times as much oil and 2.9 million times as much coal. Atomic reactors use the large amount of energy released by uranium-235 fission to heat water into steam which runs electricity-generating steam turbines. The fission reaction is speeded up by bringing quantities of uranium into close proximity so that a neutron released by fission of one atom is likely to bombard another atom and induce it in turn to split. In an atomic bomb, this chain reaction gets going so rapidly that the whole thing explodes. In an atomic reactor, explosion is prevented by inserting graphite rods to absorb some of the neutrons and thus keep the chain reaction under control.

The proven and probable reserves of cheap uranium are relatively small. Using current technology to produce electricity at current prices, the reserves in the United States would be sufficient to meet projected demand for only a few decades. However, two changes could give nuclear power a much longer usefulness. First, if the price of electricity doubled, the reserves of expensive uranium in the United States are probably sufficient to provide power equivalent to 2½ centuries of power consumption at the current rate. Second, improved technology, which is now under development, would extract about 50 times as much power from the available uranium fuel. This is the technology of breeder reactors, in which the neutrons produced during fission are used to convert uranium-238, which cannot be induced to undergo fission, into plutonium-239, which can be induced to undergo fission and release energy. Since there is much more uranium-238 than uranium-235 in natural ores, the breeder reactor's ability to tap the energy in uranium-238 atoms results in a large increase in the energy yield for a given supply of uranium. Large supplies of thorium can be used in a similar way in breeder reactors, provided only that a radioactive trigger like uranium-235 is available. Thus breeder reactors would make much more efficient use of the available fuel. On the other hand, difficult safety problems and technological problems due to the high temperatures remain to be solved. Breeder reactors are now in the pilot project stage of development and should be ready for use by the 1980s or soon thereafter.

Looking further into the future, scientists are working to control nuclear fusion, the process that occurs in the stars and in hydrogen bombs, a process which is potentially the most powerful and promising source of energy that could be developed. A typical fusion reaction is the fusion of the nuclei of two hydrogen atoms to form the nucleus of the next heavier element, helium. Only the heavy form of hydrogen, known as deuterium, will work in this reaction. Deuterium can be extracted from water, where it occurs at 34 parts per billion. The fusion of a single gram of heavy hydrogen releases 57 million Calories. The technology of fusion reactors has developed slowly because of the extremely high temperatures needed for a maintained reaction. These temperatures are high enough to vaporize any known substance on earth, so physicists are currently trying to develop ways of containing the reacting gases in a vacuum by using very strong magnetic forces. It is not yet clear whether this technology can be developed to provide a useful source of energy.

Energy Resources and Consumption in the Future
Because energy is related to affluence, at least in the sense of physical conveniences, human aspiration as well as population growth can be expected to result in increased demand for energy in the future. Predictions of future demands are difficult, since so many factors remain unknown. Will nonindustrial countries succeed in industrializing and therefore use much more energy than they now do? Will industrial countries continue to strive for ever greater material consumption or will other goals acquire prime importance? How fast will population grow? A lower estimate of energy demand in the year 2000 can be derived by assuming that per capita consumption will remain constant and by using a low projection of population growth (Chapter 19). An upper estimate for energy demand in the year 2000 can be derived by assuming that world per capita consumption will rise to current United States' levels of consumption and using a high projection for population growth. The low and high estimates of projected demand are respectively 60 and 470 million billion Calories per year. An intermediate estimate of 170 million billion Calories per year is derived by assuming that total energy use will continue to increase at current rates.

It seems likely that we will be able to meet these energy demands for a considerable period in the future. However, it must be admitted that there is at least as much uncertainty in predicting future energy resources as there is in predicting future energy demand. Will breeder reactors and fusion reactors be developed? How many underground reserves of fuels remain to be discovered? Table 9–3 gives estimates for

Table 9-3 ESTIMATES OF TOTAL POWER RESERVES
FOR THE WORLD

SOURCE OF POWER	ESTIMATED TOTAL RESERVES (MILLION BILLION CALORIES)	COMMENTS
Geothermal	25	These estimates are minima based on the assumption that dams become useless after 200 years due to silt accumulation, tidal plants similarly last only about 500 years and geothermal steam sources are not renewed by inflow of new water to the steaming regions. The available power will be greater to the extent that these assumptions are overcome, for example, by dredging reservoirs, building new dams at new sites or injecting water into geothermal sites.
Tidal power	250	
Water power (at dams)	4000	
Oil shales	400	These estimates are based on known reserves plus estimates of the fraction of oil fields, coal mines, and so on, which remain to be discovered. Further geological exploration may result in changes by as much as a factor of two for these estimates.
Tar sands	400	
Natural gas liquid	200	
Natural gas	3000	
Crude oil	3000	
Coal	100,000	
Uranium	100,000	This is a minimum estimate for the assumption that breeder reactors will be developed. A more probable estimate would be about 100 times as large.

Source: Calculated from data in M. K. Hubbert. 1969. "Energy Resources" pp. 157–242 in *Resources and Man* (San Francisco: W. H. Freeman and Company,; Environment Policy Division, Legislative Reference Service, Library of Congress. 1970. *The Economy, Energy and the Environment.* Washington: U.S. Government Printing Office.

each of the major sources of power together with comments on the reliability of the estimates. Hubbert has estimated lifetimes for fuel reserves based on expected increase in usage to be only about half a century for oil and gas, and about two centuries for coal. The estimates for the power available from uranium reserves are less reliable because the inadequacy of geological information is compounded with uncertainty about future technological developments. If breeder reactors are developed as expected, the uranium reserves should supply hundreds or perhaps even thousands times more energy than all the fossil fuel reserves. If it becomes possible to use fusion reaction power generators, then even 1 percent of the deuterium in the oceans would provide more than half a million times the energy of all the fossil fuels currently known to exist. But for the present, the technology of fusion power is too uncertain to count on it in our plans.

In conclusion, it seems likely that we will have the resources available to meet total energy demand for at least a few centuries into the future. Although energy demand probably can be met, there will be serious problems, including the difficulties of developing new technologies for power production and new technologies to use the new sources of power for the many special purposes that oil and gas now serve. Probably even more serious will be the problems of controlling the pollution that results from power production and power use.

Energy and Pollution

Power generation produces several unfortunate by-products which fall into three general classes: heat, chemicals and radiation. At the present time, the total production of heat by man is not a serious threat on a global scale, because we produce less than one-hundredth of a percent of the total heat striking the earth from the sun. The major problem is that of concentration, because the heat which we produce is discharged into a relatively small area, generally near population centers. When discharges of hot water from power plants and other industries raise local water temperatures, the metabolism of fish and other organisms is speeded up so oxygen consumption increases. At the same time the oxygen content of the water decreases and the affinity of hemoglobin for oxygen decreases. In these circumstances some fish and other organisms will not be able to survive. However, if local changes in temperature can be kept small, the effects on the environment are rarely critical. Releasing heat is generally not so deleterious in air as in water, because air mixes rapidly and heat is not confined to a small area for any appreciable length of time. Hence it is generally desirable to cool water by releasing its heat to the atmosphere before discharging the water into streams.

The major sources of air pollution in the United States are presented in Table 9–4. Motor vehicles are the primary source of carbon monoxide, nitrogen oxides and hydrocarbons. Carbon monoxide binds strongly to the hemoglobin in the blood, and thus displaces oxygen and reduces the oxygen-carrying capacity of the blood. Carbon monoxide is produced by internal combustion engines because the fuel does not burn completely, so it forms carbon monoxide rather than carbon dioxide. This can be partially corrected by afterburners

Table 9–4 SOURCES OF AIR POLLUTION IN THE UNITED STATES IN 1966 (MILLIONS OF TONS PER YEAR)

| | POLLUTANT | | | | |
SOURCE	carbon monoxide	hydro-carbons	nitrogen oxides	sulfur oxides	particu-lates
Motor vehicles	66	12	6	1	1
Industry	2	4	2	9	6
Power plants	1	1	3	12	3
Space heating	2	1	1	3	1
Refuse disposal	1	1	1	1	1
Total	72	19	13	26	12

Source: From U.S. Congress, Joint Committee on Atomic Energy. 1969. *Selected Materials on Environmental Effects of Producing Electric Power*, 185. Washington: Government Printing Office.

in the exhaust systems of cars and other smog control devices provided that they are properly adjusted.

Nitrogen oxides and hydrocarbons react chemically in sunlight to produce smog constituents that damage plant leaves and cause eye irritation. Nitrogen oxides are produced by the burning of the nitrogen in the air in the internal combustion engine. Many of the proposals to reduce carbon monoxide through increased burning efficiency will also *increase* nitrogen oxide emissions. Nitrogen oxides may possibly be reduced by catalytic mufflers but their elimination will require engines that have lower compression ratios and lower combustion temperatures. Hydrocarbons escape into the air because of sloppy fuel transfer practices, leakage of storage tanks and incomplete combustion.

Industry and power plants pose different types of problems. Coal and oil are burned at a slow controlled rate, producing carbon dioxide which is a natural component of the atmosphere. However, each year man consumes more than five billion metric tons of fossil fuels, equivalent to approximately 3 percent of the total primary production of the earth. As a result, the carbon dioxide content of the atmosphere has risen noticeably in the last several decades (pg. 42).

The major industrial pollutants are the sulfur oxides and particulate matter or "fly ash." Inhaled particles can irritate the respiratory tract. Particulate matter may also aggravate the effects of other pollutants. Other pollutants are adsorbed on the particles, which increases the exposure of the lungs to these pollutants, since particles of certain sizes penetrate deeply into the lungs and may be stored there. The emission of fly ash can be controlled effectively by proper burning techniques and electrostatic precipitators.

Sulfur oxides give the atmosphere a pungent, irritating odor. Sulfur dioxide forms sulfur trioxide, which in turn combines with water to form sulfuric acid. This highly corrosive acid is found in rainwater and on any wet surfaces which have direct contact with the air, for example, our lungs. As a result, even marble buildings are slowly being eaten away. Sulfur dioxide, at the concentrations found during severe air pollution, causes constriction of the airway and increased mucous secretion, and appears to exacerbate chronic respiratory disease. Sulfur dioxide pollution may be reduced by reduction of overall energy consumption, by the use of new processes which convert heat energy to electrical energy more efficiently so less fuel is burned in power plants, by the use of fuels with low sulfur content, by removal of sulfur from fuels and by the removal of sulfur from power plant exhausts. Low sulfur fuels are currently used by such power generators as the Philadelphia Electric Company. However, the scarcity of such fuel brings premium prices and thus increases the cost of electricity. Sulfur can be removed from fuel oil for about 25–50 cents per barrel, roughly 10 percent of the price of the oil at the refinery. It is difficult to remove sulfur from solid coal, but coal can be chemically processed to yield essentially sulfur-free gas. Sulfur may also be removed from effluents by a variety of processes costing (including capital investments) between $0.36 and $2.45 per ton of coal. If the maximum extra cost were added to the price paid by the consumer for electricity, the increase in price would be less than 4 percent. These estimates assume that sulfur by-products are sold to industry. The by-products from coal-burning electric plants could supply all the sulfur used by industry in the United States and thus our energy requirements could be reduced slightly by eliminating the mining of raw sulfur. On the other hand, the cheapest method of removing sulfur dioxide, absorption by dolomite, does not produce any salable by-product and produces millions of tons of solid waste.

The use of fissionable materials to produce electricity presents another problem, that of radioactivity. Since fission produces almost two million times as much energy per gram as does the combustion of coal, the total quantity of material pollutants will be far less than for equivalent power generated from coal. But the amount of radioactive wastes will be much larger. It is well established that radioactivity can damage the genetic material and thus induce cancers in the irradiated individual and genetic defects in his or her offspring. Genetic defects are transmitted to each succeeding generation and are irreversible, at least with any technology now available. Very little is known about how much damage will be produced by low doses of radiation which persist over long periods of time. Responsible estimates of the effects of radiation levels permitted by regulations in force in 1970 range as high as a 5 percent increase in cancers. Regulations are made by the Atomic Energy Commission, the same agency which is responsible for promoting the use and development of atomic energy. Given this conflict of interest and the absence of any adequate data on safety, the AEC has been inclined in the past to avoid making safety regulations so stringent that they might hamper the development of atomic energy. It should be added that the average United States citizen receives much less radioactivity from nuclear power plants than from medical x-rays, and that medical x-rays could be reduced, for example, by substituting tuberculin skin tests for chest x-rays in TB screening programs.

Nuclear power plants produce radioactive waste of three kinds: emissions to the atmosphere, radioactive substances carried off in the water used to cool and clean the reactor, and spent nuclear reactor fuel. By far the biggest amount of radioactivity is in the spent fuel. A conventional atomic reactor produces primarily strontium-90 and cesium-137, which still have half of their radioactivity after 30 years of storage. Strontium-90 is chemically similar to calcium and is therefore concentrated into milk from which it is concentrated into the bones of growing children. Thus even low levels of strontium-90 in the environment can result in high levels of radiation near human bones. Current plans are to store the radioactive materials underground for long periods until their radioactivity has reached a safe low level. Such storage can only be safe if it is based on accurate and reliable predictions of seepage of underground water, container durability, earthquake improbability and the like. Smaller amounts of radioactivity escape from nuclear power plants with the gaseous and water effluents. These low level releases directly to the environment will constitute an increasing hazard as the use of atomic reactors increases.

More dramatically frightening is the possibility of a major accident resulting in the release of large amounts of radioactive material. Some of the mishaps and near-mishaps of the early years of atomic energy were the result of primitive technology which has since been corrected. But possibilities remain for a major accident and emergency safety systems have not been thoroughly tested under realistic conditions. In addition, the possibility of accidents during transport of radioactive fuels and wastes will increase as the number of nuclear power plants increases.

Hazards from radioactive pollutants will be much reduced if nuclear fusion reactors can be developed, since fusion reactors would use little or no radioactive fuel and would produce much less radio-active waste than fission reactors.

Proposals for the Future

As energy consumption rises, pollution is increasing and some sources of energy face exhaustion in the near future. In order to cope with these problems several steps must be taken:

1. Population growth must slow down and eventually stop. Almost half of the current increase in energy consumption in the world is the direct result of population increase.
2. We should reduce per capita energy consumption in countries like the United States, where energy consumption is very high. Where possible, we should substitute goods and services that require less energy. For example, efficient public transportation and reduction of commuting distances by more imaginative city planning could reduce the tremendous outpouring of energy and wastes by automobiles used in daily commuting in the United States. The same purpose could be served by substituting natural products for manufactured products (for example, cotton for nylon) wherever sufficient agricultural resources are available to spare for growing nonfood products. This would reduce energy problems, because plant growth makes use of the major underexploited, pollution-free energy source, sunlight, whereas manufacturing processes use fuels and produce pollutants.

    Another way to reduce energy demand per capita would be to reduce consumption of goods per capita, for example, by producing goods that lasted longer and would not have to be replaced so often. Similarly, if we could reduce our military expenditures (almost 10 percent of Gross National Product currently), per capita energy requirements would be reduced proportionately. Finally, energy demand could be reduced by more efficient use of energy. For example, the heat produced in the manufacture of steel might be used to power electric generators before being dispersed as waste into the environment.
3. Gaseous emissions from the combustion of fossil fuels should be reduced as close as possible to carbon dioxide and water, the natural by-products of respiration. With increasing fuel consumption, greater efforts will have to be made to clean up, or environmental quality will deteriorate. Technological development in this area is relatively primitive. Research is urgently

needed to develop cheap methods of removing pollutants from effluent gases and to develop methods of burning fuels so that fewer pollutants are produced.

4. Alternatives to the combustion of fossil fuels and the use of nuclear reactors should be vigorously explored and exploited. Solar, tidal, geothermal and hydropower all provide energy with minimal pollution, and solar power, in particular, taps a major underexploited energy source. In general, research in the use and transformation of energy should be given very high priority, equally for the development of new energy sources and for the refinement and perfection of current methods of providing power and reducing energy demands.

All these proposals will require that preservation of environmental quality take precedence over maximization of immediate profits. Government intervention has already begun to move in this direction, for example, by requiring reductions in the pollutants contained in auto exhaust. However, government policy remains highly inconsistent. For example, late in 1971, Congress and President Nixon removed the 7 percent excise tax on automobiles in order to reduce consumer prices and thus increase sales of autos. This action will increase air pollution and solid waste problems and will deplete supplies of iron, gasoline and other resources. However, despite their expressed concern for the environment, President Nixon and Congress have enacted this change because it will increase profits and employment in automobile factories, steel mills, iron mines and gas stations. In Chapter 11, we will show that policies can be found which could both provide adequate income for all *and* preserve environmental quality.

BIBLIOGRAPHY

Environmental Policy Division of the Legislation Reference Service of the Library of Congress. 1970. *The Economy, Energy and the Environment.* Washington: U.S. Gov't. Printing Office.

Gough, W. C. and B. J. Eastland. 1971. The prospects of fusion power. *Scientific American,* February: 50–64.

Hubbert, M. K. 1969. Energy resources. pp. 157–242 in *Resources and Man.* San Francisco: W. H. Freeman and Company [an excellent summary of energy resources for the future, with comparisons to past use].

Seaborg, G. T. and J. L. Bloom. 1970. Fast breeder reactors. *Scientific American,* November: 13–21.

Secretary of Health, Education, and Welfare, Third Report to Congress. 1970.

Progress in the Prevention and Control of Air Pollution. Washington: Senate Doc. #19–64, U.S. Gov't. Printing Office.

Stern, A. C., ed. 1968. *Air Pollution,* vol. I *Air Pollution and Its Effects.* N.Y.: Academic Press, Inc.

Tamplin, A. R. and J. W. Gofman. 1970. *Population Control through Nuclear Pollution.* Chicago: Nelson-Hall [a skeptical view of the safety of nuclear reactors].

chapter 10

minerals and related resources

We have seen that energy is a nonrenewable resource. Once it is used and released as heat, it usually cannot be reused. Energy must constantly be supplied anew from high energy sources to satisfy the power demands of civilization. Mineral and other resources differ in that they are at least potentially available for recycling after they are used. When iron, for example, is incorporated into an automobile, it is still iron. And when that automobile finally gives up the road, the iron in the wrecked automobile may be recovered for reuse. In fact, the scrap iron industry is a major source of that metal. All too often, however, metals and other resources are not recovered, with the result that wastes build up in our environment and that the supplies of some resources have become critically short.

Resources should be conserved by recycling, but expansion of supplies depends on mining new ores. How large are mineral reserves relative to probable future demand? The known reserves of good quality ore are not large; for many metals, these reserves would not last much beyond the end of this century even at current rates of consumption. But new discoveries are expected, and larger supplies of most minerals could be made available by using more energy to mine relatively inaccessible ores or to extract metals from low grade ores (with small proportions of the desired metal). Also synthetic materials can substitute for some scarce minerals. How long can we expect these resources to continue to provide the raw materials we need? We really do not know. In this condition of ignorance, it would seem wisest to conserve resources as though our minimum estimates of availability were correct, while carrying out the research to maximize our knowledge of the available resources.

Known Reserves of Readily Accessible Minerals Are Small
Discouraging results are obtained when future demand is compared to minimum estimates of mineral reserves. These minimum estimates include only ore deposits which are known to exist or are very probable on geological grounds. These estimates also exclude those known deposits which are so costly to extract that they could not be profit-

ably mined at present. Such reserves will run out before the end of the century for copper, lead, zinc, tin, gold, silver and platinum, even under the unrealistic assumption that rates of consumption will not increase. Reserves of aluminum, nickel, cobalt, manganese and molybdenum would last about a century more, and iron and chromium an additional two centuries. Actually population is growing and per capita consumption is increasing so these "highly probable" reserves will run out even faster. However, for almost all these minerals, actual reserves are probably significantly larger than these "highly probable" reserves, because new deposits are likely to be discovered and because very deep, remote or low grade ores could be mined if the cost in terms of additional fuel, equipment and labor were paid.

Some metals are found either in fairly rich deposits or at extremely low concentrations, so costs will jump enormously once the rich deposits have been exploited. Others, like iron and aluminum, are present at progressively lower and lower concentrations, so very large quantities can be extracted, at progressively higher and higher costs. The increase in costs may be partially offset by improvements in technology, but probably not entirely. This can be illustrated by the history of copper mining in the United States. Since 1925, the average grade of ore has dropped from 1.6 percent to 0.6 percent copper content. Until about 1950, the price of copper (adjusted to eliminate the effects of inflation) held fairly steady at about 24 cents per pound, because improved technology offset the effects of decreasing ore grade. However, after that the higher costs of extracting copper from poorer ores has resulted in a price rise to more than 42 cents per pound in 1968. We are now turning more and more to other countries like Chile which still have high grade copper ore. It has been proposed that low grade ores could be exploited more cheaply in the future because fusion reactors will provide low cost energy. However, the cost of fuels is such a small part of the total cost of energy that cheaper fuel supplies, which might come with fusion energy, will probably not substantially lower the cost of generating power. Furthermore, we have no guarantee that fusion power will ever become a reality.

When we consider the possibility of tapping the huge mineral stores in the oceans, costs of extraction are even higher and apparently prohibitive for most minerals. Only a few minerals are abundant enough in the ocean to be extracted profitably at present. These include common table salt, bromine and magnesium. The value of 17 other critical metals (including copper, gold, uranium and zinc) in a cubic mile of seawater is less than $1 million at current prices. The expenditure required to extract these metals from that much water (more than two million gallons per minute for a year) would be far more than the value of the resources it contains.

Far more probable as future resources are the minerals which occur in the bed of the sea. Oil and gas currently account for most of the wealth which we now obtain from the sea, and offshore wells produce 17 percent of all oil and 6 percent of all natural gas. However, problems with oil leakage, pointed up by the disastrous Santa Barbara oil spill, leave one to wonder about the advisability of exploiting this resource until more reliable methods of oil recovery are used. Quite a lot of mining is carried out under sea by way of mine shafts which are dug from the land out underneath the sea. Subsea mining can be conducted economically for certain ores as far as 15 miles from the shoreline, and significant amounts of coal, iron ore, nickel-copper ores, tin and limestone are obtained in this way. The floor of the ocean is relatively poor in mineral resources.

In conclusion, known resources of readily accessible minerals are very limited. Improved technology and higher costs will make more available. But the crucial question of how much more minerals at how much higher cost cannot be answered yet.

Some Substitutes for Scarce Minerals Can Be Found

Many optimists insist that as the supply of minerals runs out, "technology" will find new replacements for them. This has been spectacularly true for rubber. Synthetic rubber was first made on a commercial scale in Germany during World War I when a British naval blockade prevented the importation of natural rubber. World War II provided a second impetus when Japan cut off the United States' supply of natural rubber from southeast Asia. Synthetic rubber is now produced in roughly comparable amounts to natural rubber. However, the natural raw material for most synthetic rubbers is petroleum, which is being burned at a high rate for energy rather than being conserved as a mineral resource. Consequently, we can expect to face supply problems within the next century. Since plastics are also made primarily from petroleum they face a similar raw material shortage. The much larger reserves of coal might provide an alternative raw material, but the synthesis of plastics from coal will probably be more costly. Another factor that limits the potential for substituting synthetic materials for scarce minerals is the need for certain special properties, such as high electrical conductivity, which some metals have and synthetic materials lack.

Scarce Resources Should Be Recycled

Resources are not recycled more than at present primarily because of economic considerations, or short-term profit motives. The recovery of metals from manufactured objects costs money, often more than to extract them from mined ores. As natural resources of metals become scarce, prices of metals will rise, there will be a greater incentive to reclaim minerals from worn-out objects, and recycling will become more and more prevalent. There are a number of things that we could and should do to increase recycling of materials before that critical stage has been reached. For example, our tax structure should be changed. At present it gives a financial advantage to many of the industries that mine mineral deposits relative to industries engaged in recycling. This is because the former receive a tax advantage, in the form of the depletion allowance, which the latter do not receive. If we wish to conserve scarce resources, we should impose a heavier tax burden on miners and a lighter tax burden on recycling processers.

In many cases, it would be possible to manufacture items in such a way that their components could easily be separated and reused. However there has been no strong incentive for manufacturers to develop this type of product, and in some cases, such a product is more expensive or less desirable to the consumer. The beer can is a good example. Until recently, beer cans were made entirely out of steel which could be reused quite easily, provided that the cans were not tossed along the road where collection is difficult and expensive. The introduction of the "soft" aluminum top, however, meant that cans were made out of two metals. As a result, to recover either the iron or the aluminum, the tops of the cans must be separated from the rest, and the process is not economically worthwhile. This becomes significant when one considers that we dispose of more than 50 billion cans of various sorts each year in the United States. The recent development of the all-aluminum can will alleviate this problem. However, the substitution of aluminum for steel will aggravate energy resources problems, since twice as much power is used to produce the aluminum as to produce the steel it replaces.

For certain minerals such as lead, copper and aluminum, ore reserves are already sufficiently expensive to mine, and recovery from manufactured items is sufficiently easy, that large amounts of these metals are supplied by "secondary production" from scrap. In Figure 10–1, several mineral industries in the United States are schematically diagrammed. In each case, secondary production of the metals from scrap represents a large proportion of the total production. A more relevant statistic from the standpoint of recycling, but one which is harder to obtain, is the proportion of the total waste metal which is recycled. For automobiles in 1966, about six million were scrapped with extraction of metal for recycling, while a quarter of a million were left in "graveyards" or along roads. For most other products, the proportion recycled is probably lower.

Figure 10–1 PRODUCTION, RECYCLING AND STANDING CROP
FOR SELECTED MINERALS IN THE UNITED STATES.

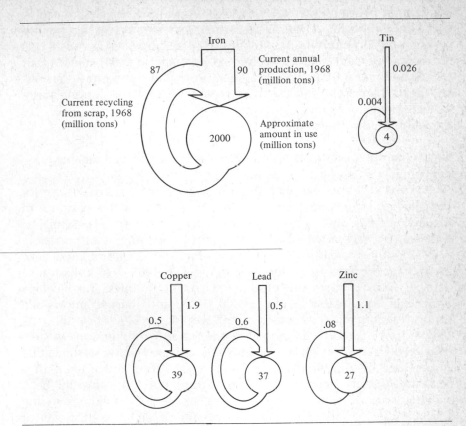

Iron

87   90   Current annual
production, 1968
(million tons)

Tin

0.026

Current recycling
from scrap, 1968
(million tons)

0.004

Approximate
amount in use
(million tons)

2000

4

Copper   Lead   Zinc

1.9   0.5   1.1

0.5   0.6   .08

39   37   27

Source: Data for 1968 from *U.S. Mineral Yearbook.*

Plant resources are continually replenished by plant growth, but our use of forest products has increased to such an extent that widespread conservation programs are necessary to ensure sufficient forested areas. Increased recycling should replace widespread burning of paper and wood "trash" in order to conserve resources and reduce air pollution. Each year in the United States we use about 55 million tons of paper stock, representing the cutting of a billion trees. Paper pulp is taken primarily from temperate and northern forests that, over the surface of the earth, have a productivity of more than 100 times our current use of paper stock in this country. This appears to be a vast abundance of raw material relative to its consumption until you consider that the United States has only about a tenth of the population living in these regions, over half of a tree cannot be used for pulp, large amounts of wood are used for lumber and large areas of forest in mountainous regions are inaccessible. Only about 20 percent of the total paper used in the United States is now recycled, meaning that 44 million tons are lost as trash each year, more than 400 pounds for each person. Burning this amount of paper provides as much heat as about 5 percent of the coal burned annually in this country. Thus far only a small proportion of the heat produced during trash burning has been harnessed for useful purposes. Therefore, current trash-burning practices contribute to thermal and air pollution as well as to depletion of forest resources.

Large Quantities of Metals Are Currently in Use and Not Available for Recycling

If recycling were perfect, then the most important measure of use for comparison to resource reserves would be the standing crop of material, that is, the total amount actually in current use. Steel, for example, is used primarily for automobiles and other transportation, and in building construction (office buildings, factories and large commercial establishments). In the United States in 1967, 16.5 million tons of steel were used in the production of automobiles. The average lifetime of cars in this country is 5.6 years, and thus, if automobile production remained constant, there would be 5.6 times 16.5=92 million tons of steel in automobiles. The other 66 million tons of steel produced in 1967 went largely into construction. If we assume that the average building lasts 30 years before it is torn down, then, after 30 years of construction use at the current rate, there would be a standing crop of almost 2 billion tons of steel in buildings in the United States, or about 10 tons per person. To achieve this level of material affluence for the entire world would require about 35 billion tons of steel. Currently world production of steel is only about 0.6 billion tons a year. Similar calculations for the world at United States' levels of affluence indicate that a standing crop of 500 million tons of lead, 330 million tons of zinc, and 50 million tons of tin would be required. The present yearly world production of these commodities is only 3.2 million tons of lead, 5.0 million tons of zinc, and 0.23 million tons of tin.

If the calculated standing crop levels were set as production goals, it is entirely possible that world reserves might be able to meet such a demand for iron and that it could be produced within a century. However, a shortage of other minerals that are alloyed with iron to make steel might develop. Shortages of lead, zinc and tin would probably develop since the "highly probable" reserves in non-Communist countries are only 50, 70 and 5 million tons respectively, with at least 20 percent more in Communist countries. In all three cases, new discoveries are likely to increase reserves substantially, but it remains dubious whether the earth can support even its present population at the level of affluence which we have in the United States.

Reducing the Demand on Limited Mineral Resources

That limited resources should not be wasted is a truism. That waste nevertheless persists where profitable is nearly a truism. The case of helium (presented in Box 10–1) illustrates how rapidly reserves can be dispersed by wasteful procedures, and describes a faltering government program to eliminate the waste and conserve the resource.

That the finite resources of the earth cannot support population growth indefinitely is also a truism. Indeed, the data in this chapter, as well as the preceding chapters indicate that it would be wise to begin now to reduce population growth.

Box 10–1 **HELIUM CONSERVATION**

Helium, the lightest gas after hydrogen, is a unique element that is rapidly being wasted. Helium is found in quantities which are economical to use primarily in natural gas deposits, where it occurs in concentrations as high as 2 percent. We are rapidly using our natural gas reserves as an energy source, and as the gas is burned, the helium has been allowed to escape into the atmosphere where it becomes so dispersed that it is extremely expensive to extract.

Helium has several properties which make it a unique and potentially critical element. It is currently used largely to pressurize rocket fuel tanks because it will not react chemically with the fuels and has light weight and good expansion and temperature characteristics. Its nonflammability, rapid diffusion and rareness in the atmosphere make it ideal for leak detection. It can be cooled to very low temperatures without freezing, and thus it is the only suitable substance for low temperature superconductance which makes possible, for example, the very powerful magnets likely to be used in fusion reactors. Many other uses are known and more are expected in the future.

Because of its uniqueness and the fact that it was being wasted, the government started a program in 1960 to stockpile helium in underground reservoirs near Amarillo, Texas, and contracted with four natural gas companies to extract helium for this purpose. In order to pay for the stockpiling program, the government bought helium from its producers for about $12 per 1000 cubic feet and sold it at an artificially high price of $35 per 1000 cubic feet to all government agencies and private users. This method of financing assumed a government monopoly, but the legislation provided no way of enforcing a monopoly. Two private companies extracted helium and sold it to private industry for $10–15 less than the government price. As a result, most of private industry bought its helium from private companies, and the government revenues that were to pay for the storage program fell short of expectations. As a consequence, the storage program cost approximately $50 million in 1969. There is currently enough helium stockpiled to meet demands for roughly 30 years, and many people wondered whether this expensive project was worth the price. Recently the program was cancelled.

It is very difficult to forecast the needs for helium in the future, for many of its potentially large uses are now only in the development stage. Antagonists of the program contend that there is plenty of helium in storage or in gas reserves to meet demands for half a century and that when shortages come, either new reserves of helium will be found, or new ways of extracting helium from extremely dilute sources such as the atmosphere will become economical because of new technological improvements and cheap sources of power. To abandon the storage program on these assumptions represents an irreversible gamble with large risks, since it costs about $10 million to extract a year's supply of helium now from limited natural gas reserves, whereas it would cost almost $10 billion to extract a year's supply of helium from the air using current technology.

In considering how to limit mineral consumption, there is one other factor which those of us in the United States particularly need to consider, namely inequality of consumption. The United States, with 6 percent of the world's population, currently consumes about a third of the world's mineral production (Table 10–1). Modern communication has brought knowledge of our affluence to many people with much lower levels of consumption. Economists have found that a person who knows that particular products exist and are possessed by others often aspires to attain the same for himself. This "demonstration effect" is sufficiently important that high consumption and predicted increases in the United States (Table 10–1) should be expected to have a worldwide impact on demand. World demand is bound to increase in any case as population grows and people strive to attain minimal material necessities, but the demonstration effect will certainly accelerate the increase. The responsibilities of the United States are even more serious, since it imports from other countries so much of the resources it consumes (Table 10–1). We could obtain all our minerals from North America, since almost all the minerals are available either in the United States or in Canada although at a higher cost. But, given our current purchasing patterns, our mineral policies should take into consideration worldwide resource needs and limits.

Table 10–1   UNITED STATES' MINERAL CONSUMPTION

MINERAL	U.S. CONSUMPTION AS A PERCENT OF WORLD PRODUCTION (1968)	U.S. IMPORTS AS A PERCENT OF U.S. CONSUMPTION (1968)	PROJECTED ANNUAL GROWTH RATES IN CONSUMPTION (1968–1985)
Manganese ore	12	82	2.1
Iron ore	20	33	1.6
Bauxite (aluminum ore)	33	78	5.5*
Copper	32	53	3.8
Zinc	34	49	3.1
Tin	36	73	NA
Lead	41	33	0.4
Molybdenum	60†	0	5.6

*—Projected increase for aluminum consumption
†—Excludes production in Communist countries
NA—Not available

Source: Data for 1968 from *U.S. Mineral Yearbook.*

Solid Waste Disposal

Many of our activities produce prodigious amounts of wastes that cannot easily be reused and must be disposed of somehow. Many cities in this country are finding themselves critically short of space for the dumping of solid wastes and do not have alternative plans. New York City, for example, is expected to run out of land space to dump wastes in 1975, and is already barging a large amount of wastes to points off the coast of New Jersey where they are dumped into the sea.

Solid wastes are disposed of in many different ways. The cheapest is the open dump, but this is also the worst from the standpoint of public health. Unfortunately, open dumps are one of the prevalent "solutions" to the waste problem, especially in small towns. Dumps are sometimes set on fire to make room for more waste, but the low temperature burning, often with insufficient oxygen, produces dirty smoke that adds substantially to the pollution of already overloaded air in some urban areas. Sanitary land fills, in which trash is dumped for a short period into a trench or over a shallow bank and then covered with a layer of dirt, eliminate much of the public health nuisance of the open dump. They also use a considerable amount of space, however, so much that some large cities are running out of room. Sanitary landfills also present water pollution problems, because rainwater filtering through the dump can leach out many chemicals which eventually find their way into streams. Landfills have other serious drawbacks. Frequently, landfills are put into areas which are otherwise deemed unusable for human purposes. Marshes, one of the most highly productive habitats on earth, unfortunately bear the brunt of this ill-informed planning. In five years, one-eighth of the wetlands surrounding Long Island, New York, were destroyed by landfill projects. This area constituted valuable feeding ground for many commercially important fisheries. In urbanized areas, housing projects have been built on landfills before they have properly settled, resulting in sagging buildings and streets. These areas might be better set aside as parks and playgrounds.

Many large cities incinerate some or all of their solid wastes. Municipal incinerators are often a major source of the fly ash in air pollution, although fly ash can be effectively removed by electrostatic precipitators in the smoke stacks. Two important advances are under development: processes for using the heat energy produced during incineration, and processes for sorting out recyclable materials like metal and glass before incineration. One alternative to incineration is under development, namely, recycling of the bulk of the solid waste, including paper, which constitutes about one half of municipal solid waste. The other major alternative to incineration is composting of organic materials after metals and glass have been removed. The compost produced has relatively little fertilizer value but is useful as a soil conditioner and is used to a considerable extent in Europe. In the United States compost has not been able to compete economically with alternative sources of humus, especially peat and steer manure, and therefore most existing composting plants have closed.

The solid waste disposal problem in the Delaware Valley of Pennsylvania and New Jersey is described in Box 10–2.

Box 10–2 **SOLID WASTE IN THE DELAWARE VALLEY REGION**

Each year in the Delaware Valley region more than 2.7 million tons of solid waste are collected from domestic and commercial locations, with that much again being produced by industry. By 1985, this amount is expected to double. The Delaware Valley region is inhabited by just over five million people, so the solid waste production is somewhat over one ton per person per year, or about six pounds per person per day. Present annual expenditures for the collection and disposal of solid wastes throughout the region are $33.5 million, three-quarters of which goes to collection and one-quarter toward disposal costs. The trash that is collected is deposited on 108 recognized land disposal sites covering more than 3000 acres, at least 250 "promiscuous" dumps, 17 incinerators, most of which were built before 1960, and 112 hog feeding facilities that are gradually being phased out because they are no longer profitable.

Waste disposal problems in the region are rapidly mounting though they are not so critical as New York's. More than half of the land disposal sites will be filled within five years and land is running short for the development of new sites. Incinerators currently receive about 1.2 million tons of waste or less than one-quarter of the total. The out-of-date facilities are a significant source of air pollution, producing 3 of the 73 million tons of particulates released in the area each year.

One critical problem that stands in the way of improved waste disposal is the fragmented jurisdiction in the area. Although the Delaware Valley region is a natural geographical area, it encompasses parts of two states (Pennsylvania and New Jersey), eight counties, and 353 civil divisions (borough, township and city). About three-quarters of the civil divisions exercise jurisdiction over garbage collection or operate their own collection services. The area also includes an estimated 1300 private collectors. Under the circumstances, coordinated planning is difficult to achieve.

Legislation is coming, but slowly. The Pennsylvania Solid Waste Management Act required the development of a solid waste plan by January 1, 1971 in each municipality with a density of more than 300 persons per square mile. Philadelphia's new Air Management Code will reduce air pollution from burning, but incinerators are exempted for five years from meeting the new code's standards. Many proposals have been put forward for the region's wastes, including the use of offshore waters of the Atlantic Ocean that

115

already receive sewage sludge, shipping waste by rail to strip mine sites in the coal regions of northeastern Pennsylvania, and the construction of new incinerators by private firms to operate under contract to the local governments. Meanwhile, alternatives, thoughtful consideration and garbage continue to pile up.

BIBLIOGRAPHY

Benarde, M. A. 1970. *Our Precarious Habitat.* New York: W. W. Norton and Company, Inc. [a general discussion of man's pollutants and their effect on the environment].

Brown, H. S., J. Bonner, and J. Weir. 1957. *The Next Hundred Years.* New York: The Viking Press Inc. [a well-reasoned and readable prognosis, particularly for natural resources available to man].

Cloud, P. E., Jr. 1968. Realities of Mineral Distribution. *Texas Quarterly* 11: 103–26 [a well-documented, hard-nosed and somewhat pessimistic view of mineral resources in the future].

Flawn, P. 1966. *Mineral Resources.* Chicago: Rand McNally and Company [gives the estimates of reserves].

Grinstead, R. R. 1972. Bottlenecks. *Environment* 14(3): 2–13 [a good description of the prospects and problems for recycling materials from solid waste].

Park, C. F. in collaboration with M. C. Freeman. 1968. *Affluence in Jeopardy: Minerals and the Political Economy.* San Francisco: W. H. Freeman and Company.

United States Department of the Interior Bureau of Mines. 1969. *Mineral Yearbook.* Washington: U.S. Gov't. Printing Office [a wealth of useful information on mineral and fuel resources].

Wenk, E., Jr. 1969. The physical resources of the ocean. *Scientific American,* September: 166–76.

chapter 11

possibilities for our society to live well with limited material resources

In the preceding chapters we have discussed limitations on the available resources and have proposed ways to make optimum use of the limited resources. In the first part of this chapter, we draw together some of the general principles that should be used in adapting to the limitations of our environment.

One of these principles is that, given the limitations on resources, individual material consumption cannot rise indefinitely. This principle is not one that most people find appealing for the immediate here and now. The majority of people we know wish to increase their income and personal consumption, and almost without exception, governments are pleased when the national economy is growing rapidly. Some of these attitudes are beginning to change as people become more aware of environmental problems. But there is still a widespread feeling that economic growth brings greater well-being, and a consequent reluctance to forgo economic growth.

In the second half of this chapter we present two lines of argument that indicate that improvements in well-being need not be linked to economic growth. First we show how one objective measure of well-being, namely health, varies independently of national wealth for nations above a certain moderate level of income. Second, we show that a stable economy need not be stagnant, that full employment, increased leisure and a variety of other benefits can be achieved in an economy where material consumption is not increasing. Anyone with ecological awareness must hope that these suggestions will have appeal and that, in well-to-do countries like the United States, a general preference will develop for the good things in life that do not depend on increasing material consumption. Only then can democratic choices lead to ecologically sound policies.

Ways to Conserve Scarce Resources
Finite supplies of minerals will inevitably run out unless minerals are continuously reclaimed from worn-out products and made available

for reuse. We have already given examples of how recycling could increase the supply of useful resources and reduce the flow of waste products into the environment.

More durable goods would require less recycling. Planned obsolescence moves in the opposite direction toward increasing consumption of raw materials and increasing accumulation of waste materials. An obvious example of this problem in the United States is disposable packaging of all sorts.

A considerable increase in goods available for individual consumption could be achieved by converting the industries that now produce spaceships and weapons into industries that produce prefab housing, pollution control devices, fertilizer and machinery for use in non-industrial countries and so on. The world's resources are so limited that, if we continue to devote 7 percent of global production to military expenditures, some vital problems are bound to go unsolved. Peace has become a necessity not only to save lives and avert the massive environmental destruction produced by war, but also to release scarce material and human resources to solve urgent problems.

Ways to Preserve Our Limited Supplies of Clean Air, Water and Land

Until very recently, air seemed limitless and free—free for all to breathe and free for all to use as a dump for waste gases. Rivers and oceans, too, were seen as limitless, free receptacles for wastes. We are now beginning to realize that neither air nor water nor land has limitless capacities to absorb our wastes.

But wastes continue to accumulate in increasing quantities. The individual producer generally finds it more profitable to continue to pollute than to control waste emissions. His calculation of profits does not, however, include the costs to others of the smog-filled air or undrinkable water that results from his activities. Owing to such omissions, his calculations of private profit often lead to decisions that do not promote the maximum public good. Private and public calculations could be made more congruent if the private producer were charged for the major costs due to the pollution he produces. This could be done by placing taxes on waste production or by imposing fines for violations of regulations that limit waste dispersal into the environment. Such procedures would reduce the emission of pollutants. Recycling of materials would become relatively more profitable. For example, disposable bottles would probably become less profitable than returnable bottles, if the manufacturer had to pay for the ultimate disposal as well as the initial manufacture of the bottle.

If automobile drivers were taxed for the air pollution that they produce, they would be motivated to make more use of public transportation. In public transport systems one engine moves many people, and therefore less air pollution is produced per passenger-mile. Decreased use of autos should also be encouraged by improving public transportation. A good beginning could be made with technically simple improvements like cleaning the subways and equipping them with rubber wheels to reduce the noise (as has been done successfully in Montreal and Paris).

These examples illustrate how pollution could be reduced by the substitution of a less polluting product for a more polluting product. That such substitutions could make a major contribution to the reduction of pollution is suggested by an analysis of the factors responsible for past increases in pollution. In the United States from 1946 to 1968, various pollutants are estimated to have increased by 200 to 1000 percent. During that period, population increased 43 percent; per capita GNP (corrected for inflation) increased 59 percent; and total production increased 126 percent. Therefore less than half of the increase in pollution was due to increased volume of production and over half the increased pollution must have been due to an increase in the amount of pollution per unit of production. How did that occur? Production shifted from less polluting goods to more polluting goods. Nonreturnable beer bottles and cans replaced returnable beer bottles. Autos replaced railroads. Synthetic materials like plastic and nylon replaced natural materials like wood and cotton. Growing plants use sunlight to produce natural materials, whereas fuels must be burned to provide energy for the production of synthetic materials, with the result that air pollution and heat pollution increase. Furthermore, after a product is discarded, microorganisms and fungi can rapidly disintegrate natural materials, but they are frequently unable to metabolize synthetic materials. The convenience and other advantages of the new products must be weighed against their increased environmental impact in order to determine which technological advances are truly advantageous.

Higher Costs and More Sophisticated Plans Will Be Necessary

Many of the methods of reducing pollution will involve costs, such as increased inconvenience to the consumer or requirements for more labor and raw materials to produce the same amount of consumable goods. In general, the closer we approach the limits of the available resources, the more resources we must expend to maintain even the same material conditions. When the first pioneer family settled on the Delaware River, they could dump virtually all the sewage they could produce into the river and expect biological and physical processes to

119

purify the water before it had flowed a mile downstream. Now the load of sewage produced is much too great to be handled by natural processes; sewage plants are a necessity. When copper was first used, it could be picked up from the surface of the earth in some places; now we must dig for it and extract it from ores which contain less copper and more of other materials. When growing populations have been forced to use marginal land that has low fertility and poor rainfall, more effort must be expended to grow adequate food. Thus, as we approach the limits of available resources, we must spend more and more to accomplish the same objective.

We will also need to make much more sophisticated and comprehensive plans. When many resources are in short supply, it is all too easy to aggravate one resource problem by a scheme designed to alleviate another. For example, desalinization plants could provide needed water but would increase fuel use and pollution. Proposals for solving the various environmental problems must be examined together in detail to make sure they are compatible and will complement each other, not cancel each other out.

Standard of Living Should Not Be Defined Solely in Terms of Consumption

In proposing solutions, we have assumed that maximum material consumption should not be an overriding goal, as it has sometimes seemed to be in the United States. Rather the goal of increasing material consumption must be balanced against the goals of conserving natural resources and improving social and psychological aspects of the quality of life. This point of view leads us to challenge the traditional definition of standard of living, which is based on the assumption that the amount of consumption should be the sole criterion for standard of living.

A common measure of average standard of living in a country is the Gross National Product per capita, in other words, the annual production per person of consumable goods and services and capital goods. Higher GNP per capita means that more material resources are available for better health and educational facilities. In consequence, life expectancy and literacy are generally higher where GNP per capita is higher (Table 11–1). These correlations increase the validity of GNP per capita as a measure of standard of living. However, for countries where GNP per capita is above approximately $1000 per year, life expectancy and literacy reach a plateau and do not increase with further increases in GNP per capita. Once a moderate level of consumption is attained, improvement in health and many

120

Table 11–1 CONDITIONS OF LIFE IN SELECTED COUNTRIES
DURING THE EARLY 1960s

COUNTRY	GNP PER CAPITA (1966)	LIFE EXPECTANCY (1960–1965)	PERCENT LITERATE AMONG THOSE 15 YEARS AND OLDER (APPROXIMATELY 1960)
Guinea	$80/yr.	36 years	10–20%
India	$90	46	25–30%
United Arab Republic (Egypt)	$160	47	20–25%
Taiwan	$230	66	55–65%
Mexico	$470	60	65–70%
Japan	$860	69	98–100%
USSR	$890	69	98–100%
Puerto Rico	$1090	70	80–85%
Sweden	$2270	74	99–100%
United States	$3520	70	97–100%

GNP or Gross National Product per capita is the annual production of consumable goods and services and capital goods divided by the population. Data on literacy are especially unreliable because the definition of literacy varies. Nevertheless, it is clear that literacy and life expectancy tend to increase as GNP per capita increases, except among the richest countries, for which literacy and life expectancy are not correlated with GNP per capita.

Source: United Nations data as compiled by the Population Reference Bureau, Washington, D.C. (printed with permission) and United Nations, Population Division, Department of Economic and Social Affairs. 1971. *Estimates of Crude Birth Rates, Crude Death Rates and Expectations of Life at Birth, Regions and Countries, 1950–1965.* New York: United Nations.

other important conditions of life seems to depend less on further increases in consumption than on other developments. Most people would agree that intangible factors such as love, security, peace of mind and self-esteem are essential for the quality of life. We do not wish to propose how to measure these, but your experience probably corroborates our impressions that these intangibles are not closely related to income or per capita GNP, at least above some minimum level. There are many other indications that GNP per capita may not adequately measure standard of living. We present next some examples from the field of health where objective data demonstrate that increasing GNP per capita can, under some circumstances, be associated with deteriorating conditions.

Some Problems that Will Not Be Solved by Increasing Material Consumption

Death rates in the United States have risen recently despite constantly growing GNP per capita (Table 11–2). From 1961 to 1966, death rates increased for white males and females and for nonwhite males at nearly all ages between 15 and 59.

What are the causes of the increase in deaths during this period of rising affluence? The major rising causes of death seem to indicate increasing stress and increasing misuse of material goods in our society. Both stress and excess consumption of fat apparently contribute to arteriosclerotic heart disease. Increased smoking and increased air pollution are probably the major causes of the rise in lung cancer. Rising alcohol consumption is the major cause of the increase in cirrhosis of the liver. Motor vehicle accidents have increased for all age-sex-race categories. Homicide has increased, especially for nonwhite males. Suicide rates have risen by roughly 50 percent since 1955 for adults of reproductive ages, with a larger increase at the younger ages and a smaller increase at older ages. Since we were unable to get a breakdown of war deaths by age, we have not included them in Table 11–2. The addition of war deaths would increase the death rate for young males by roughly one-fourth in the late 1960s. Taken together, the causes of increasing deaths form a pattern which suggests increasing stress and increasing destructive use of material resources in our society.

These conditions probably explain why life expectancy in the United States is so close to Puerto Rican life expectancy, despite a threefold higher per capita GNP in the United States (Table 11–1 and Figure 11–1). Deaths due to infectious disease are higher in Puerto Rico where medical care is poorer, but heart disease and cancer are higher in the United States. The material benefits of an affluent society are apparently offset by the effects of stress, pollution and other problems.

Another example of incongruity between income and health measures of standard of living emerges from a comparison of conditions in Sweden and the United States. Although Sweden has only two-thirds the per capita GNP of the United States, she nevertheless has significantly better health with the lowest death rates in the world (Figure 11–1). We presume that Sweden's advantage must be due in part to her governmental programs to assure adequate medical care for all. One major reason that death rates are high in the United States is the very poor health among low income groups. In Philadelphia, for example, death rates for young and middle-aged adults are twice as high in the poorest quarter as in the richest quarter. Infant mortality in the poorest health district is three times that in the most affluent.

Table 11–2   RISING DEATH RATES IN THE UNITED STATES
FROM 1961 TO 1966

20–24 YEAR OLDS

	all causes	motor vehicle accidents	suicide	homicide
Males—White	163/183	72/89	11/14	5/7
Nonwhite	271/315	62/83	12/14	67/94
Females—White	58/62	13/19	3/4	2/2.5
Nonwhite	(133/134)	14/19	3/4	16/19

35–39 YEAR OLDS

	all causes	motor vehicle accidents	homicide	cirrhosis of the liver
Males—White	246/259	28/36	6/8	9/12
Nonwhite	595/697	45/54	75/106	24/45
Females—White	(147/147)	9/12	(3/3)	5/7
Nonwhite	(428/442)	12/15	20/23	20/29

55–59 YEAR OLDS

	all causes	arteriosclerotic heart disease	malignant neoplasms of the respiratory system (lung cancer and so on)	cirrhosis of the liver
Males—White	1727/1836	699/754	125/140	50/61
Nonwhite	2358/2788	534/648	126/173	40/64
Females—White	793/831	174/181	17/24	19/24
Nonwhite	(1794/1760)	350/368	22/27	18/32

Death rates are given for the three leading causes of increased deaths for three representative age groups. Numbers indicate deaths per 100,000 people in the specified age group. The 1961 data are to the left of each slash and 1966 data are on the right. Parentheses indicate that the change was less than 5%.

Death rates for "all causes" do not include war deaths; inclusion of war deaths would increase deaths due to "all causes" by roughly one-quarter for young males in the late 1960s. Deaths due to some causes not listed and total death rates for young children and older people declined in this period.

Source: U.S. National Office of Vital Statistics, PHS Dept. HEW. 1961 & 1966. *Vital Statistics of the U.S.*

Figure 11–1 CHANGES IN HEALTH WITH HIGHER MATERIAL
CONSUMPTION

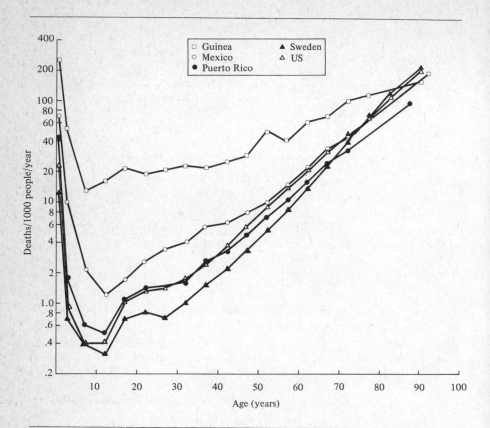

Health has been measured by age-specific death rates, which are the number of deaths per thousand people in a given age group in a given country in the year 1965 or the year 1966. Note that a logarithmic scale has been used for the death rates. With a logarithmic scale, a doubling of death rates corresponds to an equal vertical distance anywhere along the scale. This scale allows us to plot clearly death rates of less than 1 per 1000 for children and more than 100 per 1000 for old people, all on the same graph.

This figure, when taken together with Table 11–1, illustrates how health improves as national income rises. The figure also illustrates that, among the richest countries, differences in health are not associated with differences in GNP per capita. For example, Puerto Rican children suffer more from infectious disease than children in the United States, but this is balanced by less heart disease and cancer among Puerto Rican adults. In consequence, life expectancy is the same in the United States and Puerto Rico, despite a three-fold difference in GNP per capita.

Source: U.N. Department of Economic and Social Affairs. 1968. Demographic Yearbook, 1967. New York: United Nations.

The disparity in health is due primarily to comparably large disparities in health care, diet, housing and education. Under these circumstances, greater equality would seem at least as worthy a goal as increased total production.

Even this brief review of health statistics suggests that many of the serious problems in the United States can be solved without an increase in material consumption. More equal distribution of existing resources would relieve the problems of the poor. We do not need more material goods to end war deaths in Vietnam or to reduce highway deaths. The stresses revealed by rising suicide, cirrhosis of the liver and so on call primarily for changes in social and psychological conditions.

Although our discussion of major problems in the United States is sketchy in the extreme, it illustrates our belief that the resolution of the United States' most pressing problems is entirely compatible with decreased growth in material production and consumption. This is fortunate, since equilibrium with our environment seems to demand not only that we eventually stop growth of both material consumption and population, but also that we begin to move in this direction soon. We seem to be so close to the finite limits of the earth's resources that it is doubtful whether the contemporary United States' rate of material consumption could be achieved even for the world's current population. To complete our argument that policies for stabilizing material consumption are both necessary and desirable, we will respond next to the common fear that if production does not grow we must expect increased unemployment and stagnation.

We Can Stop the Growth of Material Consumption without Causing Unemployment

A very common response to proposals that the United States should stabilize material consumption, reduce the use of autos, cut military production and so on is the argument that such policies will lead to increased unemployment. If production is not increasing, fewer workers will be hired to build new factories and machines. If through-flow of material goods is reduced by building fewer autos and ICBM's, workers will be out of jobs. These seem like realistic objections in the current situation. However, these objections could be overcome if workers were hired to produce whatever people really need, rather than to produce whatever can be sold at a profit. Initially, workers would be needed to build public transport and antipollution devices and to manufacture equipment needed for economic growth in the poor countries (which have certainly not yet reached a level of affluence where a stable GNP per capita is a desirable goal). In the long run, the emphasis of our economy would have to shift from material-intensive production to labor-intensive services. People who previously worked in auto factories would switch to automobile maintenance and repair. People would be needed to do the sorting and cleaning involved in recycling. Large numbers of teachers, doctors, craftsmen, artists, entertainers, city planners, gardeners and so on would be recruited to provide the services needed to raise the standard of living without increasing material consumption.

Furthermore, it would seem desirable to begin to substitute increased leisure for increased consumption. This would have two advantages. A shorter work week would increase the number of jobs and make it easier to develop a program to guarantee jobs for all those who want them. Also, increased leisure time could substantially enrich our lives. With time for learning and time for doing, creativity and initiative could develop and find expression in arts and sciences, in crafts and athletics. Perhaps there is already a trend in the United States to prefer time to spend as you please over the added consumption that longer work hours would make possible. Such a trend would be encouraging since it would bring us closer to a stable economy and equilibrium with our environment.

Preservation of the Environment Will Be Possible only if the Economy Is Fundamentally Reorganized

In a free enterprise system, the primary motive of the entrepreneur is to maximize his profits and stimulate the growth of his enterprise. This basic motive is often in direct conflict with policies needed for the conservation of resources. For example, workers have not been hired for recycling or for production and operation of public transport, when mining and sales of autos can produce bigger profits. More durable goods will not be produced if their longer lifetime results in lower sales and profits.

Most fundamentally, the entrepreneur's attempt to increase profits and assets is in direct conflict with the ecologically necessary goal of stabilizing the level of material consumption. Despite much clamor about environmental problems, in 1970 more than $20 billion was spent on advertising to increase sales, which must increase material consumption, with attendant exhaustion of resources and increases in pollution. In the same year, less than half that amount was spent on pollution control. It does not seem reasonable to expect this fundamental conflict to be resolved by government regulations that leave the basic structure unchanged, particularly when experience has shown how successful industries have been in acquiring substantial influence over the government agencies that are supposed to regulate them. Instead, we will need basic changes in economic organization, so that fulfillment of human needs rather than maximization of profits becomes the guideline for decisions.

We conclude with a specific suggestion for reorganization to solve one problem that will arise in any nongrowing economy, namely, how to provide capital for new businesses or to finance the purchase of a house. In our society this is now accomplished by lending money for interest. In 1968, 3.9 percent of United States' national income was paid as net interest on loans and investments. If such payments were made in a nongrowing economy, they would result in a decrease in affluence for borrowers and an increase in affluence for lenders. We would expect most of the borrowing to be done by poor people and most of the lending by rich people, with the consequence that the rich would get richer and the poor would get poorer. On the other hand, several existing programs provide models of how to make capital available without running into these problems. Loans to meet the costs of college education are often available with little or no interest, with payment deferred until after graduation when earning starts. Similar programs could provide money to buy a home and to meet the other expenses of starting a household. The National Science Foundation provides money to scientific entrepreneurs who submit applications outlining how they propose to spend the money and what they plan to accomplish with it. Similar programs could provide capital for purposes other than scientific research, for instance, to start a school or to build a plant to manufacture solar energy collecting devices. For some types of enterprises, funds should be repaid once the endeavor is established. Criteria and methods for selecting workable proposals would have to be developed. This approach would eliminate money-lending as a source of profits, so we would expect it to arouse strong political resistance from some groups. But some such change is necessary for any long-range solution. Furthermore, the possibilities for initiative, creativity and independence are exciting. Hope stimulated by such possibilities is as much our reason for urging change, as fear stimulated by gloomy prospects if we continue on our current course.

BIBLIOGRAPHY

Commoner, B., M. Corr, and P. J. Stamler. 1971. The Causes of Pollution. *Environment 13:* 2–19 [presents the evidence for the importance of the post-World War II shift to more polluting types of goods].

England, R. and B. Bluestone. 1971. Ecology and Class Conflict. *The Review* of *Radical Political Economics 3:* 31–55 [explains why major economic reorganization will be necessary for preservation of the environment].

Eyer, J. 1972. *The Rise in Stress with Modern Development.* (Ph.D. Thesis, Department of Biology, University of Pennsylvania, Philadelphia) [an analysis of health and reproduction statistics and what they reveal about the quality of life].

Zwick, D. and M. Benstock. 1971. *Water Wasteland.* New York: Grossman Publishers [describes how industries can and have blocked effective regulation of water pollution].

chapter 12

effects of population growth on economic growth

More and more people are challenging the widespread assumption that economic growth is intrinsically good. In the previous chapter we have described situations (typified by the contemporary United States) in which an increase in production and consumption of material goods seems likely to subtract from the general well-being at least as much as it will add. In such situations, important goals are improved social and psychological conditions, fair distribution of goods, and production technology that does not damage the future well-being of people and their environment.

However, for countries where material consumption is very low, increased material production is a reasonable and important goal. Progress toward this goal has been slow. By 1965 the yearly production per person (GNP per capita) had reached only $170 for Asia, Africa and Latin America combined. (Japan, South Africa and Israel are excluded from the statistics.) Production per person has increased about 2 percent per year; this is equivalent to a doubling in 35 years. The sluggishness of the increase in GNP per capita is often blamed primarily on population growth, which has averaged over 2 percent per year.

There are several ways in which population growth may interfere with economic growth. If natural resources like land are in short supply and population doubles, then each farmer has only half as much land to work, and production per capita might be expected to decline. This factor is counteracted to some extent by the tendency of farmers in these circumstances to adopt new and more productive technologies (Chapter 15).

Rapid population growth can also interfere with economic growth by increasing the demand for man-made resources such as houses and schools. When this happens, more resources must be diverted from building and operating factories, railroads and dams to building and operating schools, hospitals and houses. The diverted resources will include capital, both local capital and foreign exchange for imports, and human labor, both skilled and unskilled. Labor, however, should increase in proportion to the population increase, although with a lag, since each person begins working only after some period as an unemployed child.

The lag between beginning to consume and beginning to work is the cause of another problem related to population growth. When population growth is rapid and each generation is larger than the last, the proportion of children is high. Thus, there tend to be more consumers for each producing adult. However, this effect is partly cancelled out because the proportion of people too old to work is smaller in a rapidly growing population. The net difference in the proportion of the population at working ages (15–59) is small: 51 percent for a representative group of countries with rapid population growth compared to 58 percent for a group with slow population growth. Furthermore, the critical shortage in most poor countries is not total labor supply, but rather the supply of skilled labor. In this respect a younger population will be an advantage, if the educational system is expanding and improving so that younger workers have more skills and higher literacy.

Thus arguments for negative effects of population growth on economic growth must be balanced against arguments for positive effects. Our knowledge is insufficient to predict which set of factors will outweigh the other. Since the theoretical arguments prove inconclusive, we need an empirical test of whether population growth does or does not retard economic growth. If population growth has a significantly depressing effect on economic growth, then countries with rapid population increase should have slow economic growth. As Figure 12–1 shows, there is only a slight tendency toward such a negative correlation between population growth and economic growth. It seems that the effect of population increase on economic growth is small, and that other factors must be responsible for most of the variation in economic growth rates. Crucial among these other factors are natural resources, the ability to find export markets and obtain foreign exchange to finance imports, education, and political and economic organization for effective use of available resources.

These observations have several implications for policy. First, the funding of a birth control program can be only a small part of a program to achieve economic development. This is particularly true since such programs will almost certainly fail to reduce birth rates significantly, unless the programs occur in a context of increasing education, improved health and other broad social changes. (Chapters 16–18 give evidence for this assertion.) Indeed, since these social changes will be difficult to achieve without some increase in per capita consumption, we conclude that economic growth is necessary, not only for humanitarian reasons, but also to provide the situation in which birth rates will decrease.

These arguments lead to the second policy implication: that there

Figure 12–1 RELATIONSHIP BETWEEN POPULATION GROWTH
AND ECONOMIC GROWTH

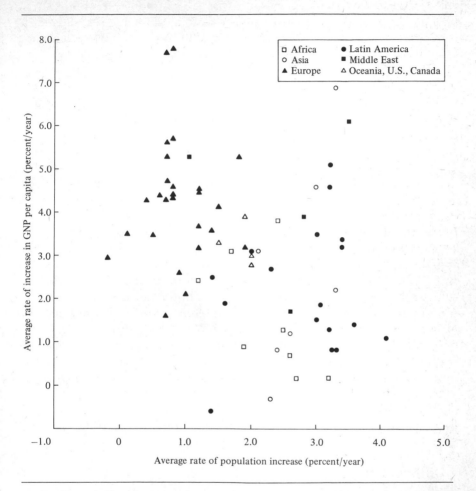

Each symbol represents one country. There is a slight tendency for rapid
population growth to be correlated with slower increase in production per
capita. This shows up as slightly more symbols in the upper left-hand and
lower right-hand corners. However the correlation is not very strong for this
period (1958–1966 for population data, 1960–1965 for economic data), and is
even weaker for similar comparisons for earlier periods. This implies that other
factors affect economic growth more than population growth does.

Source: U.N. Demographic Yearbook, 1966; Agency for International Development,
Statistics and Reports Division, Office of Program and Policy Coordination. 1970.
GNP: Growth Rates and Trend Data by Region and Country; Joint Economic
Committee. 1970. *Economic Development in Countries of Eastern Europe.*

131

is an urgent need to provide more of the resources needed by poor countries for economic growth. The whole question of what resources will be necessary for economic growth is enormously complex and beyond the scope of this book. One example will suffice to illustrate how more resources could be made available, and thus how economic growth could be speeded up.

For many poor countries a major bottleneck in economic development is a shortage of foreign exchange. Since the biggest source of foreign exchange is payments received for exports, two significant barriers to economic growth are (1) the United States' and European restrictions on imports, especially manufactured imports, and (2) the successful efforts by rich countries and their manufacturers to increase the price of their exports relative to the price of their imports. A second source of foreign exchange is government aid. United States' economic aid to Asia, Africa and Latin America has declined in recent years and is relatively small. In 1969, the United States sent $3 billion of economic aid and received $1 billion in repayment of former loans. The net flow amounted to less than 5 percent of United States' military spending. Private investment currently does not provide a net flow of foreign exchange to the nonindustrial countries. The United States sent $2 billion in loans and investment, but received $4 billion as repayment and profits. Of course, the problem of how foreign exchange is used is as important as the quantity available. Thus, there is a need not only for more foreign exchange, but also for many nonindustrial countries to reorganize their public and private institutions to increase motivation and skills in using resources to optimize economic growth.

In conclusion, the prospects for economic growth in Asia, Africa and Latin America are not good at present. But we cannot look to population growth as the main villain. Other problems are crucial and must be solved if economic growth is to occur.

BIBLIOGRAPHY

Easterlin, R. A. 1967.   Effects of Population Growth on the Economic Development of Developing Countries.   *Annals of the Amer. Acad. of Polit. and Social Sciences*. Jan., 1967, pp. 369–71 [presents both sides of the argument re the extent to which economic growth is slowed by population growth].

Myrdal, G. 1968.   *An Asian Drama, An Inquiry into the Poverty of Nations*, vol. II. New York: Pantheon [an in-depth analysis of why most Asian countries remain poor].

Weisskopf, T. E. 1971.   Capitalism, Underdevelopment and the Future of the Poor Countries, in *Economics and World Order*, ed. by J. N. Bhagwati. New York: Crowell-Collier and Macmillan, Inc. [a set of concise arguments about why poor capitalist countries stay poor].

population regulation

In the preceding chapters we have presented abundant evidence that the resources of the earth are finite and that man will soon face insoluble resource problems if resources continue to be wasted, if consumption per person continues to increase *or* if population growth continues. All three of these conditions must change if our grandchildren are to have a world with adequate food, water, clean air, fuels and minerals.

How should population growth be stopped? Even if no effective action is taken, we can expect population growth to slow down eventually—when food becomes so scarce, air so polluted and conditions so generally deteriorated that death rates rise. However, rising death rates are not an acceptable solution, so our only alternative is to reduce population growth by reducing birth rates. It is this alternative which we will explore in subsequent chapters.

We begin by considering the processes of population regulation in nonhuman animals (Chapter 13), with a special focus on the relationship between population growth and social behavior in Chapter 14. In Chapters 15 to 18 we discuss the early history of human population growth, the effects of industrialization on population growth in Europe, social and economic factors affecting family size in the United States and the current situation in the nonindustrial countries. In Chapter 19 we examine predictions of population growth, how they are made and their reliability. In Chapter 20 we evaluate the various proposals for reducing birth rates and thus stopping population growth.

section four
natural processes

chapter 13

population regulation processes in animals

Charles Darwin, the father of modern evolutionary thought, recognized more than a century ago that most types of animals produce sufficiently many offspring that their populations would soon cover the earth, if each descendant survived to reproduce. Populations do grow very rapidly when first introduced into a favorable environment. However, natural populations do not increase indefinitely. Rather they fluctuate within limits imposed by the environment. The balance between the intrinsic capacity of the population to increase its numbers and the limits imposed on population growth by the environment is the heart of the phenomenon which biologists refer to as population regulation. In this chapter, we will examine the intrinsic growth capacity of animal populations, the environmental factors which serve to limit this growth and how the two interact to regulate population size.

Population Growth Is Usually Exponential when Resources Are Abundant

Two simple kinds of growth may be distinguished: growth by addition and growth by multiplication. These are directly analogous to simple and compound interest on money deposited in a bank. Simple interest accumulates on the basis of a fixed deposit. The interest is merely added to the account, and does not figure in calculating the next interest payment. For example, if $100 in a bank were to receive 10 percent simple interest each year, the bank would pay $10 per year. The bank would not pay interest on the interest accumulated.

This is not the case in natural populations because offspring mature and produce their own offspring. This is multiplicative growth, equivalent to compound interest in the bank. If the 10 percent interest on $100 invested were compounded each year, $10 interest would be paid during the first year, which would then be added to the principal on which interest was paid. During the second year 10 percent of the $110, or $11, would be paid; during the third year, 10 percent of $121, and so on. In the same way, when offspring in a natural population of animals reach maturity, they too produce their own offspring; interest

Figure 13–1 EXPONENTIAL AND ARITHMETIC INCREASE

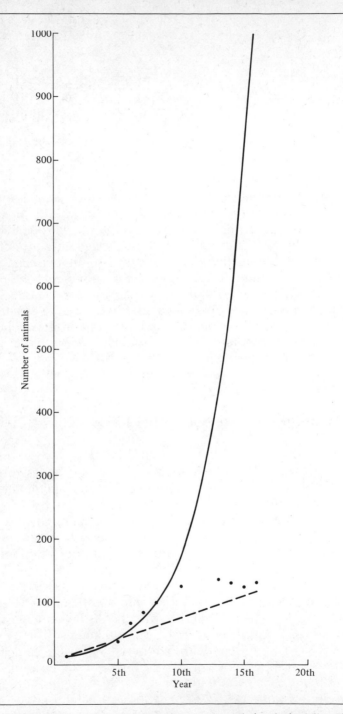

The solid line illustrates exponental increase and the dashed line illustrates arithmetic increase. The points indicate the actual growth of a population of

accumulates its own interest. Strictly speaking, not all the surviving offspring can be thought of as interest; the last two offspring represent reproduction of the "principal," not interest; reproduction of the "principal" is necessary because, unlike dollars left in the bank, parents do not survive indefinitely.

Growth by multiplication is referred to as exponential, or geometric growth, and is compared to growth by addition, or arithmetic growth, in Figure 13–1. In exponential growth each element in the series exceeds the preceding element by a constant multiplicative factor, whereas in arithmetic growth each element in the series exceeds the previous by a constant difference.

The simplest predictions of future growth of human populations are based on the assumption of exponential growth. For example, a common way of predicting world population growth is to assume that it will continue to increase by a constant multiplicative factor of 1.02 each year. Increase by a factor of 1.02 is equivalent to an increase of 2 percent per year. World population has increased by 2 percent per year recently because the average annual birth rate (34 per thousand population) has exceeded the average annual death rate (14 per thousand population) by 20 per thousand population or 2 per hundred, which equals 2 percent. The assumption of exponential growth amounts to an assumption that birth rates will continue to exceed death rates by this amount. This assumption may be approximately correct for the near future, and it is interesting to see what would happen if it were true. Most important, the population would grow by an increasing amount each year, since 2 percent of a larger and larger population would be a larger and larger addition. Probably the best intuitive way of understanding how rapid this growth would be is to calculate the time it would take the population to double if growth continued at 2 percent per year. In other words, how many times do you have to multiply 1.02 times itself to get 2.00? The answer is 35, so world population would double in 35 years if the excess of birth rates over death rates remained the same. Table 13–1 can be used to convert other growth rates to their equivalent doubling times.

Although population growth rate for the world population equals simply birth rate minus death rate, population growth rate for any smaller region equals birth rate minus death rate plus immigration

---

Figure 13–1 (continued)
bighorn sheep released on Wildhorse Island in Montana. Note that the population started to grow exponentially, and then after a decade reached a rather stable equilibrium size.

Source: Data from W. Woodgerd. 1964. Population Dynamics of Bighorn Sheep on Wildhorse Island. *J. Wildlife Management 28:* 381–391.

Table 13–1 EQUIVALENCE BETWEEN EXPONENTIAL GROWTH
RATES AND THE TIME IT TAKES FOR THE
GROWING QUANTITY TO DOUBLE

ANNUAL RATE OF INCREASE (PERCENT)	DOUBLING TIME (YEARS)
0.5	138
1.0	69
1.5	46
2.0	35
2.5	28
3.0	23
3.5	20
4.0	17
4.5	15
5.0	14

minus emigration. Situations where migration makes a quantitatively
important contribution will be described in subsequent chapters.

Population Growth May Stop when Resource Scarcity Causes Increased Death Rates or Decreased Birth Rates

For most populations, the growth rate fluctuates around an average of
zero. That is, most populations have approximately stable size. This is
because predation, disease and scarcity of food cause high death rates
and may reduce birth rates with the result that births and deaths balance to produce approximately zero rates of population growth.

The effects of food shortage on population growth can be observed
most easily when food supplies decline suddenly. One spectacular
case of periodic food shortage involves the guano-producing seabirds
along the coast of Peru. Normally these birds feed in the rich Hum-
boldt Current that flows up the coast of South America from the
Antarctic. Occasionally, this current goes far offshore and is replaced
by poor tropical waters. The result is that millions of birds die of starvation and reproductive activities are completely abandoned. A less
drastic example is the tawny owl in England which feeds principally
on rodents whose abundance varies considerably from year to year.
During years when rodents were plentiful, 75 percent of the owls
bred, raising 0.9 young per pair (including nonbreeders), whereas
during scarce rodent years, only 31 percent of pairs bred, raising 0.3
young per pair. The number of young raised was also influenced by
the density of the owls, being 1.1 per pair when 16–24 pairs were

140

present, and 0.8 per pair when 25–30 pairs were present. Thus population growth is depressed similarly by overall scarcity of food or by increased density which can result in food scarcity for individuals.

There is other evidence that birds and mammals have lower reproductive success when population densities are higher. One example is the comparisons of April and November counts of bobwhite quail over a 14-year period in Wisconsin. Low spring counts of 50 birds were tripled to 150 by November, whereas high spring counts of 300 increased by only about one-third to 400 by autumn. Furthermore, numbers decreased more during the winter after higher fall counts. Thus there must be some "density-dependent" factor (perhaps food scarcity) which causes lower reproductive success and higher mortality when densities are high.

Density-Dependent Factors Establish a Negative Feedback Which Tends to Stabilize Population Size

The observation that mortality increases and reproductive success decreases at higher densities is crucial to our understanding of why population fluctuations are generally contained within stable limits. Consider, for example, a bird population which is regulated by the density-dependent factor, food. Whenever some accident, such as a particularly long and cold winter, reduces population below its usual size, then in subsequent years there will be more food per bird, each pair will be able to raise more offspring and numbers will tend to increase to their normal level. Conversely, whenever the population is larger than usual, food will be relatively scarce, reproduction will be less successful and deaths will be higher, and the population will tend to decrease back toward its normal level. This is an example of negative feedback: where a change in one factor (population) causes a change in another factor (food) which feeds back to cause a reverse change in the first factor. Negative feedback tends to result in a stable equilibrium. The geometric models shown in Figure 13–2 illustrate the concept of stable equilibrium.

What are the density-dependent factors that provide the negative feedback to regulate population size in large vertebrates? It is difficult to obtain data on this or even to demonstrate the action of density-dependent factors in natural populations, since most populations are so strongly regulated by density-dependent influences that the population size does not vary enough even to allow us to test whether population growth rate does depend on density. In the cases where there is evidence, it seems that the density-dependent regulating factor is most commonly the shortage of some critical resource, especially food. Other factors that may be important are shortages of water, hiding places, or nesting sites, increased spread of disease at

Figure 13–2 STABLE, UNSTABLE AND NEUTRAL EQUILIBRIUM

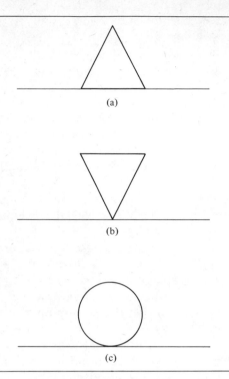

(a)

(b)

(c)

The triangle resting on its base (a) is in stable equilibrium. Any force that tends to lift the triangle off its base is counteracted by the force of gravity. Therefore, if the triangle is tipped slightly it will tend to return to its original position. Population size is in stable equilibrium if the birth rate equals the death rate, and if birth rates are lower and death rates are higher for larger population sizes.

The triangle balanced on its tip (b) is in unstable equilibrium; if it is tipped even slightly, it will become unbalanced and fall over. Population size would be in unstable equilibrium if the birth rate were equal to the death rate, but birth rates increased and death rates decreased when population size increased.

A cylinder on its side (c) is in neutral equilibrium. If it is moved slightly it will remain in its new position; gravity will not act either to return it to its original position or to pull it further from that original position. A neutral equilibrium for population size would occur if the birth rate and death rate were equal and were independent of the size of the population.

higher densities and the tendency of some predators to hunt abundant prey preferentially. These factors may interact, for example, when food shortages weaken an animal and make it more susceptible to predators or disease.

While we have concentrated on the factors that tend to result in stable population size, we do not wish to exaggerate the constancy of population size from one year to the next. Populations may fluctuate quite sharply due to the effects of density-independent factors like weather. Density-dependent factors tend to limit the fluctuations, but the upper and lower limits may be quite far apart. This is true for many small animals like insects. Sharp fluctuations in population size are also caused by the abrupt alterations of the environment that may result from man's activities. For example, mule deer on the Kaibab plateau of northern Arizona increased from about 4000 to more than 50,000 within 16 years when predators were reduced by hunting, and sheep and cattle which compete for food were also reduced. In this case population regulation worked rather poorly. Death rates did not begin to increase until after severe overgrazing had resulted in obvious deterioration of the forage, at which point massive starvation resulted in an abrupt decline to a population of about 10,000 within a few years. It is possible that a larger population of deer could have been supported in this region if initial overpopulation and overgrazing had not reduced the growth of food plants.

BIBLIOGRAPHY

Lack, D. 1954. *The Natural Regulation of Animal Numbers.* Oxford: The Clarendon Press.

Lack, D. 1966. *Population Studies of Birds.* Oxford: The Clarendon Press [these two books present the view of population regulation subscribed to by most ecologists, and conflicting arguments are thoroughly discussed in the second reference].

Slobodkin, L. B. 1962. *Growth and Regulation of Animal Populations.* New York: Holt, Rinehart and Winston, Inc. [a detailed mathematical treatment of population regulation].

Solomon, M. E. 1969. *Population Dynamics.* New York: St. Martin's Press, Inc. [a good, short introduction to population regulation].

chapter 14

behavioral aspects of population regulation

In the previous chapter we described how the size of many vertebrate populations is regulated by increases in mortality and decreases in reproduction which occur when environmental resources become scarce. In these cases regulation is external, imposed by the environment, and reflects the balance between the natural tendency of the population to increase and the limitations on the resources available to the population.

In this chapter we will discuss how social behavior such as territoriality and dominance interactions can limit reproduction. By reducing the number of births, these behaviors reduce the number of deaths needed to keep the population within the limits of available resources. Whether social interactions actually slow the rate of population growth depends on their effect on death rates. For example, some aspects of group behavior may improve care for the young. In this case decreased juvenile deaths may more than offset decreased births, so that the net effect is to increase population growth. In other cases, mortality increases as births decrease. Such a behavior may regulate population size somewhat below the limit set by the available resources.

In this chapter we will discuss behavior that is widespread among vertebrates. Behavior more specific to humans will be discussed in subsequent chapters.

Territory

Many fish, birds and other vertebrates that care for their young have breeding territories. That is, they mate and raise their young in an area which is defended against intruders of the same species. The territory is often established by the male at the beginning of the breeding season. Territorial boundaries are established by disputes between neighboring individuals. These disputes usually involve symbolic or ritualistic, rather than real, fighting. Birds, for example, sing at territorial boundaries, proclaiming in a highly ritualistic way the limits of their defended area. An established territory allows a pair to mate and rear young with a minimum of behavioral interference and resource competition from other members of the species. Males who are unable to establish a territory live in less desirable habitats and do not breed. In several experiments, when territorial birds have been removed from an area, these males have moved into the vacancies, acquired mates and bred. Thus, territoriality serves to reduce birth rates as well as to improve care for the offspring that are born.

Not all territories are defended by an individual male or a mated pair. Nor are all territories closely associated with a breeding season. Forest-dwelling monkeys, for example, generally cooperate in larger groups to defend a territory all year long. A great deal of the defense is again symbolic, for example, by noisy calls. This defended territory provides a familiar and undisturbed region for feeding and breeding. Baboons, gorillas and chimpanzees also utilize a familiar home range, but they do not defend the boundaries, perhaps because their home ranges are so large (minimally 3 square miles, sometimes more than 15 square miles) that frequent patrolling of the boundaries is impracticable. Whether defended or not, this kind of group home area does not reduce mating. Virtually all adult female monkeys and apes live in groups containing adult males, and they find mates whenever they are sexually receptive. In some groups (for example, among some baboons), subordinate males are prevented from breeding by dominant males, but this does not reduce the births since the dominant males are quite capable of inseminating all the females. In many groups, subordinate and dominant males seem to take equal part in mating. Adult males, whether they mate or not, commonly contribute to the reproductive success of the group by cooperating in watching for predators and chasing them off. This protection is especially important for the vulnerable mothers and young.

Social Behavior and Physiological Impairments in Caged Populations

Dominance interactions normally act to organize groups and reduce intragroup strife. However, there are some situations in which dominance interactions lead to impaired physiology of the subordinates with a consequent decrease in births and increase in deaths. This is particularly clear in caged populations, as illustrated by the following experiments with tree shrews (a small mammal from Asia).

The hair on a tree shrew's tail normally lies flat. However, the hair is fluffed up when the shrew sees a strange animal, when a sudden noise occurs or when the shrew is fighting with another shrew. After a stable dominance-subordinance relationship has been established the submissive animal fluffs its tail when the dominant animal approaches it or looks at it. In these experiments the percent of time spent with the tail fluffed varied depending on the social situation and

living conditions of the animal. Various aspects of health and reproduction were impaired in direct correlation with the amount of time
spent with the tail fluffed. For instance, the offspring of females who
had their tails fluffed more than 20 percent of the time often died
before weaning because of the mother's poor lactation and feeding
behavior and because she did not mark them with a scent which protects them from cannibalism by other adults. Adult males and females
who spent more than half their time with tails fluffed became sterile.
Retardation of growth and sexual maturation and increased death
rates were also correlated with increased time spent with tail fluffed.
(It should be noted that the environments in which these responses
were observed differed from the natural living conditions of the
shrews, in that they offered no possibility of escape from fights or the
attentions of dominant animals; abnormally large groups of animals
appear to have been confined within abnormally small spaces; and
the physical environment seems to have been so simplified that opportunities for exploration were extremely limited.)

The nature of the physiological impairments and the precipitating
situations are diverse, so we would expect to find a variety of physiological and behavioral mechanisms involved. Nevertheless there is
some evidence that a general physiological response to stress may be
involved in this and many similar cases. A mammal's response to an
emergency situation (for example, the approach of a predator) includes
both specific adaptive responses (for example, hiding) and some general adaptive responses (for example, increase in heart rate and conversion of glycogen to glucose so energy can be obtained rapidly when
needed). The sympathetic nervous system and adrenalin circulating in
the blood play a vital role in producing these general responses. In
the tree shrew, sympathetic activity and adrenalin also produce the
very visible tail-fluffing response, thus allowing the experimenter to
quantify crudely the duration of general activation of the emergency
responses. In this case stress is more than an intuitive concept; stressful stimuli can be specifically defined as those which activate sympathetic activity, as indicated by tail-fluffing. Stressful situations also
elicit a second, slower response. The brain triggers the release of a
hormone (adrenocorticotrophic hormone or ACTH), which stimulates
the adrenal cortex to secrete one of its hormones (a glucocorticoid).

Box 14–1 **FECUNDITY**

Fecundity is the physiological capacity to produce offspring.
Full fecundity depends on proper functioning of a whole sequence

of physiological processes which, in mammals, includes production of viable eggs by the ovaries and sperm by the testes, ejaculation, travel by the sperm up the female reproductive tract to fertilize the egg, implantation of the fertilized egg in a uterus that provides an appropriate environment for fetal development and properly timed secretions of the hormones that control these processes. Fecundity will be impaired if any of these processes is disrupted. For example, sterility will result if the oviducts, which carry the eggs from the ovaries to the uterus, are blocked; such blockage occurs when gonorrhea or the infections that follow unsanitary abortions cause inflammation and subsequent scarring of the oviducts.

One link in the reproductive process is particularly susceptible to disruption, namely the hormonal secretions which coordinate the physiological processes of reproduction and which are themselves controlled by the brain. For example, behavioral situations which cause infecundity typically act by disrupting the hormonal balance. Similarly, inadequate protein nutrition for pregnant females causes hormonal changes that result in spontaneous abortion. This hormonal response protects the mother from excessive loss of protein when dietary intake is inadequate. When a mother nurses her infant, a hormonal balance is maintained which tends to suppress ovulation and menstruation. This hormonal response reduces the risk of a second pregnancy which would cut off milk supplies for the first infant prematurely. This response increased infant survival in the centuries before adequate substitutes for mother's milk became available.

Just as infecundity can be caused by impairment of any of the physiological processes in the reproductive cycle, contraception can be achieved by intentional interference with any of them. Ovulation can be prevented by the oral contraceptive pill which disrupts the normal hormonal balance. Fertilization of the egg by sperm can be prevented by abstention from intercourse when the egg is present (the rhythm method), by withdrawal of the penis before ejaculation (coitus interruptus), by operations which block the transport of sperm (vasectomy) or eggs ("having your tubes tied") and by temporary mechanical and chemical barriers (condom or diaphragm and vaginal spermicides). Implantation of the fertilized egg in the wall of the uterus is prevented by the loop or IUD (intrauterine device). A more complete description of the mechanisms of action of these methods and of their considerable differences in reliability and side-effects can be found in the textbook on contraception referred to in the bibliography.

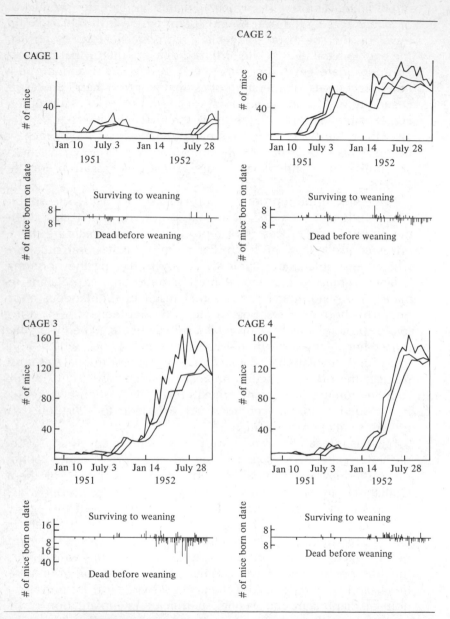

Figure 14–1 POPULATION CHANGES FOR FOUR GROUPS OF CAGED MICE

Four adult male wild-trapped house mice and four adult females were put in each cage initially. Each cage was 6 feet wide, 25 feet long, and 2 feet high, contained 48 nest boxes and was supplied with an excess of food, water and nesting material throughout the experiment. For each cage the top graph shows the total number of animals present (top line), the number of adults present (bottom line), and the number of juveniles divided into pre-weaning (top

Glucocorticoids stimulate the release of free fatty acids from fat deposits and the conversion of proteins to glucose. Both these actions increase the concentration in the blood of molecules that can be readily metabolized for energy to fuel any needed fight or flight response. However, when emergency situations become common over a long period of time, the ACTH can inhibit the maturation and functioning of the sex organs. Also, the hormones secreted by the adrenal cortex can disrupt sex hormone secretion and immune responses, thus contributing to the impaired reproduction and poor health observed in stressful situations.

Can Social Interactions Set Maximum Densities for Caged or Wild Populations?

To summarize thus far, we have described two kinds of social behavior: territoriality and dominance-subordinance interactions. Territorial behavior might limit population growth, if it reduces births more than it reduces juvenile deaths. Dominance-subordinance interactions can lead to decreased births and increased deaths, and thus can reduce population growth. If the severity of dominance-subordinance interactions increases with density, then population growth will decrease as population size increases. The maximum population size would then be the size at which population growth was reduced to zero.

In caged populations, some combination of these mechanisms often does operate to limit the size of the population. Figure 14–1 shows the results of an experiment with house mice. In each cage population growth stopped, despite the fact that food, water and nesting material were all supplied in excess and predation was eliminated. In each case a period of "internal strife" (that is, increased fighting) preceded and accompanied the leveling off of population growth. Decreased population growth was due primarily to increased deaths among suckling young and secondarily to decreased births. The social interactions that produced these impairments became severe at different population densities in the various cages, presumably because differences in personalities resulted in different

Figure 14–1 (continued)

area) and post-weaned (middle area). Note that all populations stopped increasing even though food, water and nesting material remained abundant. Personality differences apparently resulted in differences in aggressive behavior and hence differences in the population levels reached in the various cages.

Source: From C. H. Southwick, 1955. The Population Dynamics of Confined House Mice Supplied with Unlimited Food. *Ecology* 36: 212–225. Adapted with permission of the Duke University Press.

group relationships in each cage. The plateau densities are similar to those observed in some wild populations, especially those in plentiful food supplies like farmers' grain stores.

However, the question of whether territorial and dominance interactions serve to limit population growth in wild populations remains unresolved. Extrapolation from caged populations is unsatisfactory because the behavioral situation is different in the wild. When there is no cage, fights are often terminated quickly by the flight of one of the combatants. Emigration is a common response to the social situations and scarcity of resources which develop as densities increase. Emigration generally keeps population densities below those used in most caged experiments. Although emigration serves to redistribute population, it probably does not reduce overall population growth. Territorial and dominance interactions may limit population growth, but the evidence from natural populations has been inconclusive thus far.

What is the relevance of these observations for population regulation in humans? We do not wish to enter into a debate about whether war represents territorial behavior, or whether malnutrition among poor people is a consequence of their subordinate position in a dominance hierarchy. That such situations have played a role in limiting human population growth will be shown in subsequent chapters. There is also evidence that stressful stimuli resulting from social interactions are sometimes responsible for the impairment of human reproductive physiology. Perhaps the most well-recognized clinical syndrome is psychogenic amenorrhea, the failure to menstruate or to ovulate which often follows psychological stresses. The quantitative importance of such responses in influencing human birth rates has not been assessed yet.

Some people maintain that such responses will increase as human populations grow and higher densities result in greater stresses. There is some tendency for high densities to be correlated with sterility, congenital malformations and generally poorer health. However, high densities are also usually correlated with poverty, bad housing, inadequate nutrition and poor education. When people who live at high densities have adequate income, their health and fecundity are apparently not impaired. In fact, when other factors are held constant, density *per se* does not seem to have any large effect on human physiology. Similarly, there appears to be no reliable or simple relationship between changes in population size and the frequency or intensity of wars. Contemporary population densities may have some effects on human health and behavior, but these effects have not been demonstrated clearly yet, and in any case appear to be too small to play a significant role in population regulation.

BIBLIOGRAPHY

Cassel, J. 1971. Health Consequences of Population Density and Crowding in *Rapid Population Growth: Consequences and Policy Implications.* (Prepared by a Study Committee of the Office of the Foreign Secretary, National Academy of Sciences.) Baltimore: Johns Hopkins Press.

Lack, D. 1966. *Population Studies of Birds.* Oxford: Clarendon Press [argues against the importance of behavioral mechanisms for regulating the size of wild populations].

Peel, J. and M. Potts. 1969. *Textbook of Contraceptive Practice.* Cambridge: Cambridge University Press.

Sadlier, R. M. F. S. 1969. *The Ecology of Reproduction in Wild and Domestic Animals.* London: Methuen and Company, Ltd. [presents much of the data on the relationship between social behavior and reproduction in mammals, together with a well-balanced interpretation].

Tepperman, J. 1968. *Metabolic and Endocrine Physiology.* Chicago: Year Book Medical Publishers [gives good descriptions of hormones and hormone regulation].

von Holst, D. 1969. Sozialer Stress bei Tupajas (Social Stress in Tree Shrews). *Z. vergl. Physiologie 63:* 1–58.

Wright, Q. 1942. *A Study of War.* Chicago: University of Chicago Press [documents the absence of any direct relationship between war and population density].

Wynne-Edwards, V. C. 1962. *Animal Dispersion in Relation to Social Behavior.* Edinburgh and London: Oliver and Boyd, Ltd. [argues strongly for the importance of various kinds of behavioral regulation of population size].

section five
human populations

chapter 15

early history of human population growth and its relation to technological change

About two million years ago a small group of primates left skeletons quite similar to human skeletons in parts of Africa. 50,000–100,000 years ago, the descendants of these primates left human skeletons throughout the Old World. By about 10,000 years ago, human beings occupied all the continents, although still at low densities since food was obtained by hunting and by gathering roots, berries, nuts and so on. This mode of living does not support high population densities except in the most favorable circumstances. For example, groups of 19th and 20th century hunter-gatherers used ½ to 20 square miles per person under most conditions. Much higher densities (up to 100 persons per square mile) occurred only along coasts and river banks where fish were abundant.

Among contemporary hunter-gatherers, low densities are often not a direct consequence of food scarcity. In many cases births are reduced by abortion, by prolonged lactation with consequent reduced fecundity and by abstention from intercourse during certain taboo periods. Infanticide occurs often when the infant is born misshapen or if the mother still has another child who is young enough to need carrying and further breast-feeding. At the same time, health is poor and life expectancy is short due to the lack of medical technology. For many contemporary groups, the balance between limited births and high mortality seems to maintain the population below the normal carrying capacity of their area. In such cases, food resources are abundant enough that hunting and gathering are accomplished in about 10–30 hours per adult per week. Possessions are minimal but much time is free for resting, chatting, dancing and gambling. We do not know whether such situations were typical thousands of years ago.

Human Populations Have Increased as Agricultural Technology Has Improved

With the development of agriculture roughly 10,000 years ago, higher population densities became possible. Agriculture increases food production by fostering the growth of edible, high-yielding crops and animals. Perhaps the chief limitation on the development of agriculture has been the problem of maintaining soil fertility in the face of man's disruption of the natural mineral cycles (Chapter 5). The soil is gradually depleted of minerals by wind and water erosion of soil exposed during cultivation, and by removal of crops containing minerals which would ordinarily return to the soil as the crops decayed *in situ*. Initially this problem seems to have been solved by simply abandoning one area and moving on to the next when the soil had lost its fertility. An abandoned field will be invaded first by rapidly growing weeds, especially grasses and annuals. If there is enough water these are gradually replaced by shrubs, and then by trees which grow slower but taller and thus eventually may eliminate most smaller plants by blocking the sunlight. Soil fertility is restored by nitrogen-fixing bacteria, by tree roots that pull up minerals from deeper soil layers and by other natural mineral cycling processes. After about 25 years, the farmer who returns is likely to find the soil extremely easy to till with simple instruments, since it is soft and fertile from the accumulated decaying organic matter and from the ashes produced by burning the trees. The most time-consuming part of the work is to clear the trees, but even when that is included, the agricultural work week averages only 10–30 hours per week for contemporary African practitioners of this "slash-and-burn" agriculture.

Since the land is tilled only about 3 years out of every 20, this type of agriculture can support only about 50 people per square mile. Although slash-and-burn agriculture persists in some sparsely populated regions of Africa and Latin America, increasing population densities in most regions have forced farmers to use the land more often, thus shortening the restorative or fallow period. With more frequent burning, grass tends to become the predominant vegetation, since its roots survive the fires and trees are no longer such serious competitors for sunlight. The soil then becomes harder to cultivate, mainly because the net of grass roots must be broken. Typically this was accomplished with horse- or ox-drawn plows. Soil fertility, which tends to be lower with the shorter fallow, was enhanced by bringing the feces of humans and animals to the fields. Although this seems to have taken more work, averaging about 30–35 hours per week with much seasonal variation, it permitted the support of relatively high densities, roughly 100 people per square mile of agricultural land in medieval Europe.

In some regions, irrigation increases the productivity of the land, and thus increases the population density supported. Much more labor is needed, averaging 50–70 hours of agricultural work per adult per week. But with intensive cultivation, densities of roughly 200–700 people per square mile can be supported by this type of agriculture, for instance in the Chinese river valleys. Irrigation may also make it possible to expand the area under cultivation and in this way also support a larger population. It should not be forgotten, however, that soil fertility has been decreased in some places by prolonged poor irrigation practices, such as inadequate water flow and high evaporation resulting in the accumulation of salt in the soil.

To recapitulate, population growth over the last 10,000 years appears to have been closely linked to improvements in the food-producing technology. New technologies have made it possible to raise more food on the same land and have thus permitted higher population densities. Conversely, higher population densities may have provided the essential motivation for adoption of these new technologies, which often required more labor for a given yield even though they required less land. The increase in labor required probably explains why people in low population density areas often fail to adopt new technologies even when they know about them.

There are of course exceptions, that is, techniques which produce the same yield with less labor as well as less land. The most notable of these were developed in recent centuries in Europe and North America. Major improvement during the 18th century included the use of better designed, iron-tipped plows and the use of legumes with their nitrogen-fixing bacteria to maintain soil fertility. By the end of the 19th century, the use of mechanized equipment and chemical fertilizers began to spread. Population densities for agriculturally self-supporting regions using this technology range from 100–250 people per square mile of usable land. These densities are not as high as those observed in the Chinese river valleys, partly because more food is consumed per person and partly because labor that could be used in more intensive cultivation is used instead in industrial production of other goods. In very high density regions like Europe, it is possible to divert labor from maximally intensive agriculture to industrial production only because food can be imported from other areas.

Clearly, high population densities in different areas have been associated with quite different technological developments. Population pressure is but one of the factors which shape the development of technology.

Available Resources and Technology Are Not the Only Factors that Limit Population Size

Just as population densities are not the sole determinants of technological developments, the technological developments and resource limitations are not the only factors which limit population size or population growth. We have already described how hunter-gatherers limit their families by sexual abstention, prolonged lactation, abortion and infanticide. In Paris around 1820 more than a quarter of all babies were abandoned to foundling homes where about half died within the first three months of residence; this system is perhaps best described as institutionalized infanticide. Infanticide and abortion were widely practiced in ancient Greece and Rome, and indeed in very many other societies. The important role of abortion and contraception in reducing population growth in industrial societies will be described in the next three chapters.

In many times and places, population growth has been reduced or reversed by wars and disease. As a result of Mongol invasions and plague epidemics in China around 1300, the population fell to about half its former size (Figure 15–1). Earlier periods of declining population were due in part to high taxation, much forced labor for canal building (600–700 A.D.), a disastrous flood when the Yellow River broke its dikes, rebellions, and raids by nomads from the sparsely populated steppes (10–75 A.D.). The four recorded periods of major population increase occurred during long periods of unity when a dynasty managed to maintain relative peace. Usually peace was accompanied by widespread public works: building and maintaining canals and dikes that provided the basis for productive irrigated agriculture. There were also government measures to alleviate temporary food shortages by buying grain when it was abundant and selling it during times of scarcity, and by reducing taxes. Thus China alternated between war-torn destructive eras and unified peaceful eras of increasing productivity and population. This alternation was caused by a variety of political factors, such as the tendency of each dynastic government to become progressively more corrupt and expensive, ending often in rebellion and invasion.

The history of China thus illustrates how social and political factors limit productivity as much as technology and raw materials do. Therefore, social and political organization must be included among the factors that limit the size of the population that can be supported. In earlier chapters we have indicated several contemporary examples of how economic and political organization cause production to be less than resources and technology would permit. The failure to use resources optimally has affected population growth recently both by increasing deaths (for example, during the famines in Biafra during the Nigerian civil war) and by reducing births (for example, during the depression in the United States; see p. 178).

In summary, technology and raw materials set upper limits to population growth. Increases toward these limits have been interrupted

Figure 15–1 POPULATION GROWTH IN CHINA

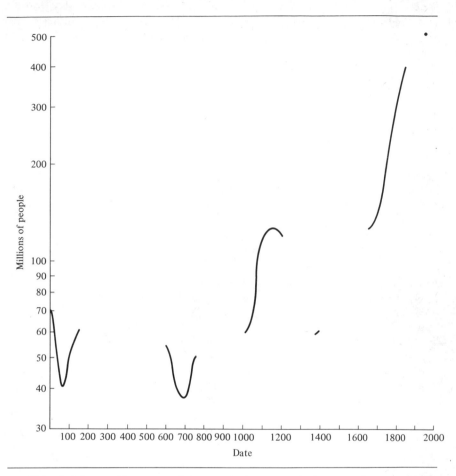

China's history illustrates that population growth has not been a steady progression to higher and higher numbers of people. As explained in the text, China's population growth was periodically reversed when political organization broke down so that existing resources and technology were not mobilized effectively for the support of the population. China's history thus illustrates how population size is limited not only by the available technology and resources, but also by political, social and economic organization which determine how efficiently the available resources are used.

China has been chosen as an illustration because it is the only country for which such a long series of censuses is available.

Source: From J. Durand. 1960. The Population Statistics of China, A.D. 2–1953. *Population Studies 13:* 209–256. He has selected the most reliable estimates for "China proper," excluding Manchuria and Mongolia. Adapted with permission of the author and editor.

at times by disease, wars and social conditions which keep production below maximum or cause gross inequalities in distribution. On the more optimistic side, population growth has been reduced in some societies by adult action to limit the number of children in their families. In the next two chapters we will examine the role of all these factors in the history of population growth in Europe and the United States.

BIBLIOGRAPHY

Boserup, E. 1965. *Conditions of Agricultural Growth*. Chicago: Aldine-Atherton [describes the development of agricultural technology, especially how productivity per man hour often decreased as productivity per acre increased].

Deevey, E. 1960. The Human Population. *Scientific American*, September: 194–204 [estimates of size and geographic spread of early human populations].

Langer, W. L. 1963. Europe's Initial Population Explosion. *American Historical Review, 69:* 1–17 [includes a description of institutionalized infanticide in 19th century Europe].

Lee, R. B. and I. DeVore. 1968. *Man, the Hunter*. Chicago: Aldine-Atherton [gives estimates of food resources, work week and describes population regulation for hunter-gatherers].

Needham, J. 1969. *The Grand Titration: Science and Society in East and West*. Toronto: University of Toronto Press [an informative discussion of the variety of factors that influence the development of technology].

Van Bath, B. H. Slicher. 1963. *The Agrarian History of Western Europe, A.D. 500–1850*. Trans. O. Ordish. London: Edward Arnold and Co. [re development of agricultural technology and productivity in Europe].

chapter 16

the decline of birth rates and death rates in europe

High Death Rates Slowed Population Growth in Early Periods

During the late 14th century, population growth in Europe was dramatically reversed (Figure 16–1). Plague swept through Europe, killing roughly a quarter of the population in the three years from 1348 through 1350. Further outbreaks of plague continued until about 1700, often in association with typhus, syphilis and "English sweat" (which was apparently a deadly type of influenza). Frequently a quarter to a half of the people in a city were killed within a year. As may be imagined, this death and depopulation had a dramatic effect on social and economic organization and on religious attitudes. It is not clear why plague suddenly swept through Europe and China at the same time (Figure 15–1, see pg. 159), nor is it clear why plague gradually disappeared from Europe.

There may have been another significant interruption in European population growth during the first half of the 17th century when famine and plague were widespread in Russia, and the whole of north-central Europe was caught up in the Thirty Years War. The enormous distress which must have been involved in slowing population growth this way can only be imagined by considering that during the first half of the 20th century, Europe's population continued to grow despite two world wars and the Depression.

The steady rapid growth of Europe's population after 1700 masks several major changes which are most clearly seen in the records of individual countries (illustrated for Sweden in Figure 16–2). Three basic periods can be discerned. In the first period, birth rates and death rates are both high and quite variable. In the second period, death rates begin to decline and sometime later birth rates also decline. This is a period of rapid natural increase of population and considerable emigration. In the most recent period, death rates are low and rather steady and birth rates are low and quite variable.

The major peaks in death rate during the first period occur at times of epidemics, crop failures and wars. Crop failures were sometimes due to poor weather, sometimes to wars or epidemics which disrupted farming and sometimes even to previous crop failures, which

Figure 16–1 THE POPULATION OF EUROPE SINCE 1200 A.D.

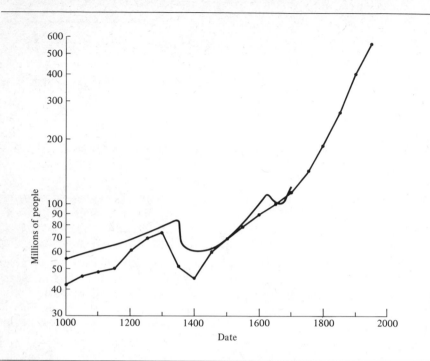

For the earlier years, estimates from two different sources are given in order to indicate the uncertainty of the data. Both estimates agree on a considerable decline in population during the 14th century, due primarily to the plague. Since 1700 the rate of population growth has been relatively constant, as indicated by the straight-line appearance of this semilog plot. This masks important developments discussed in the text.

Source: M. K. Bennett. 1954. *The World's Food.* New York: Harper & Row; U.N. Department of Economic and Social Affairs. *Demographic Yearbooks.* New York: U.N.; and from "The Black Death" by William L. Langer. Copyright © 1964 by *Scientific American, Inc.* All rights reserved. Adapted with permission.

often produced grain harvests too small to supply both food for the farming family and seed for them to plant the following year. Crop failures also contributed to the spread of epidemics, since under-nourished people are more susceptible to disease and since starving people often take to wandering in search of food, frequently carrying disease with them as they go. Wars also often bring disease, not only because they disrupt the food supply, but also because they bring large groups of men into close proximity, which provides optimal conditions for the spread of many diseases such as influenza or typhus

162

Figure 16–2 BIRTH RATES, DEATH RATES AND POPULATION
GROWTH IN SWEDEN

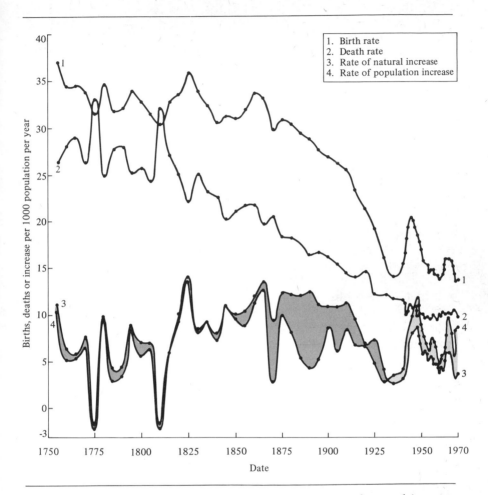

1. Birth rate
2. Death rate
3. Rate of natural increase
4. Rate of population increase

The excess of births over deaths is often called the rate of natural increase. It indicates Sweden's contribution to the population growth of the world. The shaded area between the rate of natural increase and the rate of population increase in Sweden indicates the amount of emigration or, recently, immigration. Death rates declined earlier than birth rates did. This produced a period of high rates of natural increase and high emigration.

Source: Historical Statistics of Sweden, Vol. I. Population, 1720–1950. 1955. Stockholm, Central Bureau of Statistics; *U.N. Demographic Yearbooks.*

which is carried by body lice. An epidemic of one disease tends to increase the incidence of other diseases, since sick persons have lower resistance against other infections. Thus the causes of high death rates reinforced each other.

During the early period of high birth rates and high death rates, birth rates tended to decline whenever death rates rose. To some extent this can be attributed to poorer health during these periods and hence lower fecundity. But it is also known that peasant couples postponed marriage in years of bad harvests, thus to some extent adjusting population growth to the available resources. In a few areas couples apparently limited births within marriage, presumably by abstinence, coitus interruptus (that is, withdrawal), or abortion. These practices are best documented for northwestern Europe, a region which was peculiar in this first period for its relatively low birth rates and generally late marriage. For example, about half of both men and women were still single at age 25 in Sweden in 1750. Late marriages apparently became customary in western Europe during the 16th century about the time of the Reformation. The consequence was infrequent intercourse during much of the woman's most fertile period (20–30 years old) and lower birth rates, generally less than 35 births per 1000 population, as compared to birth rates around 40/1000 in late 19th century eastern Europe and as high as 50/1000 in the late 18th century in the United States.

Population Growth Increased when Deaths Due to Infectious Diseases Declined

Death rates in Europe have decreased markedly in the last century. Figure 16–2 illustrates this decline for Sweden, where the decline was exceptionally early and steady. Improved survival has been due primarily to a decrease in infectious diseases, while "degenerative" diseases such as cancer and heart disease have shown little or no decline.

Infectious diseases are those diseases which are caused by parasitic organisms (for example, viruses, bacteria and tapeworms) which grow and reproduce within the human body. These infectious organisms can harm the body in a variety of ways. Tapeworms absorb nutrients for their growth and thus rob the human host of nutrients he can replace only if he has plenty to eat. The bacteria that cause pneumonia and diphtheria secrete toxins, that is, poisons. Some of these toxins are enzymes that break down molecules of the human body in a way which may help the bacteria grow, but which interferes with the proper functioning of the human body.

Since every person eventually dies, a parasite can only survive from generation to generation if it has some means of getting from one person to another. Methods of transmission are varied. Mucous droplets produced in a sneeze or cough can carry flu viruses or tuberculosis bacteria from the respiratory passages of one individual to another. A louse can pick up typhus bacteria by biting an infected person and can inject these bacteria into the next person it bites. The bacteria that cause cholera and typhoid fever colonize the bowels. These bacteria are carried in feces into rivers and other water supplies. When the water is drunk, the bacteria are carried into the bowels of previously uninfected individuals. Bacteria which cause diarrhea and enteritis also colonize the digestive tract. During food preparation, these bacteria may be carried by dirty hands from the anal regions of infected workers into the food, which can then carry the bacteria into new digestive tracts to colonize.

A major means of decreasing infectious disease has been to interfere with the transmission of disease organisms from person to person. For example, the transmission of cholera and typhoid fever bacteria in the drinking water can be eliminated by sanitary disposal of sewage, and by filtration and chlorination of drinking water. These practices became common in European cities during the late 19th and early 20th centuries and contributed to the decline in death rates at that time. Pasteurization of milk at about the same period reduced transmission of live tuberculosis bacteria from cows. Pasteurization and improved handling techniques for milk were also crucial in preventing transmission of the bacteria that cause diarrhea and enteritis, which were formerly major causes of death among infants. Improved bodily cleanliness reduced the louse population and thus reduced the spread of typhus. Less crowded housing with better ventilation reduced transmission of airborne parasites such as tuberculosis bacteria. The spread of tuberculosis was further reduced by well-organized detection efforts which resulted in early isolation and treatment of infected individuals. The spread of many other diseases has been reduced by effective detection, isolation by quarantine or in hospitals and rapid cures with modern drugs which reduce the number of infected carriers.

Deaths due to infectious diseases can be reduced not only by reducing the transmission of the diseases but also by preventing the growth or harmful effects of disease organisms after they have infected a person. The body has natural defenses against parasites, and these defenses can be enhanced by immunization techniques. When a new substance is introduced into the body, the natural defense system produces molecules called antibodies which bind to the foreign substance. Some antibodies bind to toxins and can prevent their harmful effects. Other antibodies bind to bacteria and viruses and immobilize them, after which they are eaten and broken down by white blood cells. The second time a foreign substance is introduced into the body, more antibodies are produced faster than the first time, so the defense is more effective. In vaccination, a first exposure is given under controlled conditions, typically with small doses of toxin or of killed bacteria; then any natural infection is met with the more effective second antibody reaction. Vaccination against smallpox became relatively common during the early 19th century. Toward the end of the 19th century, Pasteur's discovery of bacteria as a cause of many infectious diseases resulted in the rapid development of techniques of immunization against typhoid fever, diphtheria and so on. Vaccination contributed primarily to better survival of young children who were generally most susceptible to infectious diseases; most adults had caught any common infectious disease and therefore developed their own immunity; infants were protected by maternal antibodies received through the fetal circulation and mother's milk.

While vaccinations have played the largest role in reducing growth of disease organisms in infected individuals, two other factors have played an important role. First, there was a reduction of acute food shortages, due to improved techniques for food production (Chapter 15) and improved transportation. This helped to reduce infectious disease, since malnutrition can lead to the breakdown of some of the body's natural defenses, such as the membranes which keep infectious organisms out of the body. However, the net contribution of changes in nutrition is not entirely clear, since average consumption of meat and some other foods seems to have declined in European cities during the first half of the 19th century.

Second, since World War II antibiotics such as penicillin have been widely used to curb bacterial growth. The first antibiotics used were chemicals which are produced by fungi to kill the bacteria with which the fungi compete for the dead organic matter on which both feed (in the process known as decay; see pg. 37). Antibiotics interfere with specific chemical functions of the bacteria, such as the synthesis of proteins or the formation of the cell wall. The bacteria that cause pneumonia, staph infections, or venereal diseases are commonly controlled with antibiotics, so commonly, in fact, that these bacteria have evolved increasing resistance to the most popular antibiotics (just as insects have evolved resistance against widely used insecticides; see pgs. 18 and 67).

In conclusion, declining death rates were caused by: (1) improved public health and medical technology especially for curing and preventing infectious diseases; (2) the developing organization to apply this technology, including hospitals and medical schools, sanitation and water systems, public health programs for immunization, education and detection of disease and (3) improved nutrition, more sanitary housing and increased general literacy with consequent greater awareness of health principles.

Decreased deaths resulted in a wider gap between birth rates and death rates with a consequent acceleration of the rate of natural increase of European populations. How was it possible to support the increasing population? A significant fraction of the increase produced by excess births over deaths did not stay in Europe but rather emigrated, primarily to North America. From 1850 to 1940, the emigrants from Europe numbered about a tenth of the excess of births over deaths. In North America and Australia, the emigrants displaced the native populations and acquired access to the resources of two continents. For those that remained in Europe, the increasing food needed by the growing population came from cultivating new land (for example, by farming in colder areas and by draining swamps), from increasing productivity per acre (for example, through the use of potatoes which give three times more yield per acre than grain, legumes which add nitrates to the soil and chemical fertilizers) and by importing food. Imports of food and other raw materials continued to expand because of improved methods of shipping, because Europe developed an industrial technology which produced suitable goods for trade, and because European countries developed the military power to enforce trade on reluctant partners (such as China) and to extract taxes and other payments from colonized regions (such as India).

The importance of these factors is thrown into relief by considering an exceptional case, that of Ireland. Due to earlier conquests, most Irish land was owned by English landlords who typically felt small love for the "shiftless and rebellious" Irish and who often lived in England, not Ireland. These factors probably contributed to a general willingness to oust an Irish tenant if a higher rent was offered by another farmer. The incumbent tenant therefore had little inducement to improve his land, since he had no assurance of being able to stay on the land and every likelihood that his rent would be raised, especially as land became scarce while population grew during the late 18th and early 19th centuries. The English landlord also failed to invest in land improvement in Ireland. One of the factors responsible for the lack of industrialization in Ireland was the flow of large amounts of investable money (rents) to England. The only increase in productivity which served to support the growing population resulted from the introduction of the potato. The potato became the main food for most Irish, since plots were too small to grow sufficient quantities of anything else. When disease struck the potato crop in the late 1840s more than one million out of nine million Irishmen died of starvation and the typhus, dysentery and cholera which spread in the wake of the famines. Another million emigrated to North America; many of these died en route. Many tenants who failed to pay their rent were evicted and were thus left without means of support. Other tenants sold grain to pay their rent; during the famines considerable grain was exported for sale in paying markets. After the famines, population continued to decline due to continued emigration and to decreasing birth rates which resulted from postponed marriages, with as much as a quarter of the population never marrying. Ireland's calamitous history is exceptional in Europe. But it indicates one possible course of population development, especially to be expected where rapidly growing populations cannot command access to the resources of other regions and lack the means to increase productivity at home.

During Late Industrialization Birth Rates Declined and Population Growth Decreased

Birth rates began to decline by 1880 in most of northwestern Europe. With few exceptions this decline coincided more or less with the period of late industrialization for each country. In southern and eastern Europe where industrialization came later, birth rates generally began to decline later, sometime around 1900. The most striking feature of this decrease in births is that increasing numbers of married couples began to use contraception to limit the size of their families. They did this despite the opposition of both Protestant and Catholic churches, and despite the lack of modern chemical and mechanical contraceptives, which meant that couples were forced to use primarily the difficult technique of coitus interruptus.

What was behind this widespread decrease in births? Several plausible arguments can be made, although it is difficult to evaluate the relative importance of many factors which typically change simultaneously during late industrialization. On small farms and in early industrial societies, children typically begin work at relatively young ages. During late industrialization, most work involves complex machines and can only be accomplished by educated adults. During this period, education spreads and laws prohibiting child labor are introduced. Children must then be supported until older ages and thus become more of an economic burden. In cities, lack of space also tends to make children more of a burden. The steady stream of new goods produced by industrial manufacture may have commanded an increasing proportion of family budgets. Furthermore, family ties tend to break down in cities, so that grown children are less likely to support aged parents. All in all, there may have been reason to want fewer children.

In addition, childhood mortality had declined in many places so that fewer births were needed to produce even the same size family. The notion of controlling family size and information about techniques for avoiding births may have spread more rapidly as education increased, as cities and improved transportation brought people into wider contact with each other and as more people worked with a technology that emphasized manipulation and control of nature instead of working with nature as in the patterns of preindustrial agriculture. The importance of education and participation in a planning-oriented culture is indicated by the observation that birth control spread first among the bourgeosie and only later among the workers and farmers. In contrast, deteriorating conditions and delayed marriage seem to have caused decreased births for some people. In some cases, also, decreased births may have been due to decreased fecundity, particularly in the cities where venereal disease seems to have increased. In the next two chapters, we will give further evidence about the relative importance of these various factors.

During the most recent period, birth rates and death rates have both been low. Death rates have generally declined, with the most notable exceptions occurring during the First World War and the associated flu epidemic and during the Second World War in countries where fighting occurred. Birth rates, although generally low, have varied with economic conditions. During the Depression of the 1930s, births were markedly less than during the economic boom after World War II. The reduction in birth rates has brought the rate of natural increase down to approximately that of the first period discussed. However, population increase has not been negligible. Despite the low birth rates and despite 70 million European deaths attributed to the two world wars and related events, Europe's population has grown about 1 percent per year during the 20th century. This corresponds to population doubling in less than a century. Proposals for decreasing this rate of growth will be discussed in the last chapter.

BIBLIOGRAPHY

Glass, D. V. and D. E. Eversley. eds. 1965. *Population in History.* London: Edward Arnold and Co. [main emphasis on population growth in pre-industrial and early industrial Europe; articles by Hajnal, Meuvret and Utterstrom are especially useful].

Humphrey, J. H. and R. G. White 1964. *Immunology for Students of Medicine.* Philadelphia: F. A. Davis Company [re antibodies and vaccination].

Langer, W. L. 1964. The Black Death. *Scientific American,* February: 114–21 [re the medieval plague epidemics and their social effects].

United Nations Department of Social Affairs, Population Division. 1953. *The Determinants and Consequences of Population Trends.* Population Studies,

#17. New York: United Nations [evaluates the causes of declining birth rates and death rates in recent times].

Woodham-Smith, C. 1962. *The Great Hunger: Ireland 1845–1849*. New York: Harper and Row, Publishers [general description of the potato famine including discussion of relations to England, grain exports, epidemics, and so on].

chapter 17

the united states: what determines family size?

In this chapter we will analyze the causes of variation in fertility in the United States, and will also deal briefly with the other determinants of population growth: deaths and migration. We will begin with data from the recent past, and then deal with earlier historical periods for which the scarce data can best be interpreted by using our much more complete understanding of contemporary behavior. Our detailed examination of factors affecting fertility leads us to proposals about how to reduce birth rates.

Educated, Employed, Urban Women Have Fewer Children
Why do some couples have many children and some few? We will investigate the reasons by comparing the number of children born to couples in different socioeconomic circumstances, the number they say they want, the methods they use to achieve the desired family size and some of the psychological interpretations of this behavior. Differences in fecundity (the physiological capacity to bear children) will also be explored. To facilitate comparisons, all figures on family size are the average number of children born to women of the specified type who had ever been married and were 35–39 at the time of the 1960 census. Unfortunately the available data on number of children wanted and contraceptive practice are for a somewhat different group, namely white wives, ages 18–39 when surveyed in 1960. Because these data were gathered near the end of a baby boom, they indicate generally larger family sizes than will the results of more recent surveys when these are made available (see Figure 17–2).

One cultural factor generally believed to lead to large families is religion, especially Catholicism. It is true that in 1960 over half of Catholic couples either used no contraception or used only the relatively ineffective rhythm method, in accordance with church doctrine. However Catholic-Protestant differentials in contraceptive use have decreased since then. Furthermore, lesser contraceptive practice among Catholics is to some extent balanced by later marriage (about 1–2 years later for women). In consequence, the difference between

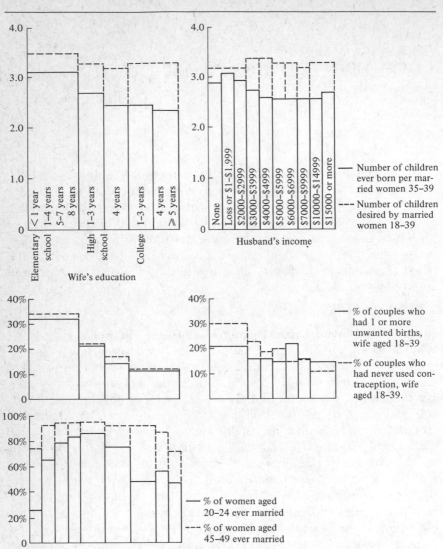

Figure 17–1 RELATIONSHIP OF EDUCATION AND INCOME TO CHILDBEARING

Couples with low income and poor education have slightly more children, primarily because they use contraception less effectively and have more unwanted births. Despite the unwanted pregnancies (about ⅓ of all pregnancies for the poor), the actual births average less than the wanted births because many couples have fewer children than they want, primarily due to infecundity. Also, ¹⁄₁₀ of women in the 35–39 age group will still have more children. Note that couples at *all* income and education levels averaged more children than the 2.2 per couple that would result in a stable, nongrowing population.

The data are for whites in the United States in 1960. A birth was defined as unwanted if conception occurred when either the husband or wife did not want a pregnancy, when contraception was not omitted for the purpose of conceiving and when the wife already had at least two pregnancies.

average Catholic and Protestant family size is small (Table 17–1). This difference increases slightly as Catholic women have more children after ages 35–39, but to a large extent the effects of religious teaching have been countervailed by other socioeconomic factors such as greater urban residence among Catholics.

Poverty, like Catholicism, is commonly thought to be associated with large families. Figure 17–1 shows that couples with low income and/or little education do have somewhat larger families. Why do these couples have more children? Contrary to middle class myth, it is not because they copulate more frequently. Nor is it primarily because they want more children. Rather, they practice contraception less and not as effectively, and consequently have more unwanted births (Figure 17–1). Among groups of higher income or higher education, contraceptive practice is more prevalent, unwanted births are fewer and, in consequence, average family size is smaller.

There are two exceptions to the general trend of decreasing family size with increasing income. First, the poorest group, listed as having no income, has smaller families than the next poorest group, presumably because any reduction in contraceptive use is outweighed by higher infecundity due to inadequate nutrition, poor medical care, and so on. Second, at the very highest incomes there is a slight increase in both children born and children wanted. This is not surprising since the most common reason given for not wanting more children is lack of sufficient money, a factor which is less important for wealthy doctors and business executives.

From this discussion we can identify three major causes of differences in family size, namely differences in physiological capacity to bear children, differences in number of children wanted and variable effectiveness of contraception to avoid unwanted pregnancies. Lower income and education tend to be associated with less effective contraception and larger families. But lower income can also have the conflicting effect of tending to reduce family size by causing poorer health or by motivating a desire for smaller families to fit limited resources. These last two effects were especially important in producing low birth rates during the Depression (pg. 178).

Now we turn to the question: why are lower income and lower education associated with less effective contraception? Causation

---

Figure 17–1 (continued)

Source: Data from Kiser, C. V., W. H. Grabill and A. A. Campbell. 1968. *Trends and Variations in Fertility in the United States.* Cambridge: Harvard University Press; O. Harkavy, F. S. Jaffe and S. M. Wishik. 1969. Family Planning and Public Policy: Who Is Misleading Whom? *Sci. 165:* 367–373; Whelpton, C. K., A. A. Campbell and J. E. Patterson. 1966. *Fertility and Family Planning in the United States.* Princeton: Princeton University Press.

seems to work in both directions. Early and rapid childbearing tends to interfere with education and reduce income. Conversely, low incomes and low education tend to result in poor family planning. This is partly a problem of resources: legal abortions, for instance, have been available mainly for the well-to-do. The importance of abortion as an alternative in case of contraceptive failure is clear when we realize that women typically have their last wanted child before 30 and are still somewhat fecund at 40, thus leaving more than ten years in which to make a mistake! This problem is even more severe for

Table 17–1 FAMILY SIZE FOR VARIOUS SOCIOECONOMIC GROUPS IN THE UNITED STATES

SOCIOECONOMIC GROUP	FAMILY SIZE (AVERAGE NUMBER OF CHILDREN BORN TO WOMEN IN THE SPECIFIED CATEGORY WHO HAD EVER BEEN MARRIED AND WERE 35–39 AT THE TIME OF THE 1960 CENSUS)
Roman Catholics	2.8
Protestants	2.6
Jews	2.1
Others	2.5
Nonwhites	3.1
Whites	2.6
Rural farm residents*	3.5
Rural nonfarm residents	3.0
Residents of towns and small cities	2.5
Residents of suburbs of larger cities	2.4
Residents of central cities in urbanized areas with over 3 million people	2.2
Women who have never worked	3.5
Women who last worked 6 or more years ago	3.0
Women who last worked 2–5 years ago	2.6
Women who are unemployed but worked within the last year	2.7
Women who are unemployed but looking for a job	2.5
Women who work less than 35 hours a week	2.5
Women who work 35 hours a week or more	2.0

*This one series is for women aged 35–44.

Source: Data from Kiser, C. V., W. H. Grabill and A. A. Campbell. 1968. *Trends and Variations in Fertility in the United States.* Cambridge: Harvard University Press.

women who marry young, as women with no more than a high school education typically do. Low income couples also have poorer access to contraceptives and medical advice about their use.

Among the less educated, lack of knowledge about reproductive physiology tends to make contraception seem mysterious and magical. This often leads to irregular and therefore ineffective use of contraceptives. Contraceptive success is believed to be a matter of luck, a belief which is part of a general image of oneself as a victim of fate. Such attitudes are common among the "lower-lower" class, which includes families where the father is intermittently unemployed, or absent from the home with welfare as the major source of income. This is the group in which unwanted pregnancies are most common. For members of racial minorities, any tendency toward fatalism is strongly reinforced by conditions in the United States where, for example, Negroes at each level of educational attainment earn less than two-thirds the income for comparable whites. It is not surprising that poor family planning is especially prevalent among Negroes, and that they have more children than whites although they want slightly fewer (Table 17–1).

Less effective contraception seems to be one reason why rural couples have larger families (Table 17–1). Other factors are also important, including the desire for slightly more children among farm women, earlier marriage in rural regions and lower prevalence of venereal disease and associated infecundity outside of cities. It seems plausible that women in cities want fewer children both because it is more difficult to raise children in urban environments and because there is more opportunity for alternative activities outside the home.

Wives who have worked want and have fewer children than those who have not (Table 17–1). The difference in actual family size is partly due to the tendency of infecund women with small families to seek employment. But even among fecund women who could have more children if they chose, women who have worked five or more years since marriage average only 2.5 children as compared to 4.1 for women who have not worked since marriage. Limited time and energy seem to be the main factors which motivate working women to limit their families. This is reasonable, since housework takes more than 40 hours per week for families with children under ten and this work falls predominantly on the woman, whether or not she works. The working wife does approximately 75 percent of the housework compared to 85 percent for nonworking wives.

What motivates a woman to seek work outside the home? For some it is the intrinsic interest of the work and the need to achieve in some publicly recognized work. This tends to be the case for women from upper socioeconomic classes to whom more interesting jobs are open.

Education is most important, with 71 percent employed among women with five years or more of college compared to 30 percent among women with elementary school education (for women more than 17 years old in 1968). Professional women, such as doctors, lawyers, professors and business executives, show the highest commitment to their work, and often will refuse marriage to a man who does not accept their career. Women in most other occupations generally plan to stop work in order to rear a family. For many the available work is insufficiently interesting or rewarding to offer much competition as an alternative to childrearing and housework. Nevertheless, many women do work even when they have young children, especially if there is no husband in the home or the husband's income is low. The main attraction for most of these women seems to be the money, rather than the job *per se*. The most common explanations that women give for working involve financial motivations. If more interesting occupations were available, there would probably be other strong motives for seeking activity outside the home. Indicative of this is the considerable restlessness expressed by mothers confined to the home while rearing young children. For example, when mothers were asked "how a woman's life is changed by having children, by far the most common reply was that children meant less freedom."[1]

Many young women who would appreciate the rewards of self-fulfilling work coupled with adult companionship on the job fail to seek work, not only because of general difficulty in finding satisfying work, but also because of social disapproval of women who do not devote themselves to family-rearing. For married women, the attitude of the husband appears to be critical. In a sample from one suburban community, among women whose husbands had no objections to their working, 43 percent worked and 43 percent planned to work, whereas among women whose husbands objected to their wife working, only 5 percent worked and 10 percent planned to. This apparently is not just a case of like-meets-like and marries to live in happy agreement. More young men than women think a woman's place is in the home; 61 percent of male students entering universities in 1967 agreed to the assertion "married women belong at home," as opposed to 38 percent of the entering female students. This leads to the crucial question of how such disagreements are resolved either before marriage or within marriage. The same kind of question is of considerable importance when husband and wife disagree about the desired number of children. Limited data suggest that in the middle class the partner who wants fewer children usually has a veto, and this is usually the

---

[1] From E. Pohlman and J. Mea, *The Psychology of Birth Planning*. (Cambridge, Mass.: Schenkman Publishing Company, 1969), by permission.

husband; among the "lower-lower" class, the husband typically is the one who wants a large family and his wishes are satisfied roughly half the time. Further data are needed.

We have explored the question of women's employment at considerable length because it presents one of the more hopeful prospects for reducing birth rates in the United States. If more women can find meaningful and satisfying activities outside the family, then they will be more likely to want two children rather than three. In a similar vein, if resources are used to provide poor people with better possibilities for education and employment, then they can be expected to take a less fatalistic attitude and use contraceptives more systematically and effectively. There may well be other factors which influence family size and which could have significance for policies for reducing birth rates. We have discussed the factors that show large correlations with family size in studies in the United States, but we expect that other important factors are yet to be discovered, since the known factors are by no means sufficient to predict accurately how many children a given couple will have.

Despite Differences, Nearly All Segments of the Population Have Enough Children to Cause Substantial Population Growth

While we have emphasized differences between groups, there is one crucial similarity among almost all these groups. In nearly all cases, the average family size is large enough to make a substantial contribution to population growth. Consider, for example, the white middle class couples who average 2.6 children. How fast would the United States' population grow if all couples averaged 2.6 children? If no one died before reproducing, and if everyone married, the offspring of the average couple would then constitute $2.6/2 = 1.3$ couples. Therefore the population would increase 30 percent in each generation. However, only 49 percent of the children born are girls, about 3 percent of the girls die before age 25, and of those surviving, roughly another 5 percent marry not at all or too late to have children (and do not have children before they marry). Adding about 10 percent to make up for these losses, we find that married couples need to have 2.2 children on the average if they are going to just replace themselves as a reproducing couple. Thus our average middle income couple with 2.6 children has produced about $2.6/2.2 = 1.2$ reproducing couples, an increase of 20 percent per generation. Since median age of childbearing is roughly 25 years, there will be about four generations in a century. In that time the population will increase by a factor of $1.2 \times 1.2 \times 1.2 \times 1.2 = 2.1$. That is, the population will double in slightly less than a century. Note the importance of age at reproduction for the rate of population growth. If the couples had their children at age 20, four generations would take only 80 years and the population would double in slightly less than 80 years.

Thus we see that all income groups have more children than required to produce a stable population. Indeed, we have somewhat underestimated the contribution of middle income people to population growth, since their death rates are lower than those of poorer people, so that more of their children survive to reproduce. Furthermore, the majority of American couples have the moderate incomes associated with about 2.6 children born, and their large numbers makes their contribution to population growth most important. The criterion of 2.2 children per couple indicates that all groups studied are contributing substantially to population growth except Jewish women, women in central cities of large metropolitan areas and working women (Table 17–1).

If married women had the 3.3 children they said they wanted under the conditions of 1960, or the 3.4 children they said would be ideal for the average American family, or the 3.7 children they said they would want if they could relive their lives under ideal conditions, then United States' population would quintuple, sectuple or octuple in a century. If married women had an average of 3.1 children, as they said in 1967 that they expected to, then population would quadruple in a century. Thus it is clear that a stable population in the United States will require substantial changes in the attitude and behavior of the majority of Americans, not just among the poor or the minority groups frequently accused of producing too many children.

During Prosperous Periods More Babies Are Born

In Chapter 13 we emphasized that the increase of nonhuman populations is often limited by the availability of resources such as water, food or nest holes. In the first section of this chapter, we described how increased income can lead to increased birth rates either by providing sufficient food, housing and other resources so that health and fecundity improve, or by supplying the resources for easier care of large families. Strong evidence of similar phenomena is seen in the recent history of birth rates in the United States.

Figure 17–2 shows that birth rates were very low during the Depression and rose sharply to produce the "baby boom" during the post-World War II economic boom. Birth rates rose as wages increased and unemployment fell. Increased housing construction and veterans' benefits after World War II made home ownership easier. Under the stimulus of rising prosperity, people's concept of the ideal family size rose from about 3.0 in 1941 to 3.4 in 1955. Couples using contraception planned and had larger families. Family size increased by more than a third, from 2.5 children for women who bore children during the Depression to 3.4 for women who bore children during the postwar boom. Women married at younger ages; median age at first marriage for females fell from about 21½ in 1940 to less than 20 in 1960. Such younger marriages generally lead to increased childbearing, particularly because of the high fecundity of women at those ages.

The fertility of nonwhites was also low during the Depression and rose markedly during the 1940s and 1950s, roughly paralleling the behavior of the white birth rate, though at a higher level. This is quite striking in view of the fact that marriage increased only slightly for nonwhites, and contraceptive use appears not to have been widespread. This combination of fluctuating birth rates with relatively little evidence of planning of births appears to be roughly representative of the experience of some other groups of poor in the United States. Apparently, the fluctuations in birth rate are due to changes in fecundity. The most persuasive single piece of evidence for widespread infecundity among nonwhites during the Depression is the large increase in childlessness among married women. Childlessness rose from 6 percent when first recorded for nonwhite women who had ever married to a peak of 28 percent for those born in the first decade of this century. The peak of childlessness for white women also occurred at this time, but only 17 percent of native white women who had ever married were childless. A survey of native white women born at about this period indicated that about 11 percent of them were childless due to physiological impairments, and about 8 percent were childless by choice and contraceptive effort. (The survey was limited to married, urban Protestants with at least an eighth grade education.) It is implausible to suppose that a higher proportion of nonwhite women were childless by choice and contraceptive effort. Therefore, we conclude that about 20 percent of nonwhite women were childless due to physiological impairments. If one out of five nonwhite couples were so infecund as to produce no children, then a significant proportion of the others must have been subfecund.

The causes of this low fecundity were presumably poor nutrition due to limited incomes, ill health due to poor sanitary conditions and poor medical care and the prevalence of venereal diseases. Gonorrhea causes inflammation of the mucous membranes of the genito-urinary tract. Severe infections in females can cause sterility by producing scars which block the oviducts which normally carry the egg from the ovary to the uterus. Accurate estimates of the prevalence of this disease are difficult to obtain, partly because approximately 90 percent of females who have the disease do not have any noticeable symptoms. The available evidence indicates that gonorrhea reached a peak fre-

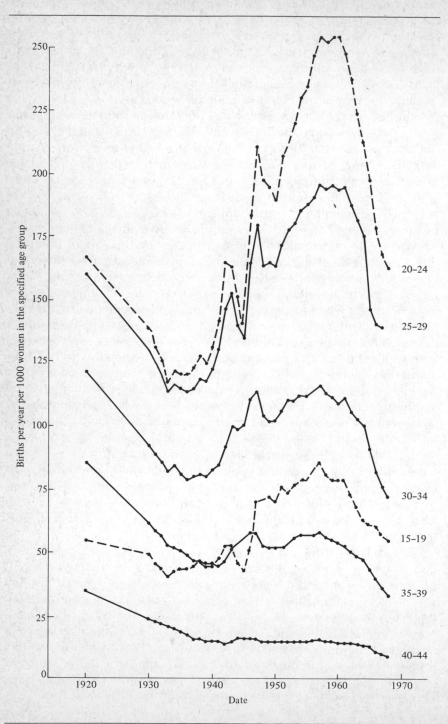

Figure 17–2 AGE-SPECIFIC BIRTH RATES FOR NATIVE WHITE FEMALES IN THE UNITED STATES

quency just after World War II, then decreased for about a decade under the influence of widespread and effective penicillin therapy, and then increased during the sixties. The decrease in venereal disease has no doubt contributed to decreasing childlessness, which for nonwhites was down to 14 percent for females aged 25–29 by 1960. On the other hand, decreasing gonorrhea cannot have been the only important cause of increasing fecundity. Birth rates for nonwhites began rising about 1936, at a time when gonorrhea case rates were still rapidly rising. The most reasonable conclusion is that decreasing unemployment, more adequate nutrition and other improvements that came with the end of the Depression led to improved health and greater childbearing.

Birth Rates Have Declined Sharply in the Last Decade

Since 1958 birth rates have fallen rapidly, returning recently to the low levels of Depression years (Figure 17–2). This decline has been quite general, affecting all ages of women, whites and nonwhites and a variety of occupational groups.

Why have birth rates fallen in the last decade? Certainly the dramatic decrease in birth rates has not been paralleled by an equally dramatic deterioration of economic conditions. Some indicators do, however, point to worsening material conditions. Housing construction has remained more or less constant, while demand has increased as large numbers of young people born during the postwar baby boom reach family formation ages. With rising housing costs and high mortgage rates, people with low incomes are more often living in trailers. In 1970, about half of all new single-family homes and 95 percent of those purchased for less than $15,000 were "mobile homes." Considering both old and new single-family homes, about three-quarters of those purchased for less than $15,000 were "mobile homes." Approxi-

---

Figure 17–2 (continued)

During the Depression and during the most recent period, couples married later and used contraceptives more, and thus had fewer children. Reduced birth rates during the Depression were also due in part to increased infecundity. Birth rates for older women are generally low, primarily because of infecundity. Birth rates among the youngest women are also low, primarily because of infrequent copulation among single women. Box 17–1 explains the relationship between these age-specific birth rates and the "crude" birth rates shown in Figure 17–4. (After 1955 the data for this figure includes immigrants as well as native whites, but this has little effect.)

Source: Vital Statistics of the United States (various years), National Office of Vital Statistics, Department of Health, Education, and Welfare.

Figure 17–3   AGE-SPECIFIC DEATH RATES IN THE
UNITED STATES

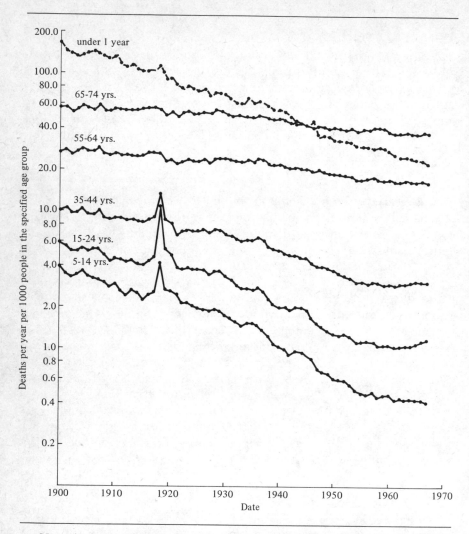

Note the log scale, and the fact that the probability of death is more than
10 times as high for infants and old people as it is for people aged 5–24.
Death rates began to decline approximately two decades before 1900. The
decline in death rates has been greatest for children, and very small for old
people. The 1918 peak in deaths was due primarily to an influenza epidemic.
This graph does not include war deaths.

Source: Data from *Vital Statistics of the United States* (various years), National
Office of Vital Statistics, Department of Health, Education, and Welfare.

mately as many housing units were rented as sold, and approximately three-quarters of these rentals were apartments. Young couples must find these trailers and apartments too small for large families. In addition, fewer households have diets that meet the standards for "good" nutrition (50 percent in 1965 compared to 60 percent in 1955). This is apparently due to decreased consumption of milk, fruits and vegetables. One final sign of deteriorating conditions is the increase since 1961 in death rates for young and middle aged adults (Table 11-2, pg. 123). Increases in war deaths, motor vehicle accidents and lung cancer all indicate increasingly unhealthy use of material resources. Increased suicide, cirrhosis of the liver and heart disease all suggest increasing stress and discontent, although we cannot yet specify the exact causes of the stress. It seems plausible that all these deteriorating conditions may have induced people to postpone and reduce family plans.

There seem to be additional causes of the recent decline in birth rates. The postwar baby boom may have contributed to the decline in birth rates in two quite separate ways. Perhaps older women are having fewer children now because they already have rather large families due to their high birth rates during the baby boom. Young women are marrying later and this may be partly due to the fact that baby-boom women outnumber men in the slightly older age groups from which husbands are usually drawn. The rise in marriage age is also due in part to increased enrollment in college, although much of the rise cannot be attributed to this cause. Another cause of decreased births may be the increase in employment among married women, especially at ages 20–30 when fecundity is maximum.

The introduction of contraceptive pills has resulted in improved ability to avoid unwanted births and has thus also tended to reduce births. Improved contraceptive efficiency cannot, however, be the only cause of birth rate declines. Contraceptive pills came into general use in 1962, several years *after* birth rates began to decline. The use of pills has not been sufficiently widespread to explain more than half the birth rate decline. It seems reasonable to conclude that social and economic conditions have motivated people to want fewer family commitments, and that contraceptive pills and, more recently, intrauterine devices have served to increase the effectiveness with which people can avoid pregnancies when they wish to do so.

These explanations of the recent decline in birth rates are subject to revision as more data become available, and the explanations may become more clearcut as we understand them better. At present it is impossible to predict how permanent the decline is likely to be. To the extent that factors like increasing education and improved contra-

Box 17–1 **RELATIONSHIP BETWEEN AGE STRUCTURE AND BIRTH RATES**

Age-specific birth rates give the number of births per 1000 females in a specific age group. Crude birth rates give the number of births per 1000 people in the total population. Crude birth rates depend on the proportion of females of childbearing age as well as on the age-specific birth rates. Crude birth rates can be calculated from the age-specific birth rates as demonstrated below for 1950 and 1960.

AGE GROUP	NUMBER OF FEMALES OF THIS AGE PER 1000 PEOPLE IN U.S.		PROPORTION OF WOMEN IN THIS AGE GROUP WHO HAD A BIRTH IN THE GIVEN YEAR (THAT IS, AGE-SPECIFIC BIRTH RATE)		NUMBER OF BIRTHS PER 1000 PEOPLE CONTRIBUTED BY WOMEN OF THIS AGE GROUP
		1950			
15–19	35.1	x	81/1000	=	2.8
20–24	38.6	x	198/1000	=	7.6
25–29	41.3	x	165/1000	=	6.8
30–34	39.0	x	102/1000	=	4.0
35–39	37.9	x	51/1000	=	1.9
40–44	34.1	x	14/1000	=	0.5

23.6 = total
births/1000 population = crude birth rate

AGE GROUP					
		1960			
15–19	36.9	x	88/1000	=	3.2
20–24	30.8	x	256/1000	=	7.9
25–29	30.6	x	198/1000	=	6.1
30–34	33.7	x	113/1000	=	3.8
35–39	35.5	x	56/1000	=	2.0
40–44	34.1	x	14/1000	=	0.5

23.5 = crude birth rate

Note that the crude birth rates are approximately the same in the two years despite significantly higher age-specific birth rates in 1960. This is because in 1960 there were fewer females in peak childbearing years due to the low birth rates from 1930–1940. The baby boom of 1940–1950 has produced large numbers of females just now reaching childbearing age. This should lead to increasing crude birth rates in the next years even if age-specific birth rates remain as low as they are now.

ceptives have been causal, we may be optimistic that the decline will persist. To the extent that delayed effects of the postwar baby boom and deteriorating conditions have been causal, we may expect or hope that the causal conditions will be removed. Even if age-specific birth rates do remain at current low levels, total births will increase in the next decade as large numbers of women born during the baby boom reach ages of maximum fertility (Box 17–1 and Figure 19–2, pg. 200).

Population Grew Most Rapidly in the Earliest Years of United States History

We turn now to the 19th century, a period for which United States demographic history is quite atypical. Birth rates started higher and began to decline earlier than in almost any other country. (Compare Figure 17–4 with Figure 16–2, pg. 163.) Fertility was especially high in newly settled regions of the United States in the 19th century. Abundant land, nearby and inexpensive or free, provided the means for supporting many children and the possibility for them in turn to have prosperous lives. Plentiful land also tended to result in higher wages, since a worker dissatisfied with his pay could leave his job and take up farming.

As population increased and land was no longer plentiful, births declined from about eight per woman born in the mid-18th century to about four per woman born around 1870 (for white women who survived to the end of reproductive years). The age at marriage rose from about 21 to about 23 for white women; this rise was responsible for about one-quarter of the decline in family size. Fecundity may have declined also. Childbearing was presumably also reduced by the use of withdrawal and the contraceptives and abortifacients which were advertised in newspapers from about 1820 until such advertisements were outlawed in 1873.

Both urban and rural birth rates fell during the 19th century. Until 1840, more than 90 percent of the population was rural, and declining rural birth rates were therefore the predominant factor in declining general birth rates. After 1840, increasing numbers of people migrated to urban regions where birth rates were roughly two-thirds as high as rural birth rates throughout the century. If we make the assumption that the fertility of couples who migrated to the cities was lowered by an amount equal to the difference between average rural and average urban fertility, then we conclude that the increase in urban population from 35 percent in 1890 to 56 percent in 1930 was responsible for half the decline in birth rates during that period (for native white women). Scattered data suggest that later marriage and lower fertility within marriage both contributed significantly to lower urban fertility. In 1910, the median age of marriage for all urban women was

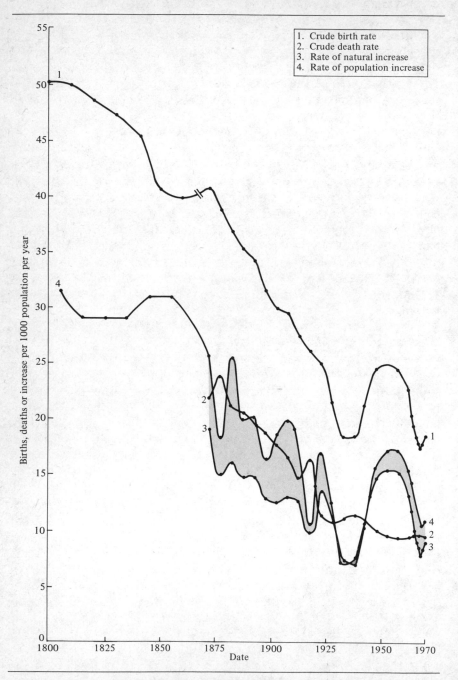

Figure 17–4 BIRTH RATES, DEATH RATES AND POPULATION GROWTH IN THE UNITED STATES

1. Crude birth rate
2. Crude death rate
3. Rate of natural increase
4. Rate of population increase

Births, deaths or increase per 1000 population per year

Date

The rate of natural increase is the excess of births over deaths. Net immigration equals the difference between rate of natural increase and population increase; it is indicated by the shaded area. Birth rates before 1870 are for whites only; all other data are for the whole population.

about 23 as compared to 21 for all rural women. Factors which may have induced later marriage of females in cities include the need for urban women to work outside the home in order to contribute to income, and the migration of more women than men to cities where jobs for single women were available, while single men more easily found work in rural regions or migrated to the frontiers. The reasons that couples in cities have smaller families have been discussed in Chapter 16.

The movement to the cities contributed to slower population growth not only because people in this environment had lower birth rates, but also because people in cities had higher death rates. For example, the life expectancy of white males in urban regions of the northeastern United States was 44 years as compared to 54 years for rural regions around 1900. For white females, life expectancies were 48 and 54 respectively. Decreases in urban death rates played an important role in the decrease in general death rate which began sometime after 1850, probably after 1870. Causes of decrease in death rates were similar to those described for Europe in Chapter 16.

Rapid natural increase in the United States was significantly augmented by a large flow of immigrants, mainly from Europe (Figure 17–4). The number of immigrants fluctuated, rising during periods of good economic conditions and falling during economic slumps and wars and during the 1920s when legal barriers were raised. Cyclically greater material resources led to cyclically greater population increases, by stimulating more immigration in the 19th century and more births in the 20th century. As in the Chinese example (Figure 15–1, pg. 159), the cyclic fluctuations in material resources were due primarily to changing adequacy of the human social and economic organization rather than to fluctuating limitations on the available raw materials.

BIBLIOGRAPHY

Brown, J., J. F. Donohue, N. W. Axnick, J. H. Blount, N. H. Ewen, and O. C. Jones. 1970. *Syphilis and Other Venereal Diseases.* Cambridge: Harvard University Press.

Figure 17–4 (continued)

Source: Data from Yasuba, Y. 1962. Birth Rates of White Population in the United States, 1800–1860, An Economic Study. *The Johns Hopkins University Studies 79.* Baltimore: The Johns Hopkins Press; Easterlin, R. A. 1968. *Population, Labor Force and Long Swings in Economic Growth: The American Experience.* New York: National Bureau of Economic Research, Columbia University Press; U.N. *Demographic Yearbooks.*

Easterlin, R. A. 1968. *Population, Labor Force and Long Swings in Economic Growth: The American Experience.* New York: National Bureau of Economic Research, Columbia University Press [demonstrates increase in immigration and birth rates during economic booms].

Farley, R. 1970. Fertility among Urban Blacks. *Milbank Memorial Fund Quarterly, 48* (Part 2): 183–214 [presents evidence that poor health was a major cause of low birth rates for blacks during the Depression].

Kiser, C. V., W. H. Grabill and A. A. Campbell. 1968. *Trends and Variations in Fertility in the United States.* Cambridge: Harvard University Press. [our main source of data on family size and its socioeconomic correlates, as reported in the 1960 U.S. census; also gives historical data on childlessness, and so on].

Parsons, T., and K. B. Clark, eds. 1965. *The Negro American.* Boston: Houghton Mifflin Company [a general assessment of the position of Negro Americans, including the datum that blacks earn two-thirds the income of whites with the same educational attainment (p. 84)].

Pohlman, E. with the assistance of J. Mea. 1969. *The Psychology of Birth Planning.* Cambridge: Schenkman Publishing Company [re psychological reasons for wanting and not wanting children, including limitations on the mother's freedom and many factors not discussed here].

Rainwater, L. 1960. *And the Poor Get Children: Sex, Contraception and Family Planning in the Working Class.* Chicago: Quadrangle Publ. [includes evidence of a fatalistic attitude among the poor, who often consider contraceptive success a matter of luck].

Whelpton, C. K., A. A. Campbell, and J. E. Patterson, 1966. *Fertility and Family Planning in the United States.* Princeton: Princeton University Press [contraceptive practice, desired and actual family size from a 1960 survey of white wives, and from several earlier surveys].

Yasuba, Y. 1962. *Birth Rates of White Population in the United States, 1800–1860, An Economic Study.* Baltimore: Johns Hopkins University Studies 79.

chapter 18

rapid population growth in asia, africa and latin america: an end in sight?

These three continents contain many nonindustrial countries with very low income and education, generally poor health, high birth rates and rapid population growth. In this chapter we will discuss first the historical development of mortality and fertility, and then the prospects for future reductions in birth rates and population growth.

High birth rates and high death rates characterize the earliest recorded situation in most of these countries, as in Europe. Famines, wars and epidemics of infectious diseases such as influenza, typhus and cholera produced the peaks in the high and fluctuating death rates.

Birth rates were high, but in many countries significantly less than the near maximum fertility of colonial North America. In part this was due to poor health. About 10 percent of pregnancies end in stillbirths in countries like Egypt and Mauritius, as compared to 2 percent stillbirths among women with good medical care in Hawaii. An even greater number of pregnancies are terminated by spontaneous abortion, that is, expulsion of a dead fetus before it is sufficiently developed to acquire the status of a stillbirth, usually before the sixth month of pregnancy. Many spontaneous abortions are difficult to detect, so reliable data are not available for nonindustrial countries or earlier periods. However, in Haiwaii 24 percent of pregnancies are terminated by spontaneous abortions, and it is safe to assume that the generally poorer health in nonindustrial countries has led to even higher rates of spontaneous abortion.

Birth rates in nonindustrial countries have also been kept below maximum by a variety of customs which restrict intercourse or prolong lactation. For example, copulation is commonly proscribed and relatively infrequent outside of marriage, so that young girls and unmarried widows are unlikely to become pregnant. In India, Hindu codes formerly forbade the remarriage of widows, and also forbade intercourse for married couples on many ritual days of abstinence.

Prolonged breast-feeding is common among Moslem women, and fecundity is reduced due to the hormonal concomitants of lactation. Such customs are widespread and definitely have had the effect of lowering birth rates, although in some cases this effect is not explicitly recognized by their practitioners.

Control of Infectious Disease Has Led to Decreased Deaths and Rapid Population Growth

For most countries, the first change in this situation of relatively high birth rates and death rates was a decrease in death rates. Gradual declines in death rates had begun by 1920 in some countries, and rather rapid declines began after World War II in most countries (Figure 18–1). As in Europe, reduced infectious disease has been the major cause of declining death rates. The decreases in Asia, Africa and Latin America have been much more rapid than in Europe, primarily because considerable medical understanding and technology had already been developed and could be rapidly imported, often at relatively low cost and with the assistance of international expertise.

For example, deaths due to malaria have dropped to a negligible low level in many tropical countries where, before World War II, 10–20 percent of all deaths were due to malaria, with another 10–20 percent of deaths in which malaria was a contributing cause. Malaria has disappeared primarily because DDT has been used to kill the particular mosquito which spreads the disease. These mosquitos pick up the malarial protozoa when they suck blood from an infected individual and later inject this parasitic protozoa into other people when biting them. DDT-spraying campaigns often involve repeated spraying of the insides of all houses in infected areas. This results in considerable human exposure to the insecticide and raises the possibility of damage to human health (Chapter 7). Massive exposure to DDT has also resulted in the evolution of increasing resistance on the part of the mosquitos. In some cases the resistance is due to the presence of enzymes that inactivate the DDT and in other cases it is due to behavioral changes such that the mosquito does not rest on the DDT-sprayed house walls after feeding. These observations suggest that it would be wise to resume alternative programs to control the mosquito, for example, the drainage of swamps to eliminate mosquito breeding grounds. Such programs had been relatively effective in some countries before World War II and would seem a good long-run investment, although their initial cost is higher than a DDT program.

A similar choice between relatively quick and cheap modern medical technology and initially expensive, but probably ultimately better, public works must be made in the control of digestive tract parasites (the protozoa and bacteria which cause diarrhea, dysentery,

Figure 18–1 BIRTH RATES, DEATH RATES AND POPULATION
GROWTH IN TAIWAN

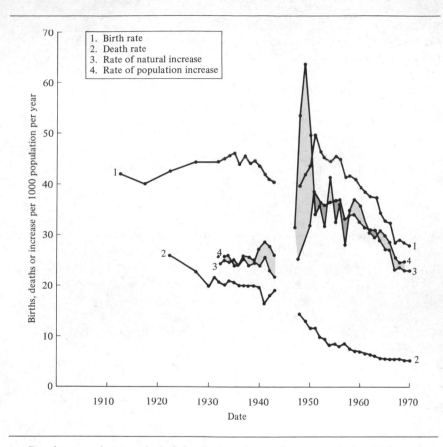

1. Birth rate
2. Death rate
3. Rate of natural increase
4. Rate of population increase

Death rates decreased slightly during the earlier part of the 20th century
and rapidly after World War II. The war, a surge of immigration from mainland
China and a postwar baby boom make it difficult to estimate precisely the
time when birth rates began to decline. Nevertheless this decline was clearly
well under way before the beginning of the national family planning program
in 1964.

Source: Trends and Differentials in Mortality. 1956. New York: Millbank Memorial
Fund; U.N. *Demographic Yearbooks.*

typhoid fever and cholera; tapeworms and so on). If large resources
are available, the primary method of control should be careful disposal of sewage and the establishment of sources of drinking water
isolated from the disposed sewage, so that disease organisms cannot
spread from one individual to another. Where human excrement is
used to fertilize agricultural land, it should be properly processed to

kill parasites so they cannot infect agricultural workers. Spread of diseases should be further reduced by chlorination of water supplies, pasteurization of milk and immunization against diseases for which effective vaccines are available. With effective programs to prevent the spread of disease, only a few individuals would contract infections of the digestive tract, and these few could be treated with appropriate medical techniques. Unfortunately, in some countries the high initial cost of sanitation works has led to heavy reliance on treatment rather than prevention of these diseases.

Tuberculosis and pneumonia are the other most important causes of death in many regions. These diseases can be controlled only by multifaceted programs including early detection and isolation of cases to prevent spread, drug treatment and (for TB) a moderately effective vaccine.

Most of these programs depend on a considerable organizational effort involving large numbers of people. It is therefore not surprising that life expectancy in a country is roughly correlated with the extent of literacy, average income and the number of medical personnel in the country, despite the fact that imported technology can occasionally produce dramatic decreases in death rates in a few years during which literacy and income have not changed much.

In most Asian, African and Latin American countries the birth rate has remained high and populations are growing rapidly. Averages for the three continents in the late 1960s are:

	AFRICA	ASIA	LATIN AMERICA
Average number of children born to a woman who lives to age 45	6.1 children	5.2 children	5.7 children
Life expectancy	43 years	51 years	60 years
Birth rate	47/1000 population per year	38/1000/yr.	38/1000/yr.
Death rate*	20/100 pop./yr.	15/1000/yr.	9/1000/yr.
Rate of natural increase	27/1000 pop./yr. =2.7 % per yr.	23/1000/yr. =2.3 % per yr.	29/1000/yr. =2.9 % per yr.
Time for population to double	27 years	31 years	24 years

*The death rates given here are misleading as an indication of health. High birth rates result in many children and young adults relative to the number of old people, so the population has a high proportion of people at the most healthy ages and therefore a low average death rate.

The dilemma of population increase is clearly more serious here than it was during the most rapid periods of European and North American population growth. One reason is that the rapid decrease in death rates without a similarly rapid decrease in birth rates has resulted in very high rates of increase. Another reason is that there are few, if any, sparsely settled regions that these growing populations can emigrate to and conquer from the indigenous inhabitants.

Birth Rates Have Declined where Health and Education Have Improved Sufficiently

In a few countries birth rates have declined: Argentina, Uruguay, Israel and Japan have low birth rates; Cuba, Taiwan, Singapore and Hong Kong have moderate and falling birth rates; birth rates have recently started to fall in a few other countries, such as Ceylon, Trinidad and Tobago, Mauritius, Malaysia and South Korea. Most of these countries have undergone considerable industrialization and/or commercial development, just as European countries had during their period of declining birth rates.

Which of the many changes associated with late industrialization are most important in stimulating the birth rate decline? A definitive answer for that question is not yet available. But it is thought that increasing education and increasing life expectancy may be among the most important factors. Literacy and life expectancy correlate closely with national birth rates (Figure 18–2). Furthermore, reasonable psychological mechanisms by which education and improved health could stimulate lower birth rates are suggested by the following data.

In Haiti and Ghana, two countries of extremely low literacy and life expectancy, roughly half the adults responded to the question "What is a good number of children to have?" by saying either that they didn't know or that this was up to God. More typical are the responses of rural Indians who say they want about four or five children, although most do not see this as a goal to act on. More than half do not know any contraceptive method, and 90 percent or more have never practiced family planning. Among the better educated and in cities, fewer children are wanted, and knowledge and use of contraception are more prevalent. In consequence more educated couples almost universally have fewer children, and urban and wealthier couples also generally have fewer. A couple who plans the size of their family can be expected to plan fewer births where child survival is better and fewer births are necessary to insure, for instance, that they will have a son alive to support them in their old age. This presumably is part of the reason that countries with longer life expectancies have lower birth rates.

Figure 18–2 RELATIONSHIP OF BIRTH RATE TO LIFE EXPECTANCY AND LITERACY

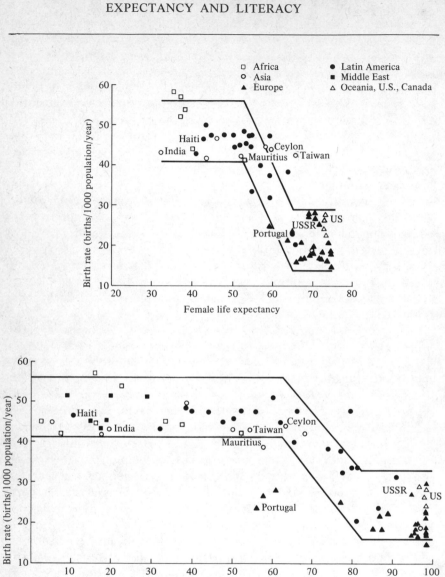

Each symbol represents one country. The lines indicate the general trend of birth rates with increasing life expectancy or literacy. The data are for the 1950s. Taiwan is an example of a country in which the birth rate has fallen dramatically since then; Ceylon and Mauritius are examples of countries in which birth rates have recently started to fall; India and Haiti are examples of countries in which birth rates remain high.

Source: Data from M. Russett *et al.* 1964. *World Handbook of Political and Social Indicators.* New Haven: Yale University Press.

It is clear from Figure 18–2 that the changes in birth rate do not develop uniformly as conditions improve. Rather there is a relatively abrupt transition between high and low birth rate countries. The duration of the transition from a high birth rate of 35/1000 to a low birth rate of 20/1000 has shortened from 40–55 years for countries beginning the transition in 1875–99 to 25–37 years for countries beginning the transition in 1925–49. The more rapid declines in birth rates recently may be due partly to more rapid economic change and partly to the availability of more efficient means of limiting family size. With contraceptive pills and intrauterine devices, couples with relatively low motivation are more likely to avoid unwanted births than when withdrawal or abstinence are the only available means. When abortion is legally and cheaply available, even poor planners can effectively limit family size.

Family Planning Programs Can Sometimes Accelerate a Decline in Birth Rates

The efforts of Asian countries to supply modern birth control methods have probably facilitated the more rapid fall in their birth rates as compared to Latin American countries with similar socioeconomic conditions. In the latter countries, strong Catholic influence has limited the supply of contraceptives with the consequence that the predominant methods for family limitation all involve considerable risk and/or effort: coitus interruptus, rhythm or other forms of abstinence, the condom and illegal abortions. The data do not, however, support those enthusiasts of national programs for distributing family planning services who see such family planning programs as panaceas for reducing birth rates. Such programs have only been effective where social and economic conditions are favorable. This can perhaps best be illustrated by contrasting the success of programs in two countries with very different conditions: India and Taiwan (see Figure 18–2).

In India the national program, begun in 1952, has emphasized vasectomies and insertion of IUD's. Effectiveness has been limited by administrative inefficiency and by unresponsiveness of the prospective clientele. In one of the more successful village programs, 80 percent of married women aged 15–45 said that they wanted to learn a contraceptive method, but only about 40 percent ever tried any method and after two years less than 20 percent were still practicing fertility control. The national program has resulted in sterilization or contraceptive use for about 8 percent of couples with wife aged 15–44, but there is as yet no evidence of a decline in birth rate. This may be partly due to countervailing influences, such as the decrease

195

in widowhood as life expectancy and remarriage of widows both increase.

In Taiwan, the national family planning program began in 1964, years *after* the beginning of the decline in birth rate (Figure 18–1). The program appears to have accelerated this decline somewhat, mainly by inserting IUD's, now carried by about 15 percent of married women aged 15–44. Some of these women would not have found equally effective alternative contraception without the program. This program also seems to have facilitated discussion of family planning and use of methods outside the program. Commercial sales of contraceptives supply about 15 percent of couples with wife aged 15–44. Illegal abortion apparently also increased. Age at marriage rose. It seems clear that conditions in this rapidly industrializing country have motivated people to want to limit births, and the family planning program has provided one of several means for them to do so. Even so, the birth rate is well above the death rate. That the birth rate is higher than replacement levels is to be expected, since additional children are wanted by 86 percent of mothers of two children and 34 percent of mothers of four children (in 1962). As in the United States, achieving zero population growth will depend on changing desires as well as improved family planning.

In conclusion, for Asia, Africa and Latin America, rapid reductions in birth rate will depend on improved social and economic conditions together with suitable family planning programs.

BIBLIOGRAPHY

Audy, J. R., ed. 1961. *Public Health and Medical Sciences in the Pacific—A Forty-Year Review.* Pacific Science Congress, 10th, Honolulu [this description of the specific causes of decreased death rates in several Asian countries makes clear the importance of organization as well as medical technology].

Kirk, D. 1969. Natality in the Developing Countries: Recent Trends and Prospects. In Behrman, S. J., L. Corsa, and R. Freedman, eds. *Fertility and Family Planning—A World View*, pp. 75–98. Ann Arbor: University of Michigan Press [fully documents the need for both improved social and economic conditions and family planning programs in order to rapidly reduce birth rates].

Maudlin, W. P. 1965. Fertility Studies: Knowledge attitude and practice. *Studies in Family Planning* #7. Publ. by Population Council, N.Y. [documents desired and actual family size and the high expressed interest and low practice of family planning in nonindustrial countries].

chapter 19

forecasting population growth

In order to make intelligent plans for the solution of environmental problems, we need to know how much population increase to expect in future years. Unfortunately, demographers have been notoriously poor forecasters, rather like weathermen. For example, the prediction for western European countries in the 1930s was that birth rates would continue to decline, and population sizes would begin to decrease within this century. The reversal of falling birth rates in the postwar baby boom was totally unforeseen. Poor predictions of population growth have been due to inability to forecast major social and economic developments, and to poor understanding of how these developments influence birth rates, death rates and migration. Recent predictions should be more accurate due to increased attention to and better understanding of the relationships between socioeconomic changes and population processes (Chapters 16–18).

But we still have only a primitive ability to predict major historical developments which will have an enormous influence on the course of population growth. Will there be nuclear or biological warfare on a large scale? How much effort will be devoted to increasing food production and averting famine? Will there be international cooperation to mobilize material and human resources to bring improved education and other developments which appear to be the preconditions for reducing birth rates in many countries of Asia, Africa and Latin America? Is the United States entering a period of prosperity or depression? What kinds of new life styles will develop which might motivate adults to want only two children even in periods of prosperity? To what extent will abortions be legalized and easily available? Clearly the future of human population growth depends in major ways on political decisions made now and in the future. We will hazard no predictions about these developments, but do wish to stress that the projections given below depend critically on the assumptions that no major calamities will befall the human species, and that public policy will improve enough to justify their "moderately optimistic" to "moderately pessimistic" point of view.

Within these assumptions, the simplest projection is that world population growth will continue at its current rate, an increase of 2 percent per year. This simple projection leads to an exponential curve (Figure 19–1) and is the basis for statements such as, "If population growth continues at the current rate, population will double in 35 years." The United Nations has made more careful projections based on detailed study of separate regions and countries. In each case estimates were made of probable social and economic developments and consequent declines or increases in birth rates and death rates. Three different projections were made (Figure 19–1) based on a range of assumptions about social and economic developments.

To make these refined projections, the United Nations also had to take account of demographic factors like the age structure of the population. If the proportion of young women of reproductive ages is high, the crude birth rate will tend to be high (Box 17–1, pg. 184). In the next decade this will be the case for the United States and for some other countries in which there was a postwar baby boom. Even if couples in the United States begin now to have only enough children to replace themselves, the population will continue to increase for decades. Although the number of young people would be stabilized immediately, the number of older people would increase due to births that have already occurred (Figure 19–2). For example, more babies were born in 1950 than in 1900, so we must expect more 60-year-olds in 2010 than we had in 1960. The size of older age groups would only stabilize after 70 years of families limited to 2.2 children per couple, during which time population size would increase 40 percent.

Notice that older people would constitute a much larger proportion of the stable population than of our current population. In a stable population, older age groups would continue to be smaller than younger age groups because of their longer exposure to mortality. But the proportion of older people would not be reduced by the other factor now operating, namely the smaller number of births in earlier periods. The higher proportion of older people might well tend to make the society more resistant to change, since older people tend to be more conservative, at least in our current society. Perhaps individual psychology and institutional structures could change so that older people would defer more to younger people in making decisions that will affect the future of young people long after the old have died. More resources would have to be devoted to retraining workers, since less of the labor force would be young people who have recently finished schooling that can adapt them for the new occupations that constantly appear as technology develops. If institutions of stable size were to be able to innovate, we would need better techniques for terminating old programs instead of simply adding on

Figure 19–1 PROJECTED POPULATION INCREASE
FOR THE WORLD

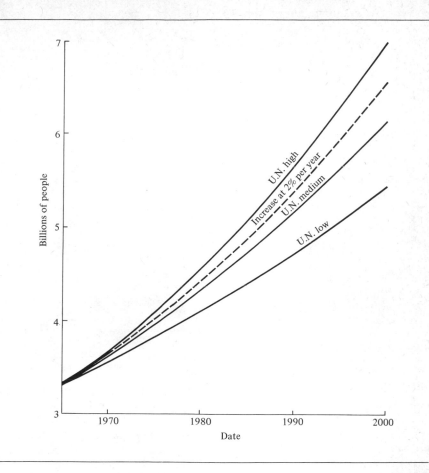

The dashed line indicates the growth of world population at a constant rate of increase. The more complex assumptions underlying the U.N. projections are described in the text.

Source: From *Resources and Man: A Study and Recommendations* by the Committee on Resources and Man of the Division of Earth Sciences, National Academy of Sciences—National Research Council. San Francisco: W. H. Freeman and Company. Copyright © 1969. Adapted with permission.

new ones. This discussion suggests some of the problems of social organization that may arise if we reach zero population growth. We should plan for them even while we strive to achieve the stable population so necessary for ecological reasons.

Figure 19–2 CURRENT AGE STRUCTURE FOR THE POPULATION OF THE UNITED STATES COMPARED TO THE EQUILIBRIUM AGE STRUCTURE WE COULD REACH BY 2035 A.D.

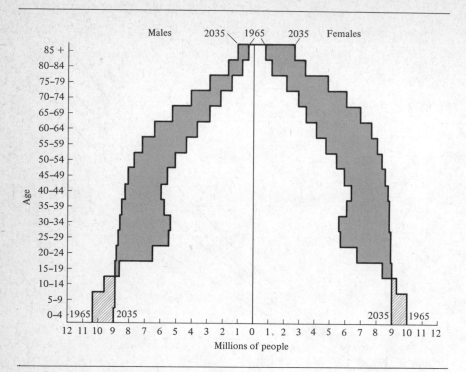

Low birth rates during the Depression resulted in relatively small numbers of adults aged 25–35 in 1965. This low proportion of women at ages of high fertility helped to produce low crude birth rates in 1965.

The figures for 2035 are based on two assumptions: (1) that death rates remain at 1965 levels; and (2) that starting immediately, the average couple has just enough children to replace themselves. This would result in fewer births than during the baby boom years around 1960, but more births than were produced by the smaller populations of parents before 1950. As these babies grew up, there would therefore be fewer children and more adults until an equilibrium of births and deaths was reached in 2035.

Source: Numbers from T. Frejka. 1968. Reflections on the demographic conditions needed to establish a U.S. stationary population growth. *Population Studies 22:* 379–97; Keyfitz, N. and W. Flieger. 1968. *World Population, An Analysis of Vital Data.* Chicago: University of Chicago Press.

BIBLIOGRAPHY

United Nations. 1966. *World Population Prospects as Assessed in 1963.* Population Studies, No. 41, Department of Economic and Social Affairs. (Sales #66 XIII. 2) [the most definitive recent projections of world population growth].

chapter 20

proposals for reducing population growth

The finite resources of the earth can be used much more efficiently than they are now, but they cannot be made to support an infinitely large human population. Our estimates of the earth's resources and the benefits to be achieved through optimum use of resources lead us to conclude that very serious problems will develop unless population growth slows down substantially within this century.

We reject out-of-hand all proposals that would decrease population growth by increasing death rates. We have heard a variety of people propose that war is now useful as a solution to the population problem, and that the starving should be let starve since they are, after all, part of our surplus population. The proponents of such solutions seem never to conceive of themselves as surplus population. Any such solution, which is proposed only for some unknown "them," but unthinkable for oneself seems to us to be morally unacceptable.

Therefore, birth rates must be reduced. There are two basic approaches. The first is to change people's motivations so they want fewer children and so they more urgently desire to avoid unwanted children. The second is to provide couples who do not want a birth with the practical means to avoid unwanted births (contraceptives, sterilization operations and abortions). These two approaches are complementary.

Specific proposals for implementing these approaches range from limited to comprehensive, and from voluntary to coercive. The chief question about most voluntary proposals and limited proposals is whether they will have a big enough impact on birth rates. How many births would be averted by legalizing abortion and improving access to contraceptives? Can TV programs about environmental problems effectively reduce the desire to have more children? The chief concern about comprehensive proposals and coercive proposals is that they may prove too costly or otherwise unacceptable. Can we mobilize enough resources for Asia, Africa and Latin America to achieve the large social changes which have historically led to smaller families in Europe and North America? What would happen to our society if we accepted various schemes for involuntary sterilization? No precise answer to these questions can be given because evidence on cost, acceptability and effectiveness is scanty. In the following discussion of specific proposals, we give indicative estimates of costs and effectiveness, and outline the most important pros and cons. On the basis of this evidence we can begin to make intelligent and well-informed choices among the various proposals for action.

Contraception and Abortion Should Be Made Freely Available

As biologists, we assume that the sexual drive is sufficiently strong and fundamental in the human animal that celibacy neither will nor should become sufficiently widespread to serve as the primary method of reducing births to an average of two per couple. This is not to deny the importance of temporary or periodic abstention. A substantial number of people postpone intercourse until marriage or abstain from intercourse during the potentially fertile half of each menstrual cycle (the rhythm method). However, most couples will find it impossibly difficult and unnecessarily trying to limit their offspring to two by such methods.

Therefore, contraception and abortion must be widely available if we are to stabilize our population. To those who find contraceptives or abortion immoral we can only reply that we consider it immoral to bring into the world a child who is not wanted or for whom the minimal necessary material resources cannot or will not be made available. Widespread acceptance of this point of view is indicated by the rapid spread of family planning programs in the last decade, by the growth in use of contraceptives, by the trend toward reduced legal restrictions on abortion, and by worldwide use of illegal abortions by women who are barred from legal abortions.

Chapter 18 presented some of the evidence that more effective contraceptives and easier access to contraceptives and abortions can decrease the gap between the desire to limit family size and the effective prevention of births. An estimate of the importance of closing this gap comes from the following data. In nonindustrial countries (which contain about two-thirds of the world's population), the average completed family has somewhat over five children. In contrast, almost half of the couples with three children say they want no more and about two-thirds of the couples with four children say they want no more. A typical couple in a nonindustrial country has roughly one birth they did not want. If these unwanted births were eliminated, population increase would be reduced by roughly a third.

The cost of providing contraceptives to people who need them is relatively low. The national family planning programs of Taiwan and South Korea have provided contraceptives (primarily the intrauterine device, or IUD) to 20–30 percent of eligible women at a cost of about $5 per user per year. These low costs, the considerable potential for effectiveness, and the general acceptability of programs to supply contraceptives to those who want them are such important virtues that family planning programs should be an important part of any plan for reducing birth rates. Abortion is less generally acceptable and more expensive, but can be more effective in avoiding unwanted births, especially among inexpert or poorly motivated family planners.

While recognizing the necessity of such programs, we should not overestimate their importance. By themselves, they cannot stabilize the size of the world population. This is obvious when you consider that such programs are designed only to avoid unwanted births. Wanted children average three per couple in industrialized countries and four per couple in nonindustrial countries. Families of these sizes would result in a population increase of about 50 percent per generation, even if allowance is made for deaths of some children before they reach reproductive age and for childlessness among some adults. A population increase of 50 percent per generation is equivalent to a quintupling each century. Obviously, if attitudes remain unchanged, voluntary family planning programs will not stabilize population size. In view of this, some scientists and politicians have proposed that we need compulsory limitations on family size.

Compulsory Sterilization Schemes Will Probably Create More Problems than They Will Solve

The schemes proposed for involuntary sterilization are of two main types. In the first type, selected adults (for example, all welfare mothers with more than three children) would be subjected to sterilizing operations. In the second type, some yet-to-be-discovered sterilizing chemical would be put in the drinking water and an antidote would be available to those permitted to procreate.

Both schemes arouse violent opposition among their intended subjects. For example, residents of an Indian village, in the belief that the visiting sterilization team was going to forcibly sterilize all men with more than two children, attacked the team with hoes and shovels, and had to be put down by the local guard. It seems very likely that violent opposition to coercive sterilization will make such schemes unworkable. Prohibition, which infringed on the much less intimate right to drink alcohol, had to be abandoned in the United States because it could not be enforced in the face of widespread opposition, and because the illegal traffic in liquor brought with it widespread violence and graft.

Even if compulsory sterilization could be imposed on people, it would have many undesirable features. If a chemical sterilant were put in the water, it seems probable that lifetime exposure would injure the health of at least some fraction of the population. In any compulsory scheme someone would have to decide who would be allowed to reproduce and how much. Would such decisions be made fairly? Could we even achieve a general concensus about what would constitute fair decisions? Serious doubts must be raised by current experience with the draft and with tax "loopholes."

If it is accepted that these objections warrant the rejection of coercive limitations on family size, then ways must be found to change people's motivations, so they will want fewer children. We will discuss three main proposals.

Can People Be Educated to Want Only Two Children?

Education with the aim of reducing births can take three forms: information about contraceptives and where to get them, propaganda in favor of small families, and general education resulting in increased literacy, longer years in school and so on. Practical information about contraceptives has proved a useful part of family-planning programs for couples already motivated to limit their families. Propaganda in favor of smaller families has generally not had noticeable success. In the reverse case, official hostility to contraception by the Protestant and Catholic churches was ineffective in stemming the birth rate decline during industrialization in western Europe and the United States. In several European countries during the Depression, birth rates remained low despite governmental exhortations to reproduce abundantly and save the nationality from extinction.

It is to be expected that propaganda campaigns and information about environmental problems will not have sufficient impact to outweigh the effects of the immediate economic, social and psychological situation of the individual or to outweigh the long-standing cultural values that often favor large families. Perhaps careful education about environmental problems can substitute the attitude that "a couple who has more than two children is selfish" for the prevalent attitude in the United States that "a couple who has fewer children than they can afford is selfish." Our authorship of this book is evidence that we think it important for people to be aware of the reality of the problems we face. But historical evidence gives little reason to hope that this knowledge by itself will produce major declines in family size.

Can Financial Incentives against Childbearing Be Effective and Fair?

Relatively little is known about the effects on reproductive behavior of the many monetary incentives for and against large families. It is difficult, for instance, to evaluate the effect of the income tax deductions for each child and the child-support payments that are common in Europe and North America. That such incentives should have an impact if large enough is suggested by the fluctuation of birth rates with changing economic conditions, most notably the decline of birth rates during the Depression and the rise of birth rates during the postwar economic boom in most industrial countries. However, economic incentives do not appear to affect childbearing when the payment is small relative to income. For example, birth rates continued to decline during the late 1920s and early 1930s in Belgium, Italy, and France despite a variety of government incentives encouraging marriage and childbearing. On the other hand, recent experience in nonindustrial countries indicates that small financial incentives to users of contraceptive or sterilization clinics increases use of the clinic, at least temporarily.

Even if financial incentives can effectively reduce births, it will be extremely difficult to administer them fairly. If the sum paid for avoiding a birth is independent of income, then poor couples will feel the impact of the incentive much more strongly than rich couples. Payments large enough to reduce births among the well-to-do would be extremely expensive. If financial incentives took the form of a reduction of income or services for large families, how could we avoid jeopardizing the healthy development of children in large but poor families? Perhaps poor couples should be given positive incentives for avoiding births and rich people should be given negative incentives in the form of heavy taxation for each additional birth.

Fundamental Social Changes Will Be Necessary

Past experience suggests that the programs discussed thus far can make a positive contribution to reduction of birth rates, but cannot have enough impact to stabilize population growth unless the more coercive proposals are enacted. Widespread and strenuous objection to coercive proposals may make them unworkable as well as undesirable. Furthermore, in the past nearly every major decline in birth rates has occurred in association with fundamental social changes such as those that accompany industrialization. We conclude that fundamental social changes must occur if we are to achieve an equilibrium population.

Fortunately, many of the kinds of social change that motivate people to want and to have fewer children are desirable in and of themselves. Increased education and abolition of child labor broaden the horizons and possibilities for individual development, and at the same time reduce births by increasing the expense of child rearing. Consistently adequate food and high health standards make life less troubled, and at the same time encourage couples to plan births with the realistic expectation that they will rear the number of children they bear. Such changes during late industrialization have led to birth rate declines by nearly a half within 30 years (pg. 194). Such a rate of decline would probably be sufficiently fast to avoid insoluble environmental problems, provided that we start to use resources more wisely than we do now.

Another proposal is to institute social security in countries that do not yet have an old age insurance program. It is presumed that this would reduce births in nonindustrial countries, since one of the primary reasons couples give for having large families is to ensure that at least one son will survive to support them in their old age. Such a program for the 550 million population of India would cost roughly $2 billion per year.

How can birth rates in industrial countries be brought down to replacement levels? Birth rates in Japan, France, the United States and a variety of other countries are currently at or near levels that would lead to a nongrowing population once the age structure stabilizes, but we are not really sure why these birth rates are so low, or whether they will stay low for long. Our detailed analysis of United States' data in Chapter 17 does, however, reveal several social and economic factors that have lowered birth rates in the past and that could provide a useful basis for future policy proposals. For example, the more effective use of contraceptives among more educated and moderately well-off couples implies that unwanted births could be reduced by improving education and by reducing poverty and unemployment. Our observations about why working women have fewer children suggest that we should develop opportunities for nonprocreative creativity for women, and for men too, so that there will be less need for children as the primary source of adult fulfillment. On a more speculative level, the desire for large families could probably be reduced by other types of social change, such as increased opportunities to interact with children other than one's own, and increased cooperation in child care, which would give a child the benefit of interaction with peers even when he has only one or no siblings.

The biggest question about proposals for major social change is whether they are feasible, whether we can mobilize the necessary human and material resources. To a large extent, the question of feasibility is a political one: will resources be reallocated to accomplish such changes? Several realities of the current situation constitute major obstacles to such a reallocation. The first is the power relationships between nations. A large chunk of the needed resources is now tied up in military expenditures. Ambitions for military power also discourage some governments from active efforts to reduce births, since they do not want to reduce the supply of future soldiers. The second major source of obstacles to needed change are questions of profitability. In the first half of this book, we have discussed many examples of investments which are needed to feed people, to reduce pollution or to conserve resources, but which have not been made yet since they are not profitable. Most of the programs we have proposed for lowering birth rates would also not be profitable. Low birth rates themselves are sometimes attacked as unprofitable, because they reduce the potential market and potential labor supply and thus reduce the opportunities for commercial and industrial expansion. The last major obstacle we want to mention is the difficulty most people seem to have in comprehending future world problems as important enough to them to warrant personal action. Somehow many people seem to feel that all the dire predictions have no real relevance for them personally. In addition, political action often seems overwhelmingly difficult. We know the feeling, but we know also that the longer we postpone action, the more difficult and urgent the problems will become.

In conclusion, the environmental and population problems we face are enormous and urgent. Useful proposals for solutions are available. Neither hopeless pessimism nor naive optimism is justified. The only sensible response is thoughtful action!

BIBLIOGRAPHY

Berelson, B. 1969. Beyond Family Planning. *Science 163:* 533–42 [gives costs and potential for effectiveness of all major proposals for reducing birth rates].

Davis, K. 1967. Population Policy: Will Current Programs Succeed? *Science 158:* 730–39 [argues that family planning programs alone are insufficient and makes some alternative suggestions].

Day, A. T. 1968. Population Control and Personal Freedom: Are They Compatible? *The Humanist,* Nov./Dec., 1968, pp. 7–10 [re pros and cons of different methods to motivate people to have fewer children].

Peel, J. and M. Potts. 1969. *Textbook of Contraceptive Practice.* Cambridge: Harvard University Press.

questions, experiments, issues
for discussion and further references

Each chapter and its bibliography should suggest many topics for discussion and for library research. The best question to ask yourself at the end of a chapter is usually, "What are the main points I want to remember from that?" This section presents some additional questions that might not occur to you, offers new data and opinions to provoke discussion, gives references for further reading on related topics and describes the methods for several experimental research projects.

Standard library reference materials will help you to find information on a particular topic that interests you, but you can often find material more efficiently by other methods. We suggest that you first use the references in the chapter bibliographies and in the figure and table legends, and then look for further references in the footnotes and bibliographies of the books and articles you read. It is often useful to browse through other articles or issues of a magazine or journal you are using, or other books on the same shelf as one you have found interesting.

United States government reports have a great deal of useful information on resources, pollution, agriculture and the census in this country. They are, however, sometimes difficult to find. Most of them can be purchased rather cheaply from the Superintendent of Documents, United States Government Printing Office, Washington, D.C. 20402. The same office will provide, free of charge, *Selected United States Government Publications* which gives brief descriptions and prices of recent government publications. United Nations' publications give much useful information on population growth and agriculture for the whole world. If these are not available in your local library, some of them can be purchased cheaply from United Nations, Sales Section, New York, New York, 10017.

Chapter 2   The Need for Ecological Balance

We have avoided the use of chemical formulas in order to make this book easier to read. However, some students have wanted to know the chemical makeup of the compounds we mention. Chapters 1–6 and 1–7 of *Biology* by H. Curtis (Worth Publ., 1968) give a good introduction to biological chemistry together with the chemical formulas for most of the compounds we mention.

questions, experiments, issues for discussion and further references

Similar material is available in the chemistry chapters of most introductory biology texts.

Some people feel that the most serious threat to world ecological balance is war, with its nuclear bombs, chemical and biological weapons and so on. Do you agree? Why or why not?

Detailed information about the potential destructiveness of modern weapons can be found in:

Nuclear Explosions and Their Effects. 1956. The Publications Division, Ministry of Information and Broadcasting, Government of India, Delhi.

R. E. Lapp. 1962. *Kill and Overkill.* New York: Basic Books, Inc. [Chapter 5—regarding effects of nuclear weapons].

J. Lewallen. 1971. *Ecology of Devastation.* Baltimore: Penguin Paperback [Chapters 2–5—regarding the effects of war in Vietnam].

J. B. Neilands, G. H. Orians, E. W. Pfeiffer, A. Vennema, and A. H. Westing. 1972. *Harvest of Death—Chemical Warfare in Vietnam and Cambodia.* New York: The Free Press.

One good way to study the mechanisms involved in ecological balance is to analyze the processes in artificial ecosystems. You will be most likely to get meaningful results if you set up several very simple ecosystems. Useful materials include a set of identical covered jars, soil, water, aquatic plants, snails and worms. Soil, water from a pond or stream, plants and animals all harbor microscopic organisms including bacteria, protozoa, eggs, small algae and spores of fungi which will become part of your artificial ecosystem.

Your goal in working with these ecosystems should be to try to set up at least one balanced ecosystem, to test what factors affect the ecological balance and to analyze the processes and interactions in a balanced ecosystem. An ecosystem is balanced when each type of organism in the ecosystem can obtain from the physical environment and from the other organisms in the ecosystem enough of what it needs to maintain a stable population. Your artificial ecosystem will be balanced when it can maintain itself stabily without further input (except the sunlight that comes in through the jar).

Keep the following questions in mind as you plan your ecosystems and make your observations. What are all the processes that must be in equilibrium for your simple ecosystem to be balanced? Does dead matter accumulate? If not, why not? (See Chapter 5.) What factors limit the numbers of each kind of plant or animal? (See Chapters 4, 5, 13, and 14.) What factors are particularly scarce at night? During the day? You may want to design an experiment to answer a particular question, such as, how do external conditions like the amount of light affect the balance that develops? What is the effect of adding small amounts of fertilizer (about ¼–⅛ teaspoon per quart) or pollutants or a continuous supply of sugar (¼ teaspoon or less per quart per day)? If two jars initially contain different numbers of organisms, will they stay different or will they eventually develop into similar balanced communities? If you established two artificial ecosystems with the same organisms and in the same conditions, will they always develop the same type of balance? If the answer to this question is no, what does that imply about how you should design experiments to answer any of the previous questions?

Since ecological balance develops rather slowly, you should make observations approximately twice a week for several months. Keep careful records so that information can be extracted even weeks later. Things that may not seem important when they occur may become crucial later when you realize what was happening and how important it was, if only you could remember it exactly!

If you have a tank of fish, you may find it interesting to add aquatic plants, snails and so on. If you can achieve ecological balance, you won't have to supply food, air or clean the tank in the future.

You may also want to try to analyze the relationships in some existing ecosystem, such as a nearby forest, although this is difficult without a great deal of time and effort.

You may find it informative to analyze your local town or city as an ecosystem, or part of one. What processes would need to be in equilibrium for this ecosystem to be balanced? What are the outputs from your community and how are they disposed of? What are the inputs to your community and how are they used? You can study the distribution of resources by looking at the variation in income, housing and health in different areas of your community. (Health can be measured by disease case rates or death rates. Be sure to use age-specific death rates; see Figure 11-1 and pg. 191). This information, together with data on birth rates, migration rates and unemployment rates, should begin to tell you something about what factors limit population growth in your area.

The information for this type of study of local human ecology is often available from local Departments of Health, Vital Statistics, Housing, Water and so on, from the Chamber of Commerce, from local citizens' groups and information groups, for example the Committee for Environmental Information. Publications of state and regional commissions will also often have useful information. Some basic information can be found in:
U.S. Bureau of the Census. 1967. *County and City Data Book*. Washington: Government Printing Office.

Further suggestions for topics of discussion and questions related to ecological balance may be found in:
C. Meleca, P. Jackson, R. Burnard, and D. Dennis. 1971. *Bio-Learning Guide*. Minneapolis: Burgess Publications [Sections 13, 14, and 15].

Chapter 3 Food Needs, Shortages and Surpluses

The following comment on the consequences of the "Green Revolution" appeared in the February 4, 1972 issue of *National Review:*

The dreaded rice glut is advancing. Japan, which used to import the staff of

Asian life, had a surplus of almost seven million tons in the past two years. India—yes, India—doesn't need to import any rice for the first time since that mountain toddled off to Mohammed. Meanwhile, the countries whose economies depend on exporting rice are in a bind. The market price is about half what it was in 1969. Looks like there's only one solution: More people.

Can you think of any other solutions?
[An additional note: The comment about India is misleading, to say the least. India had a surplus of food until about the First World War, and exported over a million tons of foodgrains per year in the early 1890s. Total food production declined by about 10 percent from 1893 to 1945 under British colonial rule. Only since independence has food production risen. (U.N. Economic Commission for Asia and the Far East. 1964. *Economic Survey of Asia and the Far East*, pp. 117–118.)]

Chapter 4   **Energy in the Ecosystem**

Imagine a pile of food equal to all the food you've ever eaten. This pile would obviously be a lot bigger than you. What has happened to all the extra atoms and energy in the chemical bonds of the molecules that the food contained but you don't? [Note: The Second Law of Thermodynamics should be a key part of your answer to this question.]

What are the basic differences between natural laws like the laws of thermodynamics and governmental laws like tax laws?

You can use methods very similar to those used by professional ecologists to estimate the efficiency of energy conversion in one step of a food chain. You will need two or three mice or gerbils that have just been weaned, a cage, water bottle and food. Weigh the mice or gerbils before you put them in the cage; use a paper cup as a container while you weigh them. Leave the animals undisturbed for a week or two. Weigh all the food you put in the cage. At the end of the experiment, weigh the leftover food and the animals.
To estimate the efficiency of energy conversion, you need to know how much energy was stored in the food that has been eaten, and how much energy is stored in the newly grown mouse or gerbil tissue. To estimate these energies, you could burn an equivalent weight of food or animal tissue, thus converting the stored chemical energy to heat energy, and could measure the quantity of heat energy in terms of how much it heats a known volume of water. It is simpler and reasonably accurate to use standard conversion factors: 1 gram of mouse food contains about 4.2 Calories of stored chemical energy, and 1 gram of mouse or gerbil tissue contains about 1.5 Calories. (The mouse or gerbil tissue has more water and, therefore, less chemical energy per gram.) The efficiency of energy conversion for this step in the food chain is the chemical energy stored in the newly synthesized mouse or gerbil tissue divided by the chemical energy stored in the food eaten. How do your results compare with those given in Fig. 4–2?

212

If you have a puppy or kitten you might want to design a similar experiment using the information that puppy or kitten tissue has roughly 130 Calories per ounce and that pet food has about 120 Calories for every ounce of protein or carbohydrate and about 270 Calories for every ounce of fat.

Chapter 5 **Nutrient Cycles**

Plants and animals have very different nutritional needs. What are the main types of nutrients needed by green plants? By people? What are the reasons for the differences?

Recycling is crucial for maintaining the supply of nutrients for plants. As shown in Chapter 10, recycling could also play a major role in conserving our mineral resources, such as copper. Why are the possibilities for recycling or reusing energy resources much more limited?

Bacteria and fungi (Figure 5–2 and pg. 37) are only a part of the soil community which plays a vital role in the detritus food chain and the recyling of mineral nutrients. You can find some of the other organisms in the soil community simply by digging up a patch of sod and carefully sifting through the dirt and roots. You can observe behavior beneath the soil surface by transferring a piece of sod to a box with glass sides which are kept darkened except when observations are being made. Other methods for finding and studying soil organisms, together with descriptions of the organisms and their role in the soil community, are given by:
R. M. Jackson and F. Raw. 1966. *Life in the Soil.* New York: St. Martin's Press.

A recent law in Suffolk County, Long Island, limits the phosphate concentration permitted in detergents. In light of what we know about the limiting nutrients for algal growth, does this seem like a useful policy to reduce eutrophication in the estuaries and bays on the coast of Long Island?

Chapter 6 **Water**

In Chapter 4 we pointed out many reasons why the food eaten by all the people on the earth contains much less energy (many fewer Calories) than is contained in the energy that comes from the sun to the earth. We also explained how some of these inefficiencies in energy use could be reduced. You should find it instructive to reformulate the list of inefficiencies in energy use, and to draw up an analogous list of reasons why the food eaten by people contains much less water than is contained in the precipitation on the earth. Which of the inefficiencies in water use could be reduced?

questions, experiments, issues for discussion and further references

Projects to improve the efficiency of water use obviously need to be planned more carefully than was the Aswan Dam (Box 6–1). Good insights into how and why such planning deficiencies arise (and therefore how they might be avoided) may be obtained by reading case studies about plans for similar projects in:

J. Harte and R. Socolow, eds. 1971. *Patient Earth*. New York: Holt, Rinehart and Winston, Inc.

One way to conserve agricultural water is to breed plants that use water more efficiently. Increases in efficiency of up to 30 percent have been achieved thus far. Possible types of water-conserving mechanisms are suggested by an examination of plants that have adapted, through natural selection, to survive in dry climates. For example, pine trees are adapted to dry climates, or to cold climates in which water is effectively scarce since plants cannot absorb water rapidly from cold or frozen soil. The water-conserving features of the pine leaf (pine needle) include both its shape (what's the advantage?) and its microscopic structure (a waxy coat and sunken stomata can be seen in cross sections).

In terms of their effect on aquatic ecosystems, what is the difference between eutrophication, and water pollution due to chemicals like pesticides or metal poisons?

If you live near a lake, stream or river, you may want to use a canoe or rowboat to conduct an investigation of sources of water pollution. Paddle close by the shore, keeping a sharp eye out for pipes that are discharging into the river. Even when effluent pipes are hidden behind bushes or under water, it may be obvious that pollutants are being added. You can test for various pollutants with kits that can be obtained from Carolina Biological Supply Company (Burlington, North Carolina, 27215).

To test the bacterial content of a water sample, put a small quantity of the sample in a petri dish containing sterilized agar on which bacteria can grow. In a few days each bacterium on the agar plate will reproduce enough to produce a visible colony. The relative abundance of bacteria in different samples can be determined by counting the bacteria on agar plates prepared with the different samples. It may be necessary to dilute the samples so that the volume of liquid needed to cover an agar plate will have few enough bacteria that each colony will be separate and distinguishable from the other colonies.

The most useful agar for pollution detection is Eosin Methylene Blue (EMB). Colonies of bacteria from the intestines have a distinctive metallic sheen on EMB agar. If a sample has any of these bacteria, the water is probably contaminated with feces. If anyone whose feces are in the water has typhoid fever or dysentery, his feces can carry disease-causing bacteria into the water. It is therefore important to compare the concentration of intestinal bacteria in various samples, for example, in samples taken above and below a sewage outlet.

You must use sterile procedure in order to avoid contamination by bacteria and fungal spores from the air, your sneezes and so on. Wash your collecting jars in very hot water or boil them before use and keep them sealed before and after you put in the sample. About 15 minutes before you start your laboratory procedures, you should close the doors and windows to reduce air circulation to a minimum. Wash your hands thoroughly with soap and water. Wash the table top and nearby surfaces thoroughly with an antiseptic, either Staphene or Lysol. Take about a cup of each sample and boil it for 10 minutes in order to kill the bacteria in it. Keeping the sterile water covered, let it cool to room temperature. Then prepare a mixture of 9 parts of sterile sample water and 1 part of undisturbed sample; be sure to use sterile measuring and mixing equipment for each step of the process, and stir thoroughly. Then prepare a second mixture of 1 part of the first mixture and 9 parts of sterile water. This will give you a series of undiluted sample, 10-fold dilution, and 100-fold dilution. Prepare at least two agar plates with each of these. Use sterile bulb pipettes or eye droppers to transfer 20 drops of sample to each plate of sterile agar. To minimize contamination, make the transfer quickly and lift the lid only slightly. Do not breathe onto the plate. Tape the lid of the plate closed and swish the sample vigorously over the surface of the agar. After you are finished, wash your hands and sterilize the table top again, so that there is no possibility that any pathogenic bacteria which might be in the polluted samples can survive to infect you or anyone else.

Meat in food stores may contain large numbers of bacteria and can be tested by similar procedures.

Chapter 7 **Pesticides**

From an evolutionary point of view, would you expect more evolution of resistance to DDT or to organophosphate pesticides? Why?

It is extremely difficult to detect harmful side effects of a new chemical that injures only a small portion of the population who happen to be unusually susceptible because of their particular physiological characteristics. Imagine a new chemical that at proposed doses would make 1 out of every 1000 people very sick. Suppose that half the people in the United States were exposed to this chemical. How many people would become sick? Assuming that you could find an animal that responded in exactly the same way that people do, how many animals would you have to test to demonstrate an effect of that chemical at that dose?

Your answers to the preceding questions should make it clear why laboratory tests typically use much higher doses than the public will be exposed to. But to interpret such tests, some assumption must be made about how to extrapolate the effects to lower doses. Some people propose linear extrapolation as the best method, but others argue that below a certain threshold concentration there should be no effect, since the cells of the body encounter the chemical so infrequently that they have ample time to repair damage in between encounters. There seems to be no *a priori* method for settling this

215

controversy, or for deciding how accurately effects on other animals will predict effects on humans.

What policies would you advocate for controlling dangers due to exposure to new chemicals? What risks would you be willing to take? What costs would you be willing to pay for testing?

In the United States, the average person consumes about five times as much milk and meat as is necessary to meet minimal nutritional requirements. (See Chapter 3 on nutritional requirements.) Chapters 4 and 7 each present one disadvantage of overconsumption of meat (what are they?), and in addition there is some evidence that the fat in meat, eggs and milk contributes to accumulation of cholesterol in your arteries and thus increases the risk of arteriosclerotic heart disease. On the other hand, we cannot assume that any improvement in nutrition above the "minimum requirements" is wasted, since the evidence is not yet available on this question. In the light of all this, what do you think is the best policy on meat-eating for you personally? For the United States as a whole?

What are the pros and cons of "Ban DDT" as a policy? In answering this question, you should consider the worldwide impact of such a policy as well as the impact in the United States.

Recently there has been a great deal of interest in "organic food," a misnomer since all food is organic although much of it is contaminated by man-made chemicals. If you want to try "organic" gardening yourself, much useful information is available in:
Sunset Guide to Organic Gardening.   Menlo Park, California: Lane Magazine and Book Company.

Chapter 8   Food Supplies in the Future

In this chapter we have proposed how the basic nutritional needs for calories and proteins could be met for the world population now and in the next few decades. Which of the proposals do you see as most important, as judged on the basis of feasibility and potential for improving the nutrition of large numbers of people? How does your answer vary when you consider different time periods?

To develop a more concrete and specific understanding of what will be involved in solving world food problems, you may want to read detailed analyses of the practical difficulties and potential of whichever proposal(s) you think most important. Useful information is available in *The World Food Problem* and other material referred to in the bibliographies of Chapters 3–8.

The per capita consumption of grain is about five times as high in the United States as in India. How is this biologically possible? [Hint: the key to the answer is in Chapter 4.]

Our proposed plans for providing adequate calories for the world population are predicated on rough equality of food consumption. Do you see this equality as desirable? If so, how should this be achieved? If not, what alternative would you propose?

The plans we have proposed are biologically and technologically feasible. Whether they are politically feasible remains an open question. Do you think that the fish meal currently exported from Africa and South America should be used to improve diets there rather than shipped to Europe as animal feed? If so, what political and economic changes would you propose to achieve this change? What would be the most effective way to achieve the kind of reordering of societal priorities that would free the resources outlined in Figure 8–1?

Chapter 9   **Fuel, Power and Pollutants**

In the next few decades, growing pollution problems may impose more stringent restrictions on the growth of power consumption than will scarcity of fuels. One consideration in the evaluation of any proposal, such as the use of desalinization to increase water supplies, must be whether the pollution due to the power use involved can be kept within "acceptable" levels. This is a quantitative question which is difficult even for professionals, but you can begin to answer the question for yourself by using the references about desalinization given in the bibliography of Chapter 6 and the references about air pollution in the bibliography of Chapter 9.

Who do you think should pay for the increased costs of production that will result from pollution-reduction practices? Costs might be paid by the stockholders in reduced profits, by the consumers in increased prices, by the workers in reduced wages or by the general public in higher taxes for government subsidies. What policies would be needed to enforce your decision about who should pay?

If you have any background in economics, you will realize that the actual economic relations are quite complex and that realistic policies will have to be very sophisticated. Some insight into these complications can be obtained from the England and Bluestone article listed in the bibliography of Chapter 11.

Figure 9–2 shows how energy is used in the United States. On the basis of this information and what you know about the United States' economy, what suggestions would you make for how we might reduce power consumption?

More detailed information about how much energy is consumed by each industry can be found in:

W. Leontief. 1963. The Structure of Development. *Scientific American,* September, pp. 148–166.

National Economics Division. 1969. *Survey of Current Business,* November, pp. 16–47.

Chapter 10 **Minerals and Related Resources**

The United States now consumes about one-third of the world's mineral production. Imports, often from nonindustrial countries, supply one-third to three-quarters of our consumption for most metals. Current data on world resources suggest that for most important minerals, United States' levels of consumption may not be attainable for the world population as a whole. In light of these three observations, what policy do you think that nonindustrial countries should adopt concerning their reserves of minerals?

How could we reduce consumption of minerals in the United States? Some idea of the quantitative importance of different uses, and thus the most important uses to reduce, can be obtained from the articles cited in the last question for Chapter 9.

Chapter 11 **Possibilities for Our Society to Live Well with Limited Material Resources**

What level of consumption do you personally want to achieve? In 1971, the average personal income in the United States was slightly over $4000 per person (before taxes). Do you aim for a higher level of income than that? If so, how do you reconcile your desires with environmental constraints like those described in the question for Chapter 10? What types of personal, social or economic change might lead you to be happy with a lower level of consumption?

[An additional note: This is not really a fair question since you can only answer it in terms of what $4000 buys now, not what it might buy if you could buy goods without having to pay for advertising, restyling, planned obsolescence, and so on. Also, the suggested limits on consumption should not apply to many kinds of services which are produced without serious depletion of material resources or pollution to the environment. Nevertheless, we have included the question because it gives some personal feeling for the types of environmental limits that we are talking about.]

Considering the same issue on a more societal and less personal level, how do you think that environmental constraints should affect material consumption in the United States? Do you think that average levels of consumption need to be reduced? If so, how? Should advertising be eliminated? How should a reduction in consumption be distributed among different income groups? Should certain types of consumption be reduced more than others? Why?

To what extent could current levels of material consumption be made compatible with environmental constraints by substituting services and goods that could be produced with less material resources and less pollution, or by producing the same goods as now, but with better methods?

How would you cope with political obstacles to these changes, for example, the lobbying activities of the automobile and highway construction industries and the kinds of economic pressures that led to the removal of the excise tax on automobiles in order to stimulate auto sales? Do you think these obstacles can be overcome without fundamental reorganization of the economy? If so, how? If not, how should the economy be reorganized?

Based on your own experience, what do you think would be a good definition of standard of living? In other words, how do you think quality of life should be measured?

Overcrowding due to an inadequate supply of land is sometimes listed as another of the problems produced by overpopulation. Actually, land to live on is abundant in the United States. The average population density is about 56 people per square mile, or approximately 11 acres per person. But half of the people live on 5 percent of the land. Almost one-third of the population lives in central cities of metropolitan areas. About one-third of the people live in central cities or suburbs of the huge megalopolises: Boston to Washington, Chicago, Los Angeles and San Francisco.

Furthermore, the trend of migration has been out of low density regions, like the Great Plains, and into high density regions, especially along the coasts. What are the reasons for this increasing concentration of population? Some of the motivations are esthetic, for example, climate. Many are economic, since jobs are more plentiful in metropolitan areas where many industries prefer to locate in order to reduce costs for transportation to and from related businesses and consumers. One proposal for reversing this flow has been to constuct "new towns", but in the United States, many of these new towns have been in or near metropolitan regions. Many of them also lack low-income housing, and have failed to offer innovative transport systems or other solutions to environmental problems. Such "failures" are to be expected since they permit higher profits for the corporations that are building the new towns (often with government loan guarantees or subsidies).

Why do you think people are concentrated in metropolitan areas? Do you see this as a problem? If so, what solutions would you propose? You should find it useful to discuss these questions both in terms of your personal experiences and in terms of more systematic information which can be found in:

Advisory Commission on Intergovernmental Relations. 1968. *Urban and Rural America: Policies for Future Growth.* Washington: U.S. Government Printing Office.

L. Downie. 1972. The New-Town Image. *The Nation,* May 15, pp. 617–621.

Lansing, J. B. and E. Mueller. 1967. *The Geographic Mobility of Labor.* Ann Arbor: University of Michigan Press.

C. Taeuber. 1972. Population Trends of the 1960's. *Science 176:* 773–777.

Chapter 12 Effects of Population Growth on Economic Growth

It is a striking paradox that for years population growth has been seen as a necessary stimulus for the United States economy, but at the same time population growth has been blamed for the lack of economic growth in poor countries. In the case of the United States, it has been assumed that more babies will stimulate more consumer demand and hence more production and more employment. In the case of the poor countries, attention has been focused not on the potential increase in production and employment, but rather on the increase in number of consumers, an increase which has been assumed to be larger than any consequent increase in production. Can you see any theoretical reason(s) to justify this difference in approach and conclusions for the two cases? Is it empirically true that there is an inverse relationship between population growth and economic growth for poor countries, and a positive relationship for rich countries? (You can test this by analyzing the relationship for each continent separately in Figure 12–1.) If there is no difference in the relationship between population growth and economic growth for rich countries as opposed to poor countries, then why has public comment emphasized such different aspects of the effects of population growth in the two cases?

Chapter 13   **Population Regulation Processes in Animals**

"A French riddle for children illustrates [one] aspect of exponential growth—the apparent suddenness with which it approaches a fixed limit. Suppose you own a pond on which a water lily is growing. The lily plant doubles in size each day. If the lily were allowed to grow unchecked, it would completely cover the pond in 30 days, choking off the other forms of life in the water. For a long time the lily plant seems small, and so you decide not to worry about cutting it back until it covers half the pond. On what day will that be?"[1]

How much will population increase in 4 generations if each couple has 2 children? 3 children? 4 children? How are these projections affected if you assume that 1/10 of the children die before they reproduce? How much increase would there be in a century if people had their children on the average at age 20? at age 25? at age 33? (If you have trouble figuring out how to begin, see pg. 177 for a sample calculation.)

Herbert came home in a bad mood last night and snapped at his wife Eloise for no good reason. Eloise was annoyed by this and curtly told him so. This made Herbert more upset, so he shouted at Eloise to stop being so bitchy and get him a drink. At this, Eloise flew into a rage and started screaming at Herbert.
Why is this episode not an example of negative feedback? What kind of interaction would be an example of negative feedback?

[1] From D. H. Meadows, D. L. Meadows, J. Randers and W. W. Behrens. 1972. *The Limits to Growth.* Washington: Universe Books with permission of Potomac Associates and Universe Books.

If you have set up the artificial ecosystems suggested on pg. 210, you can use them to observe the dynamics of population growth. Different techniques will be suitable for following the growth of different populations. Some organisms can be simply counted. Population size for very small organisms that live free in the water can be estimated by using a microscope to count the number contained in a small measured sample of water. Hemocytometer slides are most convenient if they are available. For some organisms, population growth is best estimated by taking into account weight gains as well as increase in numbers. For plants that do not get thicker as they grow, weight gains can be estimated without disturbing the community by measuring the increase in length. Do you observe exponential growth of the populations followed by stabilization at plateau levels (as illustrated in Figure 13–1)? If not, can you figure out why not? For populations that are more or less stable, how much fluctuation is there around the stable, equilibrium level?

More problems can be found in:
M. Solomon. 1969. *Population Dynamics.* New York: St. Martin's Press.

Chapter 14   Behavioral Aspects of Population Regulation

A *home range* is a familiar area which an animal or group of animals lives in, but which is not defended against intruders. An animal's *personal space* is the space immediately around him which another animal cannot enter into without making the animal uncomfortable. This discomfort can be felt subjectively when another person comes too close, and is evidenced behaviorally by threat displays directed at the approacher, by moving away and so on. What is the difference between territory and home range? Between territory and personal space?

Territorial behavior in the wild is most easily seen in birds during the early spring. With patience, binoculars, and an amateur bird-watcher for a guide, you should be able to observe how territorial boundaries are established and maintained.

A fallacy that has become commonplace recently is that all primates are territorial and have strict dominance heirarchies. This fallacy is based on unwarranted extrapolation from behavior in zoos and from behavior of a few species. Recent studies of primate behavior in the wild have shown that many primate groups do not defend territories, and many have little dominance interaction. Useful descriptions of this work can be found in:
I. DeVore, ed. 1965.   *Primate Behavior—Field Studies of Monkeys and Apes.* New York: Holt, Rinehart and Winston, Inc.
H. Kummer. 1971.   *Primate Societies—Group Techniques of Ecological Adaptation.* Chicago: Aldine-Atherton.

Many students find it difficult to believe that there is no evidence that contemporary human crowding is a major source of current social problems. Part of the reason they are dubious is that they know from experience that crowded areas, such as center city ghettos, are almost always much more unpleasant places to be in than uncrowded areas, such as suburbs. Why is this familiar observation *irrelevant* to the question of whether density *per se* has adverse effects on humans? (The lack of evidence for major effects of density *per se* is described in more detail in the article by J. Cassel and the book by Q. Wright cited in the chapter bibliography, and in:

J. L. Freedman, S. Klevansky, and P. R. Ehrlich. 1971. The Effect of Crowding on Human Task Performance. *Journal of Applied Social Psychology* *1: 7–25*.)

Another basis for the widespread belief that contemporary crowding must have adverse effects on humans is erroneous extrapolation from experiments with rats. The most famous experiment was done by J. B. Calhoun *(Scientific American,* February, 1962, 139–48) who observed behavioral pathologies in overcrowded populations of caged rats. Extrapolation from the behavior of rats to the behavior of humans is, however, unwarranted, given the enormous differences in behavioral repertoire and social structure. Furthermore, Calhoun's experiments were carried out in very simple cages where the opportunities for both escape and exploration were extremely limited. Evidence about the crucial effect of these limitations can be found in:

J. Kavanau. 1967. Behavior of Captive Whitefooted Mice. *Science 155:* 1623–1639.

D. Morris. 1964. The Response of Animals to a Restricted Environment. *Symposia of the Zoological Society, London 13:* 99–118.

T. E. Rowell. 1967. A Quantitative Comparison of the Behavior of a Wild and a Caged Baboon Group. *Animal Behavior 15:* 499–509.

After you have read these, you might find it interesting to speculate about what the behavior of rats might be like in situations as crowded as in Calhoun's cages, but with more nearly normal environmental complexity. If you have enough time, space and energy, you might want to set up colonies of mice or rats with equal densities but with environments of different complexity in order to test how environmental complexity modifies the effects of density on behavior.

Chapter 15   Early History of Human Population Growth and its Relation to Technological Change

Why are the mechanized agricultural methods used in the United States not appropriate for most areas of most nonindustrial countries, at least for the immediate future? (Relevant information can be found in Chapter 8 as well as Chapter 15.)

In this chapter we have emphasized people's ability to develop new technologies which will support larger and larger populations. However, this process clearly cannot go on indefinitely. On the basis of the information in the first half of the book, how large a population do you think could maintain itself on the earth? What size population do you think would be optimal?

How much do your estimates of maximum or optimum supportable population change when you take into account the possibility of future political failures to use resources optimally? Do you see such failures as likely to be more serious or less serious than the failures described for China's history? Why?

Chapter 16 The Decline of Birth Rates and Death Rates in Europe

Many people tend to think of Asia, Africa and Latin America as the most overcrowded continents, but actually Europe has the highest density. The average number of people per square mile is 150 in Europe, 100 in Asia, 30 in South America and in North America, 20 in Africa, and 3 in Australia. Why do you think that people often think of Europe as less crowded than Asia, Africa or Latin America? How do Europeans manage to obtain adequate food and other resources despite their high population density? What implications, if any, do you draw about policies the United States should adopt toward densely populated countries in Asia?

The Irish potato famine illustrates how disastrous the consequences can be if large numbers of people are dependent on a single crop that is susceptible to infectious disease. The risk of widespread crop failure due to epidemics of plant disease has increased recently as traditional breeds of grain have been replaced by the new breeds of the "Green Revolution." Why is the risk greater? What strategies would you propose for coping with this problem?

If you are familiar with the history of any European (or other) country, one good way to develop your understanding of how historical developments affect population growth is to plot the birth rates, death rates and rate of population growth over time (as we have done for Sweden in Figure 16–2). Look for effects of major historical events, and try to figure out historical correlates of major changes in population growth. The data for these plots can be found in U.N. *Demographic Yearbooks,* and usually in vital statistics volumes issued by the country.

Chapter 17 The United States: What Determines Family Size?

If unwanted births were eliminated, how close would the United States' birth rates come to replacement levels that would result in zero population growth (once the age structure stabilized)? There is considerable disagreement about the answer to this question, largely because different definitions of wanted family size give different results. For example, in 1965 married women aged 35 to 44 said they wanted 3.4 children on the average. However, when wanted family size was estimated by subtracting from expected family size those births which were not wanted at the time of conception, then average number of wanted children was only 2.5 (L. Bumpass and C. F. Westoff, 1970, The "Perfect Contraceptive" Population, *Science 169:* 1177–1182). The difference between these two estimates is due to (1) subfecundity among some couples who consequently have fewer children than they desire; (2) desires for a child that develop after it has been conceived or born, but were not present prior to conception; (3) differences of opinion between husband and wife which in the first estimate are resolved by including all children that women wanted and in the second estimate were resolved by including half the children wanted by only one spouse; and (4) economic pressures that may lead a couple not to want a particular birth even though they would really like to have a large family.

What factors do you think account for the differences between the various estimates of desired family size given on pg. 178? What practical predictive value do you think each type of estimate has? A sophisticated answer to the last question must be based on predictions about developments in contraceptive technology and improvements in medical care that could reduce subfecundity, predictions about age at childbearing, since postponements result in more births prevented by subfecundity, and predictions about economic developments and social changes, such as women's lib, and their effects on family planning.

In this chapter we have proposed that unwanted births be reduced by eliminating the poverty, unemployment and inadequate education that currently foster fatalism and poor family planning among the lower-lower class. In order to evaluate this proposal, you may want to improve your insight into lower-lower class life by reading the book by Rainwater listed in the bibliography, and two articles which describe how the economic and social difficulties faced by lower-lower class parents result in childbearing practices that aggravate feelings of hopelessness and fatalism in their children:

L. Rainwater. 1965.   Crucible of Identity: The Negro Lower-Class Family. In T. Parsons and K. Clark, eds. *The Negro American.* Boston: Houghton Mifflin Company.

E. Pavenstedt. 1965.   A Comparison of the Child-rearing Environment of Upper-lower and Very Low-lower Class Families. *American Journal of Orthopsychiatry 35:* 89–98.

What is the cause of the recent dramatic decline in birth rates in the United States? You can supplement the material presented in Chapter 17 by reading analyses of data from the 1970 United States' census (which should become available soon after this book is published), and by analyzing factors that have influenced the childbearing decisions of you, your family and friends.

If you were born during the baby boom, do you plan to have a smaller family than your parents did? If so, to what extent is the difference due to greater ecological awareness now? To fuller development of women's career ambitions in the context of women's lib? To economic insecurity and the need for the woman to contribute to family income? Are you striving for a higher level of material consumption than your parents had at your age, or are you having difficulty achieving the same level of consumption? Note that young adults during the postwar economic boom could rather easily achieve higher incomes than their parents had had during the Depression. If you and your friends want to postpone having children, to what extent is it because you have self-fulfilling things you want to do first, and to what extent is it due to a general feeling of depression and malaise that makes the world seem a bad place to bring children into? If malaise is involved, can you identify societal sources that could produce malaise in many young adults at this time? If your parents had a larger family than you plan to, how much of the difference is due to failures of contraception before the pill and IUD became available?

Considering all the reasons for lower birth rates now, do you think birth rates are likely to stay low or to start to rise above replacement levels in the foreseeable future?

Chapter 18   Rapid Population Growth in Asia, Africa and Latin America—An End in Sight?

It is extremely common to observe a correlation (such as the correlation between high population densities and high crime) and then make an entirely unwarranted conclusion about causality (such as high density causes crime). Correlation proves *only* that there must be *some* causal mechanism. Other types of information are needed to tell you *which* of the possible causal mechanisms are operating (for example, whether high density leads to more crime, or poverty impels people both to live in high density areas and to commit more crimes). Considering the casual mechanisms described in Chapter 18, how would you interpret the slight correlation observed in Figure 12–1?

It is rather obvious that improved child survival should lead to lower birth rates in countries where couples practice contraception and plan the size of their families. It is not obvious that the net effect will be to reduce population growth. This does, however, seem to be the case, as can be demonstrated by some rather simple calculations. Suppose that each couple wants to be 99 percent sure that at least one child will survive to support them in their old age; that is, they want to have enough children that the probability that none will survive is 1 percent or less. How many children will they have to have if the probability that any given child will not survive into adulthood is 1/2? 1/4? 1/10? 1/100? (To calculate the answer, make the simplifying assumption that the probability of dying is independent for each child, so the probability of two children dying is the probability the first will die times the probability the second will die.) On the average, how many children will survive under each mortality condition? Note that, under these simple assumptions, a decrease in mortality leads not only to fewer births per family, but also to fewer surviving children and hence slower population growth.

Chapter 19 Forecasting Population Growth

Compared to the age structure for the United States (Figure 19–2), what shape should the age structure of a nonindustrial country like India have? What is the major cause of the difference?

Chapter 20 Proposals for Reducing Population Growth

We can predict that human population size must stabilize eventually, in fact probably rather soon. Three basic types of stabilizing mechanism can be proposed: (1) negative feedback based on increasing scarcity of some limiting resource (for example, food) as population increases (Chapter 13); (2) negative feedback based on psychological and physiological responses to high population density *per se* (Chapter 14); and (3) decreased birth rates based on people's conscious decisions to limit family size. How likely is each of these mechanisms to play a major role in stabilizing human population growth? In the case of the third mechanism, do you think that the feedback loop can be completed so that people have on the average just enough children to replace themselves and not somewhat more or somewhat less? If so, how? If not, why not?

If you plan to have more than two children, what satisfactions other than children do you expect from your adult life? How could education, jobs and social conditions in general be reorganized so that you expected more of these other satisfactions? Would this motivate you to want fewer children?

In the questions for Chapter 15, we asked what size population you think the earth could maintain. How soon would we reach that population if population growth continued at the current rate? (Use Figure 19–1.) What policies would you propose to stop population growth by then? Policy proposals should be compatible with the available evidence about probable effectiveness and, we believe, with moral criteria such as not proposing policies for others that one would not accept for oneself.

Our analysis of environment and population problems leads us to a pessimistic outlook, *unless* strenuous and intelligent efforts are made to solve the problems, in which case we believe optimism is justified. Do you agree? If not, why not? If you do, perhaps the best exercise we can suggest is research, organizational work and political activity to develop ideas for solutions to these problems and to bring the available ideas into practice.

index

Index

Index

Index